Praise for *The Power of Positive Profit*

"This book is a *major* contribution to business understanding and conduct; the *MoneyMath* charts alone are worth the cover price!"

> —Walter J. Reinhart, PhD, Professor of Finance and Academic Director, Master of Science in Finance, Loyola College

"Brilliant and dynamic—nobody else knows business numbers like this!"

> —Naomi Rhode, Co-Founder and Director, Smarthealth Inc.; President, International Federation of Speaking Professionals, Phoenix, Arizona

"We need more of your books for all our dealers!"

> —Les de Celis, CEO, Tyres4U, Sydney, Australia

"The book is awesome. You must join our board of directors!"

> —Jim Marsh, CEO, Burns & Ferrall Hospitality Equipment, Auckland, New Zealand

The
POWER of
POSITIVE PROFIT

The
POWER of
POSITIVE PROFIT

How You Can Improve
ANY Bottom Line
in Sales, Marketing, and Management
with MoneyMath©

Graham Foster

John Wiley & Sons, Inc.

Published by John Wiley & Sons, Inc., Hoboken, New Jersey.
Published simultaneously in Canada.

For general information on our other products and services or for technical support, please
contact our Customer Care Department within the United States at (800) 762-2974,
outside the United States at (317) 572-3993 or fax (317) 572-4002.

Wiley also publishes its books in a variety of electronic formats. Some content that appears in
print may not be available in electronic books. For more information about Wiley products,
visit our web site at www.wiley.com.

Library of Congress Cataloging-in-Publication Data:

Foster, Graham.
    The power of positive profit : how you can improve any bottom line in sales, marketing,
and management / Graham Foster.
      p. cm.
    Includes bibliographical references.
    ISBN-13: 978-0-470-05234-1 (cloth)
    ISBN-10: 0-470-05234-1 (cloth)
    1. Corporate profits. 2. Pricing 3. Sales management. 4. Cost control. I. Title.
HD4028.P7F67   2007
658.15'5—dc22

                                2006011037

Printed in the United States of America.

10 9 8 7 6 5 4 3 2 1

This book is dedicated
with my deepest gratitude
to my dear wife Suzi

for encouraging me to write this and stick at it. She has
endured the tension of creative effort pouring from my soul.

Contents

Foreword

The term *business* is used to describe a raft of activities that culminate in the creation or distribution of wealth.

In the twenty-first century we have come to realize that the most important thing in a business is its people. Without trained staff the business will not operate. While this appears to be a modern revelation, I am sure good staff selection and the management of them was the backbone of businesses in past centuries. However, there is no doubt that people management is the most complex and difficult of tasks we have to manage in a business.

This book has nothing to do with people management. It addresses the mechanics of operating a successful business—the numbers. In my business life, I have been amazed at the number of senior people, marketing managers, sales managers, and so on, who do not understand the profit and loss statement, how costs are made up, margins, and cash flow. These are fundamental items of corporate knowledge needed to manage a business.

This book aims to demonstrate to the reader how to manage these tasks. It demonstrates the effect of price increases, cost reductions, and, very importantly, the effect of discounting. It compares the value of a 1 percent sales increase versus a 1 percent cost reduction or a 1 percent price increase.

The author, Graham Foster, is an experienced CEO and has been involved in the turnaround of several businesses. He would be the first to say that you must have good products and employ the right people, and that excellent customer service is essential—yet none of this will work if the margins do not cover the costs. Graham also discusses the morality of the executives of a business. In fact, the good character of the CEO of a business is one of my personal criteria for investing in a company.

I am sure that when you read this book you will gain knowledge and find it extremely valuable. At a minimum, you will reinforce the basic business principles we all use to operate our businesses. Having watched the author present at conferences around the world, and having participated in his business workshops for over a decade, I can thoroughly endorse this work.

Happy reading.

Kerry Cattell
CEO and Company Director (retired)
Foseco Limited ASEAN
(China, Australia, Indonesia, Thailand,
Malaysia, Phillippines, Singapore, Taiwan)

Preface

The current state of business leaves a lot to be desired: Its problems range from ethical considerations to massive failures. Mark Twain once observed, "It could probably be shown by facts and figures that there is no distinctly American criminal class except Congress." If Mr. Twain were alive today he would most likely pluralize his observation by including top management and the boards of directors of large corporations. Is it not rather fascinating that CEOs and other top managers receive huge salaries and bonuses for overseeing poor performance, up to and including bankruptcy? And if by chance they are asked to resign, albeit with a nice cover story, they receive a sizeable payout—normally more than the average worker earns in a lifetime.

The bonanza of payouts for departing CEOs is starting to migrate from the business world to universities. In the midst of a storm regarding excessive personal spending, the president of American University, Benjamin Ladner, grabbed a golden parasol of $3.7 million (not large enough to qualify as an umbrella by industry standards) and departed. This should create an awkward moment and make us wonder exactly what we are teaching in universities. (As an aside, the golden parasol is quite large when compared to an English or history professor's salary of $50,000.)

The laying off of some 20,000 or 30,000 people, or even a couple hundred, some of whom have spent a lifetime working for a firm, should also give us cause for pause and reflection. If the layoffs are localized (e.g., a plant closing in a small town) and no other industry exists, property values go into the tank and the community essentially dies as the laid-off workers go into the social service system, which is paid for by our tax dollars. If the workers are retired and have a defined benefit program, it is only a matter of time before the firm sheds the pension program by shifting it into the government-insured program. Guess who pays the pension? Right—all of us taxpayers.

These types of scenarios and social costs are often due to competitive advantage strategies relating to market share and discounting. These concerns are a primary reason why current managers and students, who are the next leaders of the corporate world, need to read Graham Foster's *The Power of Positive Profit*.

It is certainly not appropriate to lay the dismal state of business only at the altar of fairness and justice. No, it is only rational and balanced to recognize that the fearless leaders of business are most likely following the "buyer value" mantra proposed by academics in such fine educational institutions as Harvard University and Loyola College. All too often marketing and management professors teach that the primary way to increase market share* is to discount the price of the product or service being offered. By doing this you increase buyer value, but what happens to the value of the firm? As Graham so accurately points out in this book, discounting is a way of life, in both our personal lives and in business. However, by discounting, the firms allow margins to evaporate and hence there is little or no return for the suppliers of risk capital—the shareholders who are the owners of the corporation.

Graham Foster has come from industry and has been involved with his share of successes and failures, and he knows how things work in the pragmatic world. Throughout this experience the most important concept learned is the recognition of the power of positive profit. As you read the book you will see how, from personal experience, he identifies the hurdles and objections salespeople present that prevent the generation of positive profit because of a "discounting mentality." Graham also

---

*The drive for market share is what market theorists call competitive advantage or competitive strategy.

shows that the goal of a firm should not be to maximize the value of the buyer to the detriment of the firm, and that all too often the discounting mania to achieve the competitive advantage does just that. Some good examples of the discounting mentality to achieve market share include both General Motors and Ford.

Instead of focusing on buyer value, let us define *value* as the maximum possible sales price minus total cost. The question then becomes how the value of the product or service is divided between the seller and purchaser, or what price to charge the buyer. In the competitive strategy model, with competition being the driving force of all management decisions, the value generally accrues to the buyer. The emphasis on competition and gaining market share by providing value for the buyer typically means a low sales price. *The Power of Positive Profit* shows the implications of lower sales price and presents strategies to keep more value (profit) with the firm, which in turn allows for new product development, technology advances, and the wealth maximization of the owners. Graham presents and explains with tables and graphs how a change of focus from buyer value to owner value can be accomplished.

The purpose of this book is to examine the elements of finance, marketing, production, and support functions, and to present the three Ps for a successful enterprise: power, positive, and profit! While the three Ps are similar to the 4-P theme used in basic marketing (i.e., price, product, place, promotion), they more fully represent finance and production, with marketing playing a dominant role in strategic planning. This book shows how the power of positive profit is contrary to the emphasis on competition and market share normally focused on by many firms who follow the competitive strategy model.* The basic concepts behind the power of positive profit were first presented by Graham Foster in the

---

*Following the drive for competitive market share can lead to another set of three Ps—namely, pathetically-poor performance.

first edition of *The Power of Positive Profit* (Everest Books, 2004) and are based on his experience as a CEO along with thousand of presentations he has made worldwide to diverse audiences. Over time he came to more fully realize the negative consequences of competition and market share being at the core of business decisions.

Many academics, media personnel, and businesspeople will contend that three forces dominate the world today regarding economics and business:

1. Technology.
2. Globalization (which occurs due to technology).
3. The marketplace (which has the power to enable the first two forces).

Having technology with a global outlook does not permit success without knowledge of the marketplace. Knowledge of the marketplace requires education and understanding of how things work, and most importantly the recognition of the power of positive profits. A firm using high technology with a global perspective that does not recognize the importance of margin and its relationship to profits is in for rough times.

Graham Foster addresses these issues and assists us to become part of the solution instead of being part of the problem. In this book he lays out mathematical truths that businesspeople can apply in strategic plans in order to be competitive and maximize the wealth of the owners. In fact, Graham shows with basic math that a price *increase* is often more beneficial for a firm than a price discount.

I had the distinct pleasure of meeting Graham Foster on a flight from the United States to Australia in 2005. I was on my way to take a position as a visiting professor at Bond University on the Gold Coast, Queensland, while Graham was off to one of his many worldwide presentations. In our conversation we discovered a common interest—namely, the recognition that firms exist to maximize the wealth of the owners, or, put another way, to generate a stream of positive profits that allow a firm to compete and grow in an ever-changing and competitive environment while providing a return to the shareholders.

Even when a firm is facing an uncertain future, several truths hold—basic business fundamentals along with basic math do not change with time. As in the stock market, when you hear "It is different this time" it is time to sell and wait on the sidelines until the madness is over. The most recent example of this phenomenon was during the late 1990s dot-com bubble. We are starting to hear the same thing with the inverted yield curve, which has been an accurate forecaster of economic times, and with the real estate market. The only advice one can offer is "Buyer, beware—and get out sooner than later." It is not worthwhile trying to time the top.

The Power of Positive Profit could easily be adapted in any business strategy course (from marketing and management to finance) at the undergraduate level and should be a must for MBA strategy courses. Undergraduates who learn the principles herein will be able to make a positive impact on the firms that hire them and advance up the ladder. The MBA candidate should know the principles and implement them to enhance his or her career and the profits of the firm.

Don't be put off by the fact that the concepts presented here are founded on math. The objective of all firms is to maximize the wealth of the owners, which is done by a long-term stream of positive profits. Moreover, the math is basic math—one does not have to be a statistical wizard to understand the concepts presented in *MoneyMath*:

- The power of positive profit puts the math of strategic decisions into the forefront.
- The power of positive profit recognizes the objective of the firm and allows for all stakeholders to be treated fairly.
- The power of positive profit avoids the myopic obsession of market share to maximize top management benefits.

Foster's *The Power of Positive Profit* takes you through various steps using *MoneyMath* diagrams and charts (based on common sense) to help businesspeople, whether salespeople or CEOs, to understand how their actions can influence profits, and what actions should be avoided. As Graham states, math is math, and once you understand the relationships between sales price, margin, and profit, you are well on your way to being successful. If you want to be part of the solution and not part of the problem, *The Power of Positive Profit* is required reading.

Baltimore, Maryland
April 2006

Walter J. Reinhart, PhD
Professor of Finance, Academic Director
Master of Science in Finance Program
Loyola College

Introduction

In writing *The Power of Positive Profit* I have set out to address a few issues affecting the bottom-line success of businesses big and small after 9/11 and in this new Millennium. I also present some opportunity concepts for people at all levels in business, commerce, and industry to improve the bottom line where they work.

Since 1972 I have conducted business seminars and delivered keynotes on every continent. As I have moved around the globe, I've discovered that math skills, media culture, ethics, and morality affect the bottom-line outcome of companies in positive or negative ways.

On the other side of the coin, I have noticed that companies with strong understanding of math inside their ongoing operations seem to be able to handle the ups and downs of the market relatively easily. Of course when ethics and morality issues conflict with the profit motive, it seems that it's usually senior executives and directors who are most tempted to choose unwisely. Failure by leaders almost certainly kills the motivation of the employees, resulting in lower levels of customer service and then lower profits.

Some of what you'll read in the pages that follow came from the vast resources of public information on the Internet in the form of public financial statements, plus of course my own *MoneyMath* profit charts. The complete profit charts themselves are included in Appendix A along with an explanation of each. I call this the mother of all appendixes!

The stimulus to write this book came from the fact that many of my business friends said they had never seen a collection of tables and figures like the *MoneyMath* charts; they had seen some of them but not all together in one place with explanations. The math used in the charts is timeless—it never gets outdated.

Wise and foolish business decisions will continue till the end of time, but if we accept the premise that we all work to feed ourselves and our families, then making a profit is a worthwhile exercise. When we make more than we need for food, clothing, and shelter, we then have another choice—greed or philanthropy.

Success is not making the money for its own sake. It's what is done with it that matters most, because we certainly won't be taking it with us when we leave here.

I'm deeply grateful for the input, help, inspiration, and encouragement of the family, friends, colleagues, business leaders, CEOs, and others who have been there for me along the way. The names of many of them appear in the Acknowledgments section, with my deep thanks to them, along with my apologies to those people I may have inadvertently omitted.

My special thanks to both Bob Kelly of Wordcrafters Inc. (Sun Lakes, Arizona), who edited my first edition manuscript, and to Professor Walter Reinhart, PhD, of Loyola College, who edited the second. And unusual thanks to our family cat, Misty, who came into my office in the wee small hours and curled up beside me, offering comfort. He has since won a photographic contract for good-looking cats and will go on to star in the cat world!

Deep thanks is also due to my late parents, particularly my mother, who made me study hard at math and who gave me two important books to read when I was young: *Think and Grow Rich*, by Napoleon Hill, and the Holy Bible. My ultimate thanks go to the one, true, living God, who has revealed Himself as the God of numbers: "In the beginning, God created the heavens and the earth"—day number one!

Phoenix, Arizona   Graham Foster
September 11, 2006

CHAPTER ONE

Overcoming a Shaky Start: Millennium Novum

After 9/11 . . . that presumption of continuing sales volume with discretionary income is diminished.

—Graham Foster

S hock and awe! Today's newspaper says that your employer, the star-ship *Enterprise*, is on the skids. The company you dreamed of working for is drastically out of control. Jobs are going to be lost, the company is bleeding, the top managers have been fired—oh my gosh! Why me? Where did they go wrong?

America and much of the developed world have ridden booming economies since the early 1950s. The demographic bubble called the baby boomers drove much of this growth. Another driving factor has been the information economy, coming in over top of the industrial economy that prevailed until World War II.

On September 11, 2001, I was in my room at the Hilton Airport Hotel in Melbourne, Australia, having made a presentation that day to some hungry business executives wanting to improve their bottom line. I turned to the news channel and then it happened. Terrorists hijacked four planes, and the rest is history—and remains history in the making for the foreseeable future. We can all remember where we were and what we were doing at that time. It was like the death of John F. Kennedy or the attack on Pearl Harbor, the kind of event that freezes time in our memory.

The economic damage done to the developed world in general and the American economy in particular is with us today. My guess is $1 trillion in total damage was wreaked that day. Just prior to that in the 1990s, the West had engaged in business excesses that in hindsight we would all agree had been allowed to get out of control. That trillion-dollar loss was and is an unplanned overhead for the world economy, forcing us all to reconsider how we sell and manage for profit. The fallout of 9/11 has added a worldwide cost that has simultaneously reduced both sales and profits. The loss has been compounded more recently by the Indian Ocean tsunami and Hurricanes Katrina, Rita, and Wilma, with growing insurance burdens and the continuing hike in fuel costs.

In this new millennium, we have also seen some of the biggest corporate busts in history. Some of these busts have been due to corporate greed, malpractice, and a lack of business ethics and morality. However, the majority of business failures were and still are due to *poor management and bad board direction*. It is rarely the workers who wreck a corporation from the bottom; it is the people at the top. (I have been a CEO—trust me.)

No longer can we sell with the attitude that there is no tomorrow or that if we lose the current sale there is another one around the corner. That presumption of continuing sales volume with discretionary income is diminished. No longer can the West manage as if the party will continue indefinitely.

High-salaried CEOs and their boards who cannot manage a bottom line are unacceptable. We are now being tested as to whether we can sell in or manage the tough (normal) times we find occurring every 10 years or so. It is always time to get real. Many young executives have never had to manage in hard times because they have not seen them all that often. That is why so many are being tested managerially. Above all, the philosophy by which we sell, market, and manage goods and services is being tested. We will either come up roses or push up daisies!

I believe the Ivy League university business model of chasing maximum market share by increasing sales and trampling competitors to do it is flawed. In this book I ask you to study carefully the *MoneyMath* charts that prove mathematically that price is the strongest strategy, and that a balanced company selling quality will outperform the sell, sell, sell approach.

The three industries standing out with poor management practices leading to major problems (and opportunities) seem to be retailers, airlines, and the auto industry. I hope this book will help some of them see that higher profits are possible. General Motors, for example, right up to 2006 has run discount sale after discount sale, losing billions every time and never learning the lesson. It will go broke soon unless it changes direction.

The recent corporate busts have been extraordinary in terms of financial plunder and damage done to the ordinary investor and employee. Many of those who perpetrated the plunders are still walking the streets as free people, as if they never did anything wrong. The sense of right and wrong seems to have eluded a lot of them and they carry on regardless.

Combine all these events and you have an astonishing grand entrance to the third millennium, and certainly at the level of business where most of us earn our living.

Do you want the good news or the bad news? To establish the issues and problems that I think need addressing, let's start with corporate busts first and finish with the good news in the final chapters.

Corporations Gone Bust

Table 1.1 lists 35 of the largest corporate bankruptcies that have occurred since 1970.

TABLE 1.1   Most of the Largest Bankruptcies since 1970, Adjusted for Inflation

RANK	COMPANY NAME	BANKRUPT DATE	ASSETS $ M (USD)	INFLATION ADJUSTED
1	WorldCom, Inc.	7/21/02	$103,914	$105,796
2	Enron Corporation	12/2/01	$65,503	$67,724
3	Conseco, Inc.	12/18/02	$61,392	$62,504
4	Texaco, Inc.	4/12/88	$35,892	$57,091
5	Global Crossing	1/28/02	$30,185	$31,209
6	Penn Central	6/21/70	$6,851	$29,988
7	UAL Corporation	12/9/02	$25,197	$25,653
8	Pacific Gas & Electric	4/6/01	$21,470	$22,950
9	Adelphia Communications	6/25/02	$21,499	$22,228
10	Baldwin-United	9/26/03	$9,383	$17,295
11	NTL, Inc.	8/8/02	$16,834	$17,139
12	Kmart Corporation	1/22/02	$14,183	$14,407
13	Reliance Group Holdings	6/12/01	$12,598	$13,025
14	Federated Department Stores	1/15/90	$7,913	$11,755
15	Parmalat (Italy)	12/19/03	14B Euro	$11,500
16	Continental Airlines	12/3/90	$7,666	$10,923
17	Federal Mogul Corp.	10/1/01	$10,150	$10,494
18	LTV Corp. (1st)	7/17/86	$6,307	$10,380
19	Olympia & York Development	5/14/92	$7,023	$9,749
20	Comdisco Inc.	7/16/01	$8,754	$9,051
21	Maxwell Comms Corp.	12/16/91	$6,352	$8,465
22	Columbia Gas System	7/31/91	$6,196	$8,331
23	Owens Corning	10/5/00	$6,494	$6,942
24	ANC Rental Corp.	11/13/01	$6,358	$6,565
25	LTV Corp. (2nd)	12/29/00	$6,101	$6,522
26	R.H. Macy & Co. Inc.	1/27/92	$4,812	$6,355
27	Eastern Air Lines Inc.	3/9/89	$4,037	$6,293
28	Williams Comms Group	4/22/02	$5,992	$6,101
29	Integrated Health Services	2/2/00	$5,393	$5,919
30	360 networks (USA) Inc.	6/28/01	$5,596	$5,786
31	Montgomery Ward	7/7/97	$4,879	$5,534
32	Winstar Comms Inc.	4/18/01	$4,975	$5,318
33	Allied Stores Corp.	1/15/90	$3,502	$5,202
34	Loewen Group Intl.	6/1/99	$4,674	$5,130
35	Walter Industries	12/27/89	$3,462	$5,031

WorldCom has the dubious honor of having pulled off the biggest bust in history (two times bigger than Enron as of 2006). It filed for Chapter 11 on July 21, 2002. This telecommunications company is being investigated, but it is interesting to note that the former CEO at the time resigned amid allegations about his $366 million in private loans from this public company. He has since been jailed for securities fraud, conspiracy, and filing false documents.

Enron remains the benchmark for bad management and corporate malfeasance. Although it is hard to pinpoint the exact moment the bubble burst in Enron, its operating margin had plunged from around 5 percent in early 2000 to under 2 percent by early 2001, and its return on invested capital dangled at 7 percent—a figure that does not include Enron's off-balance-sheet debt, which was huge. Not only was Enron surprisingly unprofitable, but its cash flow from operations seemed to bear little relationship to reported earnings. In their culture of arrogance, the managers maintained their immunity from detailed investigation of their results.

In the year that Enron headed toward bankruptcy, late chairman Ken Lay took out more than $100 million in pay and fringe benefits. One Enron executive continued to build his $20 million mansion while being investigated. No remorse, no shame, no change. The stock market fallout years later is still sending shudders through the retirement funds of millions of people. While thousands lost their jobs, thousands more lost their savings and retirement funds. Hundreds of other companies were caught with unsecured exposures to Enron. The damage done by corrupt and incompetent Enron executives and directors is equivalent to staging 20 Gulf Wars! They essentially threw the corporate governance handbook out the window. On top of their gross incompetence, those at the helm of Enron were corporately unethical and immoral in every way.

The power of their negative profits was inflicted on us all. The Enron bust has cost *everybody* on planet Earth the equivalent of about $10 each, or every American household $903 each. Sadly, it is mainly the Enron investors who will lose it. To paraphrase Winston Churchill,

"Never in the history of human enterprise have so many been ripped off by so few for so much."

In 2001, the biggest retailer bust in history occurred. Kmart hit the wall for $14 billion and entered Chapter 11. Being squeezed by Target on one side and Wal-Mart on the other side, top brass decided to cut prices coast to coast in an endeavor to *raise sales* in 2001 and 2002, in the trough of a recession when there was weakened demand. Unaware of the mathematical connection between their action and the bottom line, they sank themselves. Unfortunately, thousands of families were hurt in the process, thousands of jobs were lost, and many stores shut. Later I will demonstrate that mathematical connection.

The company saw its sales drop from $36.15 billion in fiscal 2001 to $30.76 billion in fiscal 2002. It closed 13 percent of its stores (283). Yet even with those atrocious figures, the board rewarded its then CEO James Adamson with a $4 million package. Although he resigned earlier in 2003, Adamson was still expected to make another $3.6 million when the company exited Chapter 11. Happy day.

Overpaid Executives

Now the top management remuneration is an issue. I'm not saying that CEOs shouldn't get paid well, but I am saying their salaries and bonuses should be earned based on *results* and performance. H. Lee Scott Jr., CEO of Wal-Mart, in 2003 received a salary of $1.14 million with a bonus of $3.16 million. While that might sound like a lot of hay, look what Wal-Mart has done under Scott. It increased sales by 12.3 percent from 2001 to 2002 and increased profits from $6 billion in 2001 to $8 billion in 2002. At least he improved the sales a bit but at 3 percent the profit remains abysmal.

McDonald's, the number one volume retailer of fast food, having let the service quality drop off in the United States, thought it was the price of their food and competition that were making things tough for them. (Why do so many businesspeople conclude that competition is about price and not quality?) So out came the one-dollar meal to save the day. McDonald's then reported its first loss in history—$44 million in the red. Having walked away from their own credo of quality, service, cleanliness and value (QSCV), they gravitated where most poor management gravitates—to *price* cutting. While Ray Kroc no doubt rolled in his grave, the then Chairman Jim Cantalupo (deceased) appointed a young service-oriented executive, Charlie Bell, as CEO. Charlie knew QSCV through and through, and he wanted the rude service with lukewarm food in dirty restaurants replaced by the original, cheerful, "Welcome to McDonald's, may I take your order?" The McDonald's training manual states, "Welcome a customer as you would a guest in your own home." (Sadly, Charlie Bell died in 2005 at age 43.)

I heard a conference speaker once say that only 25 percent of Western populations are suitable for customer service positions, and another 25 percent may be able to be trained to do service work. (Perhaps some of our homes have become places for dysfunctional relationships that produce people unsuitable for service work?)

Airlines in Agony

Airlines around the world dropped like flies after 9/11 and some are still teetering on the edge. However, they were on the edge before 9/11, yet many of their CEOs continue to reap financial rewards that are ridiculous against results. In 2002, for example, American, United, Delta, Continental, Northwest, and US Airways lost a combined $10 billion on revenues of $70 billion. That's a 14 percent loss.

Northwest Airlines' customer revenues decreased by 5.7 percent from 2001 to 2002. During the third quarter of 2002, the company had assets of $13.6 billion and liabilities of $14.1 billion. And yet the compensation package for the airline's CEO, Richard Anderson, increased to almost $3 million, up 126.3 percent in 2002 over 2001, even as

Northwest was laying off thousands of employees and asking others to take substantial salary cuts.

Continental Airlines had a net loss of $451 million on revenues of $8.4 billion in 2002, compared to $95 million and $8.97 billion, respectively, in 2001. Yet the CEO, Gordon Bethune, had a salary in 2002 of $1.06 million with a bonus of $651,563. That was an *increase* over 2001, when his salary was $794,700 and he had a bonus of $67,320. What for?

However, the airline JetBlue is a success story, not only in the airline industry but in any industry. In 2002, its first year as a public company, JetBlue had 34 planes and 3,100 employees. It also had operating revenues of $635 million and net income of $55 million, up from $320 million and $38.5 million, respectively, in 2001. In 2002, the airline had net income of $54.9 million and an operating margin of 16.5 percent, a higher margin than any of the major U.S. airlines. The company's revenue passengers were $5.8 billion in 2002, up from $3.1 billion in 2001. Its stock was at $100 on April 11, 2002, and hit $150 by December 31 of that year. With that stellar performance, JetBlue's CEO, David Neeleman, who owns almost 5 million shares of the company's stock, had a modest salary of $200,000 in 2002 along with a bonus of $90,000.

American Airlines, deep in trouble, asked their workers in 2003 to accept a pay cut while the CEO and his top 40 executives secretly organized themselves a pay raise. Can you imagine that? This was the executive program to save the bleeding airline: to suck more blood out of its dying body! The CEO was properly and summarily dismissed by the board, but most of the complicit 40 other executives stayed on! Happy day.

I recently walked into an American Admirals Club lounge. The four ladies behind the desk were all having social conversations with each other and couldn't care less about customers standing in front of the desk. There were five of us waiting for them to finish their little chat, and then they acted as if we had rudely interrupted their day! The virus spreads right through the corporate body, doesn't it?

United Airlines (UAL) went bust for $25 billion on December 9,

2002. It had the highest cost per passenger mile of any airline in the world in 2002. It is well known that the top echelon of captains there (who have a big say in running the airline) ensure that they get industry top pay while turning in the fewest number of flown hours. No wonder the fixed costs in that airline went over the top.

When UAL filed for Chapter 11 bankruptcy, they blamed 9/11 for their losses. But 9/11 had occurred fully 14 months earlier. In other words, in the 14 months after a tragic event hit sales, the management and directors still had not effectively dealt with it. Then in June 2003, the airline reported progress inside its Chapter 11 protection. In May they reported $64 million in earnings, despite the fact that the "earnings" were due to $300 million in federal government compensation over the Iraq war. In reality, it netted an operating loss of $155 million in May.

Some hope is emerging with UAL, though. In reintroducing their flights to Asia after the SARS outbreak, United said its plan was not to reduce fares to Asia. It left that stupidity to Continental Airlines management, who announced they were reintroducing their flights to Asia at reduced fares! United has since emerged from Chapter 11 and has a chance now to show it can professionally manage customers and revenue.

Continental went belly-up in 1990 for $7 billion, and it still has not learned its lesson. US Airways entered Chapter 11 first in 2002 and again in 2004—incredible! Two times into Chapter 11 in two years—I call that being slow learners. Now they have been merged with America West and the slogan is, "Building the world's biggest discount airline." The word *biggest* gives their game away and indicates that sales volume at any price will continue for them. If the slogan was about building the world's *best* discount airline, we would know that quality was at the heart of their strategy, but instead we see that the core of it is volume.

Air New Zealand purchased Ansett Airlines of Australia and promptly set about charging its fuel bill against the Australian subsidiary, such that Ansett went bust; then they handed back the broken airline to its original Australian shareholders. Happy day: 12,000 jobs lost. Now again Air New Zealand wants the government to bail them out of their plight as they continue with poor performance. The global airline business has been forced to find new solutions and in 2006 is seeing increased traffic, higher seat occupancies, and lessening overcapacity, but it intrigues me how airlines can be so successful at one end and so unsuccessful at the other.

Qantas, the Australian flag carrier, like Southwest and JetBlue made profits right through the 9/11 tragedy and the SARS outbreak. Qantas is not an economy airline like Southwest. It is a mainline international carrier, the second oldest in the world (founded in 1924—only KLM Royal Dutch Airlines is older), and has the best safety record in the world—it has never had a passenger fatality in an accident! It employs 30,000 people and has made $500 million (Australian) profit in each six months since 2002. The formula there is espoused by the staff, who say, "We are still a customer service driven airline." What that means is that there is a large section of the market that will pay for the benefit of good in-flight meals, clubs to relax in, and friendly in-flight service. The publicly reported pay of the CEO, Geoff Dixon, is $1.5 million (AU) plus bonus, which equates to $1.12 million in U.S. dollars.

Look closely at Southwest Airlines. It was the only one of the top 10 U.S. airlines that made a profit during 2002—and its total stock market value exceeded that of all other major airlines combined by 290 percent. Southwest has posted profits for over 30 consecutive years, including $411 million in 2001 and $214 million in 2002. Following the terrorist attacks of September 11, 2001, while every other major U.S. air carrier downsized, laid off employees, and grounded aircraft, Southwest added 20 airplanes to its fleet and 2,125 employees to its payroll. The airline accomplished those impressive figures because it has one of the lowest operating costs of all major U.S. airlines. While others grow sales, Southwest grows its profits.

Southwest is impressive by any standards, due in large part to its management. After 9/11, from October 1, 2001, until December 31, 2001, chairman Herbert D. Kelleher received no salary—his current compensation is around $320,000 annually—citing the severe financial challenges the company was facing as a result of the terrorist attacks. Other company officers, including CEO James F. Parker, followed suit. That's an executive role model of behavior that motivates the socks off the employees. Southwest Airlines is a role model for every company in the world, no matter what product or service it is selling. And Southwest is only the seventh biggest airline in the United States—it certainly doesn't fit the pattern of "big is beautiful."

What is the point of having six marginal or profitless airlines in the United States moving in and out of Chapter 11 with industry downturns and asking for tax dollars to bail them out, when often it is poor management that caused it in the first place? The government has no obligation to rescue airlines or any other business in a free market economy.

I recommend that every airline worker in the world read *Moments of Truth*, by Jan Carlzon (HarperCollins, 1989), which shows how Scandinavian Airlines System (SAS) was turned around by putting the customer and service quality first, not price. While airlines, retailers, and carmakers mindlessly chase volume and market share, successful bottom-line results will elude them. In addition, if senior executives and directors are only there for what they can squeeze out of the company, that will only make it worse.

Airlines that cannot cover their costs have to have the intestinal fortitude to make some tough decisions, particularly in the United States. They have to refocus their operations on margins, not sales volume, or die. They have to crank up customer service or all go down to the low end of the market with Southwest, Virgin, and the low margin players.

Since the beginning of the 2003 Iraq war and the expansion of the Chinese economy, fuel costs for cars and planes have soared. In an endeavor to rein in the extra cost, six of the seven major U.S. airlines initially agreed to impose a $20 surcharge per ticket. However, Northwest

Airlines refused to go along with it so what did the rest do? They caved in and continued to bleed.

The distance from the sun to the planet Pluto is 3.7 billion miles, but the frequent flyer miles owed to customers by U.S. airlines as of 2002 was 870 billion miles. At 10 cents per passenger mile, the cost to the airlines of redeeming those points equates to $87 billion, to come off their already red bottom lines in the years ahead. How will this happen? Taxpayer bailout? I don't think so. My guess is that there will be only three or four viable full-service airlines left in the United States within 10 years.

Automakers' Anxieties

Detroit carmakers have been taking a lower share of the total sales compared to imports over the past 15 years, down some 40 percent (see the U.S. Bureau of Transportation Statistics, Table 1-16 at www.bts.gov/publications/national_transportation_statistics. Local vehicle production in the United States has declined from 7.1 million in 1970 to 5.4 million in 2004. Despite this, Detroit continues to chase volume and market share at low margins. Television ads say things like "No deposit, interest free, $8,000 off factory invoice." Interestingly, in 2002, General Motors (GM) and Ford each reported nearly $180 billion in sales yet made paltry profits. They just love price wars! Since then they continue to make losses and Toyota remains the world's most profitable mainline carmaker.

Based on the trends in research, buyers are getting younger and their desire for imported cars is increasing. Even worse, of the "Big Three" American automakers—GM, Ford, and Chrysler—the latter is in fact owned by Daimler-Benz of Germany, making it technically a European entity now.

Despite this, America has the number one auto dealer in the world, and he has not focused much on new vehicle advertising for 30 years. He mainly advertises his astonishingly high service quality. Carl Sewell with his Dallas dealerships (Lexus, GM, Saab, Hummer) averages a customer satisfaction index (CSI) of 97 percent, and some months he achieves 100 percent CSI.

His whole business is predicated on *service* to the customer in the long term. His famous service book is entitled *Customers for Life* (Pocket Books, 1998; Currency, 2002) and is now in its second revised edition. I recommend that any businessperson read it and substitute their own industry name when the word *automobile* is used. Carl is willing to open his business to any auto dealers who wish to have a look and improve their margins. Nobody comes.

Since 1990, by my figuring, Detroit's passenger car manufacturers have all lost market share yearly and have had all these years to change the course of their management, design, marketing, and selling to suit the market. During this time, they have also made substantial financial losses, as shown in Figure 1.1.

Despite nearly two decades of these hard numbers, the brutal fact is that they continue on in their downward spiral, thrashing the volume sales story, with poor segmentation and positioning, and less vehicle appeal to the margin-rich parts of the market. I believe helpful new thinking could change this. The decline of each is astonishing, almost a death spiral downwards, and it continues today.

Great hope emerged in May 2004: The chairman of Ford declared that they would reduce discounts and aim at profits rather than focusing so much on volume. Astonishing. The results at Ford in the first quarter of 2004 proved the validity of my *MoneyMath*. Ford had lost 1.3 percent of market share but its profits at that time doubled and started to exceed those of GM. However, this brave move by Ford did not spread to the rest of the auto industry nor to the whole world of industry and commerce. The year 2005 saw GM come out with its ill-fated "Employee Discount Sale." Sadly, this scared the rest of Detroit into following along. In 2005 GM made $190 million in sales and lost $14 billion. To say they have pricing incontinence is an understatement. At the end of 2005 the

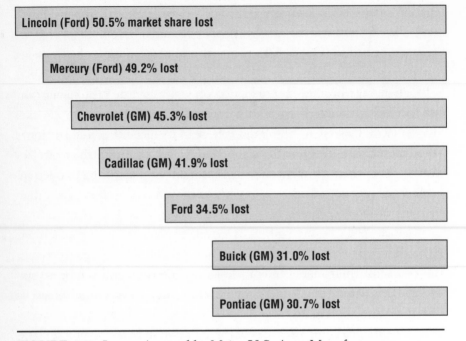

Lincoln (Ford) 50.5% market share lost

Mercury (Ford) 49.2% lost

Chevrolet (GM) 45.3% lost

Cadillac (GM) 41.9% lost

Ford 34.5% lost

Buick (GM) 31.0% lost

Pontiac (GM) 30.7% lost

FIGURE 1.1   Losses Accrued by Major U.S. Auto Manufacturers Since 1990

CEO sacked 30,000 workers just before Christmas. Why? What had the employees done wrong? The truth is that the board and the CEO are the problem and the wrong people were let go. And now Ford is on the same spiral downward following GM.

The volume problem is not exclusive to the United States. Daimler-Chrysler has stumbled since its 1993 decision to become a "volume" company rather than a quality company. Mercedes, from February to May 2003, saw its market share slip from 13.1 percent to 11.7 percent. Its profits in 2005 are nearly as low as Wal-Mart's, at 3 percent. Perhaps the volume decision at Daimler-Benz was in response to Toyota's entry with Lexus alongside their standard Toyota range. This has been a winner for Lexus, and it is now the most preferred luxury vehicle in North America. Mercedes-Benz's reliability and quality issues persist, with vehicle dependability surveys reporting a sharp rise in problems after three years of ownership. Passenger car chief Jürgen Hubbert admitted in 2004 that 70 percent of his problems are electronic. I submit that 100 percent of his problems are really customers. The chairman of Mercedes-Benz, Jürgen Schrempp, left in 2005; interestingly, he had noticed that the navigation system in his company vehicle wouldn't work.

Lexus continue to challenge Mercedes, not through motor sport but with customer service. Every Lexus service customer gets a loan car, whereas Mercedes think it is the engineering that matters. How misguided this is.

Some of the volume-based decisions of the 1995–2006 Daimler-Benz firm were:

- It decided to buy Chrysler (to get more volume). Now Chrysler may be an American icon, but a good proportion of American buyers are happy *not* to buy vehicles on which the profit is repatriated to Germany.

- It bought into the ailing Hyundai and Mitsubishi companies. The Mitsubishi CEO then announced years of poor engineering and a giant recall shortly after!

- It sold engines to Sun Yong Musso, which installed them in one of the ugliest SUV/4WDs ever built. Daimler-Benz executives quickly pulled out of that after they saw the damage to their image.

- Its last great build was the W126 series S Class. Since then "volume" has been the mantra.

Some Mercedes vehicles are delivered new with doors that do not shut tight, side mirrors that fall off, and faults that are hidden from the customer. In earlier days the company would never have tolerated this. I personally know of one brand-new Mercedes-Benz vehicle that was delivered with the wires cut on the "Base" braking system (an electronic override on the ABS braking). The dealer's explanation: "It will be fixed with a recall later." Without a non-Mercedes mechanic pointing this out, the buyer would never have known. The feature was advertised on the Mercedes brochure. Of course it's illegal in trade and commerce to misrepresent the quality or specifications of goods and services. On this same brand-new vehicle, the engine came loose off the engine mounts after three months. Is that what they mean by their slogan, "engineered like none other"? Now the Mercedes car experience is fixable only if they truly put their customers first, ahead of engineering.

I have worked with an excellent Benz dealership in Scottsdale, Arizona (Schumacher European Ltd.), on customer service issues in addition to other systems work that they needed. They moved their CSI from the low 80s to the high 90s over a period of 18 months and so far have reached 96.4. They went from number 27 out of 30 dealers in the southwestern United States to number 1 in that period. A similar thing happened with the great BMW dealership in Brisbane, Australia, run by Martin Roller. Customers are first in both these places, and both dealerships do well.

Once an auto dealership gets the vision of service replacing volume selling, as did Scottsdale Mercedes, then profitability can shift, too. It starts with the management understanding the long-term value of the customer. I love helping auto dealers move up into higher profits through superior service, not lower pricing.

A Widespread Problem

Australian insurance giant HIH went down the tubes for $5.3 billion, yet HIH kept selling low-price policies right up to the final day. Parties were held throughout the company as if nothing was wrong—expensive parties in the six-figure range. Unskilled and unethical directors went before the courts to account for their actions. Many are trying to shirk their legal obligations by saying, "I wasn't aware" or "I forgot." Some have received jail terms. Managers and directors are paid specifically to be aware and remember—that is what managing is about. It is clear that managers at HIH never put enough capital away to cover their insurance risk, and just kept selling at prices too low to sustain a viable insurance business. Because of the way insurance costs are passed off through the chain of insurance companies around the world, everybody on the planet suffers a little bit when a major corporate failure like this occurs.

How can these companies—these businesses where we ordinary folks work and derive our livelihood—avoid the outcomes described here and produce a successful bottom line, give us security in our jobs, feed our families, *and* grow, when so many still turn in such poor results, and the CEO takes out a fortune?

What should we be doing to ensure great results? How can managers, salespeople, and marketing people know that they are on the right track for good results—a positive bottom-line result both in good times and in hard times?

This book scientifically and mathematically with *MoneyMath* shows how you can help improve profits in your company. It also establishes the connection between good customer service and stronger profitability. It doesn't matter whether you are the CEO or the rookie salesperson. The benefits to you will be greater job security, understanding of strong and weak companies, and, best of all, you will be able to contribute to a stronger bottom line each time you interact with a customer.

No company is too big or too small not to benefit from putting the contents of this book into practice. No individual is too rich or too poor not to study the contents of this book to the final chapter and figure out how to change his selling approach, management approach, or marketing strategies.

The benefit to your business or corporation is that you will improve your profitability as you apply what you learn. The benefit to you as an individual is that you will be more secure in your personal remuneration as a result of understanding how your company or any company achieves its bottom line.

Application

☑ As an individual, it's a wise move to obtain and read the published financial reports of the company for which you work.

☑ If it's a small company, it may be harder, but you can ask the boss, "How are we doing? What do the margins look like?"

☑ Follow the public statements of senior executives, and look at the marketplace behavior of the company. Do they offer crazy discounts just to "kill the competition"? Are they making statements to cover their butts?

☑ Do you know the remuneration of the CEO and senior executives, and is it tied to results? What are the results?

☑ Read the following books: *Moments of Truth* by Jan Carlzon (Harper Collins, 1989); *Customers for Life* by Carl Sewell (Pocket Books, 1998; Currency, 2002); *The Nordstrom Way: The Inside Story of America's #1 Customer Service Company* by Robert Spector and Patrick McCarthy (Wiley, 1996).

LIST OF ACTIONS I CAN TAKE

_____

_____

_____

_____

_____

CHAPTER TWO

Every Business Needs It: Margin

He who loses money loses much;
  He who loses a friend loses much more;
    He who loses faith loses all.

—Anonymous

No matter what anyone tells you, *all* businesses run on margin. Margin and cash flow are absolutely essential in an operating business, whether you are the CEO, chairman, CFO, or sales representative. The term *margin* needs defining because many top-level managers believe that return on investment (ROI)—the ratio of the final or net profit to the capital employed as a percentage return—is the most important need. However, in most operating businesses, there has to be a satisfactory return on sales (ROS) *before* a return on investment can occur. It is margin that generates net profit before interest and tax. Margin can be viewed in two ways—as margin dollars or as a percentage of the selling price obtained.

When something is sold to a customer by an organization, the goal is to structure the selling price in such way that it makes a positive dollar margin. Another way to consider this is that the price needs to cover all the costs associated with the product or service sold plus a little bit more called net profit. In turn, the net profit needs to cover the interest and taxes as well as providing a return for the owners of the company. Nonprofit organizations or government departments only need to cover their costs.

This concept is more easily understood when company figures are charted into a "model of cost," as in Figure 2.1. The model of cost diagram is the best way to understand the margin needed in the daily transactions to ensure that the goods or services are paid for and the bills associated with the overhead are covered. The selling price minus the cost of goods sold (COG) equals the gross profit (GP). The interest referred to in Figure 2.1 is usually interest cost on borrowings (long-term debt) used to capitalize the organization. "Tax" refers to corporate tax, which varies according to the country, state, and city in which you locate your head office.

Concept of Margin

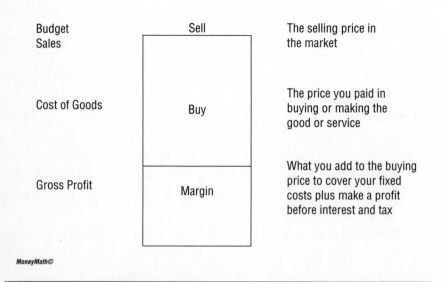

Budget Sales	Sell	The selling price in the market
Cost of Goods	Buy	The price you paid in buying or making the good or service
Gross Profit	Margin	What you add to the buying price to cover your fixed costs plus make a profit before interest and tax

MoneyMath©

FIGURE 2.1   Concept of Margin

The initial model of cost can be worked up from the company bud-get at the beginning of the year. There will be the budgeted sales value, made up from the cost of goods plus the margin needed to cover the overhead and profit. The budgeted profit also has to be large enough to cover interest payments and taxes so earnings are available to the owners or to invest back in the firm so that the business grows.

After trading has taken place, the model of cost can also be extrap-olated from the monthly profit and loss (P&L) statement using the lines of account and expenses. As costs are incurred they are recorded line by line into the accounts. All the costs associated with the operating over-heads are termed *fixed costs*. These fixed costs are married to the net profit to form the margin, or gross profit margin as it is also referred to.

In Figure 2.2 we see that the box labeled "Margin" in Figure 2.1 has now been split into two parts—the fixed costs (FC), or overhead, and

Turning Margin into Profit

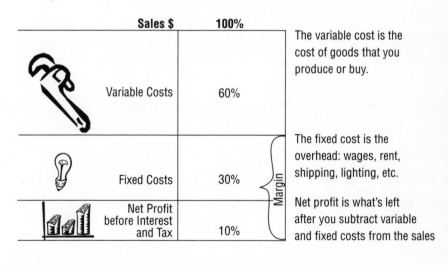

	Sales $	100%	
	Variable Costs	60%	The variable cost is the cost of goods that you produce or buy.
	Fixed Costs	30%	The fixed cost is the overhead: wages, rent, shipping, lighting, etc.
	Net Profit before Interest and Tax	10%	Net profit is what's left after you subtract variable and fixed costs from the sales

MoneyMath©

FIGURE 2.2   Turning Margin into Profit?

the net profit (NP), also referred to as earnings before interest and tax (EBIT). Nothing in the math world has changed the basic business success formula: revenue minus costs equals profit (R – C = P). Insufficient margin in your daily transactions shrinks the bottom box, the profit, because the overhead costs have to be paid as a priority and these come out of the margin first. Those overhead costs often include wages, rent, electricity, stationery, insurance, advertising, and other similar costs.

For the purposes of this discussion, the term *variable costs* is defined as the costs associated with buying or producing the item being sold. Variable costs go up or down proportionately with sales volume—that's why they are called variable. When the sales move, so do the variable costs; fixed costs remain the same in dollar terms whether you sell something or not. In the end, if the gross margin is less than the combined figure of the fixed costs and the targeted net profit margin, then some of the bills may not be paid, and that is when the creditors (those to whom you owe money) start to look closely at your operations.

From the abbreviated list of costs mentioned previously, in which ones do you have the most personal interest if you are employed? Correct, the wages—your wages and the wages of the employees and staff who work for you. If you want higher wages, you need to earn higher margin or protect the margin by cutting waste, or by operating more productively. If the margin bucket has less in it, your firm has less to play with to reward you and those who report to you. If you want increased return on your stock options, get the margins and net profit up.

Different industries have different models of cost. A typical manufacturing operation might have a 50/40/10 model (see Figure 2.3). This means that 50 percent of the costs are related to the goods they produce, to which is added 40 percent overhead costs, and the goal is a 10 percent net profit.

From Figure 2.3, an article produced for a cost of $100 would be sold for $200. Within that price is a $100 margin which covers $80 of fixed costs recovery (40 percent) and $20 net profit (10 percent).

Typical Factory Model of Cost

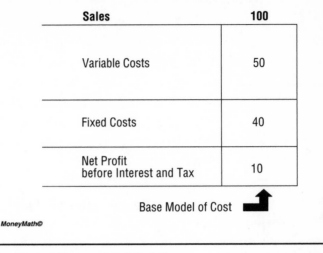

Sales	100
Variable Costs	50
Fixed Costs	40
Net Profit before Interest and Tax	10

Base Model of Cost

MoneyMath©

FIGURE 2.3   Typical Factory Model of Cost

None of this is rocket science, but it is mandatory knowledge for business survival and business success! As one might expect, the factory model does not fit all types of businesses; therefore, typical models for retail and service industries are presented in Figures 2.4 and 2.5. No two business models are ever the same.

Retailers, more than any other business, have to watch their margins on a daily basis. The reason for the close monitoring is that it could be a whole month before you notice slippage that requires action. In my opinion that is far too long to wait to find out there is something wrong. While the model in Figure 2.4 is a good one as far as retail is concerned, 5 percent net profit is actually more common. In the typical retail model of cost, the majority of costs are normally tied up with the inventory or the stock (70 percent in this figure). As a result, usually the margin is smaller than for factories and is easily eroded by discounting.

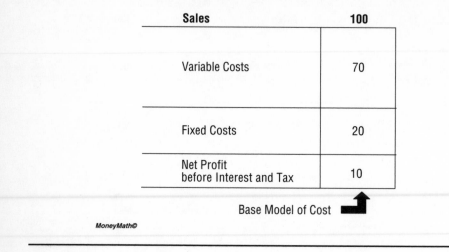

Typical Retail Model of Cost

Sales	100
Variable Costs	70
Fixed Costs	20
Net Profit before Interest and Tax	10

Base Model of Cost

MoneyMath©

FIGURE 2.4   Typical Retail Model of Cost

Typical Service Industry (Lawyers, Accountants . . .) Model of Cost

Sales	100
Variable Costs	35
Fixed Costs	40
Net Profit before Interest and Tax	25

Base Model of Cost

MoneyMath©

FIGURE 2.5   Typical Service Industry Model of Cost

By contrast, the model of cost for the service industry (referring to traditional professional offices such as attorneys, accountants, and the like) usually breaks down into thirds—one-third variable costs, one-third fixed costs, and one-third net profit. The percentages can vary quite a bit, but in general it is a good rule of thumb. To demonstrate this concept in Figure 2.5, the guide of one-third is varied slightly.

It is essential to recognize that service is an important element in all businesses and can be an important factor in generating a positive bottom line. Service can be defined in two ways. One accepted view of service is what a technician, professional, or waitperson does to keep things running smoothly. Another, and in our view more important, definition is the perception a customer has of the friendliness and helpfulness accompanying any transaction with your firm. This is more subtle, but it is measurable and can be a strong weapon for better prices, which means better profits.

Additionally, because there is often little capital cost to setting up a service business, margins can be quite healthy. This is another good reason to attach high quality service and services to commodity or "me too" products in any given market. The higher margins in the service, when added to the low-margin product, help lift the overall margin. When this is achieved, it is called *value-adding* service.

In my organization's in-house seminars for technicians in service firms, we have seen margins increase by 5 to 15 percent when quality service is loaded onto a struggling product. Here is an example using fire extinguishers:

Basic Wall Mount Model (A Struggling Product)

Factory cost	$35	87.5%
Selling price	$40	100%
Margin	$5	12.5%

With a Wall Sign Added to It (Value-Adding Service)

Sign cost	$0.50	10%
Selling price	$5.00	100%
Margin	$4.50	90%

Combination of Struggling Product and Value-Adding Service

Total cost	$35.50	78.9%
Selling price	$45.00	100%
New margin	$9.50	21.1%

Clearly the margin has gone from 12.5 percent on the basic extinguisher to 21.1 percent when it is sold together with a low-cost sign.

It is not difficult to teach service technicians how to do this kind of value-adding service. Just don't call it "sales training" or they will run a mile away!

McDonald's uses value-adding service on each transaction in its stores. In its six-step service approach to customers, this is the third step, *up-selling*: "Would you like some fries with that?" Now you might say to yourself, "If I wanted fries I would have said so!" However, while some customers become rude when asked this question, a significant number of customers are prompted in this way to spend a little bit more on their meal. The effect of this value-adding service is to increase the ticket value by about 15 percent, and the transaction margin is thereby increased. In a business with sales of over $20.460 billion a year (as of fiscal year 2005), that one little question can be worth around a cool $30.6 million in additional profit dollars.

Now, the additional profit is not the amazing thing. The amazing thing is that the employees who do this are trained to do so, and the majority of them are teenagers. In other words, McDonald's knows how to train teenagers to possibly receive verbal abuse from an irate customer and then come back smiling for more service work. That is quite an achievement. Would you keep doing it despite a rude response from some customers who resent being asked if they want fries? The effect is that it enlarges the sale and the margin for McDonald's restaurants worldwide.

Of course, lots of businesses train their staff to do this. McDonald's is used as an example here because it is a great model, and I trained and worked there at one time. What "up sell" question could your people ask? When your adult staff tell you that they cannot perform value-adding for you, remind them that teenagers are already doing it at McDonald's.

So far I have presented the concept of margin in a positive light, but what happens and what does it mean if your margin is insufficient? Insufficient margin means that your fixed costs overrun the margin, leaving you insufficient net profit. If a business does not reach the breakeven point (where the sales price covers variable and fixed costs) in its transactions, it is difficult to have a positive bottom line. Figure 2.6 presents the concept of breakeven.

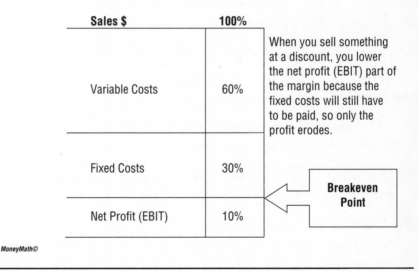

FIGURE 2.6 Breakeven Point

When you have paid your factory for what it manufactures for you or your supplier for the goods they sold you, plus any costs that run with those goods, then you have paid your variable costs, which usually approximates your cost of goods. Then when you have paid your overhead, your fixed costs, you have taken care of most of the expenses. If there is nothing left after this, then you have run your transactions up to the breakeven point. You have covered your costs but there is no profit residual left so you are basically running a nonprofit business.

Considering the fact that you could be getting a reasonable interest rate for the capital that is invested in your business, if all you do is constantly reach breakeven you would be better off parking the money in the bank instead of running the business. The deposit in the bank would at least give you a positive return. At the beginning of this chapter we noted that many businesses say return on investment is an important need. A chief lesson learned here is that an operating return on investment (ROI) is always preceded by a positive return on sales (ROS).

Okay, so we need a margin to survive, and we need sufficient margin to cover all our costs with a bit left over, which we call net profit or EBIT. Success: happy days!

Application

- ☑ As a manager do you know the average margin you need to the first decimal point? If not, search today.

- ☑ As a salesperson, do you know how to calculate your margins on the run when customers ask for an instant quote?

- ☑ To the senior executive/CEO/CFO: Do you know the margins generated on yesterday's sales? by product? by territory? by salesperson? If not, get some software that can quickly tell you.

☑ Can you afford to wait a month to discover a hole in the *Titanic*? Ask your accounting staff for a weekly P&L statement; for many companies the pace of business is now too fast for a monthly P&L to be timely.

☑ Do you have a training program for new and young hires to correct any math errors they may bring into your firm?

LIST OF ACTIONS I CAN TAKE

_____

_____

_____

_____

_____

CHAPTER THREE

Issues Affecting Healthy Margins in Sales

Mathematics, rightly viewed, possesses not only truth, but supreme beauty—a beauty cold and austere, like that of sculpture.
—Bertrand Russell (1872–1970)

A major issue affecting healthy margins is the confusion that exists between margin and markup. Confusion between them—perhaps because they both start with the same sound and both pertain to the underlying cost versus sales price—can lead to disastrous results. It is important to appreciate the mathematical fact that the numbers correlating markup and margin never ever change—not ever!

As shown in Table 3.1, markup figures are always higher than margin figures. The reason is that markup is a function of the total price while margin is the relationship between cost of goods sold and gross profit. Margin figures range from 1 to 100 percent, but markup figures range from 1 to 10,000 percent. The math issue occurs when the margin required surpasses 50 percent, or a 100 percent markup.

When operating margins required in some organizations pass the 50 percent mark it severely tests the people who are frail at pricing. They suddenly seem to stop believing in the free market principle.

Markups for a Given Margin

Margin	Markup	Margin	Markup	Margin	Markup	Margin	Markup
1%	1.1%	20%	25%	27%	37%	35%	53.8%
2.5%	2.6%	21%	26.6%	28%	38.9%	40%	66.7%
5.0%	5.3%	22%	28.2%	29%	40.8%	45%	81.8%
7.5%	8.1%	23%	29.9%	30%	42.9%	50%	100%
10%	11.1%	24%	31.5%	31%	44.9%	55%	122%
12.5%	14.2%	25%	33.3%	32%	47%	60%	150%
15%	17.6%	26%	35.1%	33%	50%	70%	233%

MoneyMath©

TABLE 3.1   Markups Needed for a Given Margin

I remember asking a young employee to price something not in the price list and asking her to apply a 400 percent markup. She instantly retorted, "I'm not going to do it. I don't agree with that. You're a capitalist pig to do that!" I was somewhat stunned at the outburst because I was the CEO, but I decided to turn it into a lesson by saying, "Okay, let's talk tomorrow about it." The next day we spoke and I said I had changed my mind: "Let's just do 80 percent margin, okay?" to which she replied, "Sure, that's much better, boss." Now you may be laughing, but I could not understand at the time why she answered that way. After all, a 400 percent markup is an 80 percent margin—it is identical math.

The difference between margin and markup accelerates as the margin gets larger. For example, at the very top end, a 98 percent margin requires a 4,900 percent markup, which sounds like a lot. The divergence chart in Figure 3.1 shows why. At 50 percent margin the markup is 100 percent, but after that crossover point the markups leap away exponen-

Margin/Markup Divergence

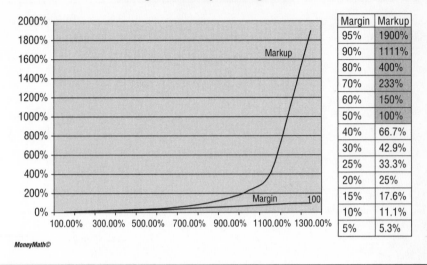

Margin	Markup
95%	1900%
90%	1111%
80%	400%
70%	233%
60%	150%
50%	100%
40%	66.7%
30%	42.9%
25%	33.3%
20%	25%
15%	17.6%
10%	11.1%
5%	5.3%

MoneyMath©

FIGURE 3.1 Margin/Markup Divergence Chart

tially toward the thousands while the margin goes steadily on a straight line to 100 percent.

There are at least three reasons why so many people, especially the younger folk, do not understand this. First, in Western societies, math skills are generally poor by comparison to Eastern societies (Asians). I believe this is because Asian students go to school primarily to learn, and there is huge loss of face in the family if a child comes home with poor results.

It is interesting to look at a comparison of the ranking of math skills at Grade 4, then Grade 8, and lastly Grade 12 in 2005, as listed by the United Nations (see Table 3.2). The leading countries are mostly Asian, whereas the United States comes in at number 28, way down the list for Grade 8. Now, what sort of management and selling skills are you going to get from employees who are weak at math?

The sad thing is that Western kids, particularly American kids, start off fairly high up the scale in Grade 4, but by the time American

TABLE 3.2   Selected Math Skills Scores, Grades 4, 8, and 12

	GRADE 4		GRADE 8		GRADE 12	
RANK	**NATION**	**SCORE**	**NATION**	**SCORE**	**NATION**	**SCORE**
1.	Singapore	625	Singapore	643	Netherlands	560
2.	Korea	611	Korea	607	Sweden	552
3.	Japan	597	Japan	605	Denmark	547
4.	Hong Kong	587	Hong Kong	588	Switzerland	540
5.	Netherlands	577	Belgium	565	Iceland	534
6.	Czech Republic	567	Czech Republic	564	Norway	528
7.	Austria	559	Slovak Repub.	547	France	523
8.	Slovenia	552	Switzerland	545	New Zealand	522
9.	Ireland	550	Netherlands	541	Australia	522
10.	Hungary	548	Slovenia	541	Canada	519
11.	Australia	546	Bulgaria	540	Austria	518
12.	**United States**	**545**	Austria	539	Slovenia	512
13.	Canada	532	France	538	Germany	495
14.	Israel	531	Hungary	537	Hungary	483
15.	Latvia	525	Russian Fed.	535	Italy	476
16.	Scotland	520	Australia	530	Russian Fed.	471
17.	England	513	Ireland	527	Lithuania	469
18.	Cyprus	502	Canada	527	Czech Republic	466
19.	Norway	502	Belgium	526	**United States**	**461**
20.	New Zealand	499	Sweden	519	Cyprus	446
21.	Greece	492	Thailand	512	South Africa	356
22.	Thailand	490	Israel	512		
23.	Portugal	475	Germany	509		
24.	Iceland	474	New Zealand	508		
25.	Iran	429	England	506		
26.	Kuwait	400	Norway	503		
27.			Denmark	502		
28.			**United States**	**500**		
29.			Scotland	498		
30.			Latvia	493		
31.			Spain	487		
32.			Iceland	487		
33.			Greece	484		
34.			Romania	482		
35.			Lithuania	477		
36.			Cyprus	474		
37.			Portugal	454		
38.			Iran	428		
39.			Kuwait	392		
40.			Colombia	385		
41.			South Africa	354		
	Grade Average	**529**	**Grade Average**	**513**	**Grade Average**	**500**

students reach Grade 12 they are way below world averages, scoring 461 against the world average of 500. Even at Grade 8, the slide is on for the American student. This is one conclusive proof that the U.S. school system is severely lacking in measurement terms, in its curriculum quality, in discipline terms, and in educational focus. Until strong measurement is applied to learning outcomes in schools, it will stay in this weakened state of affairs. This is sad for kids and even sadder for their business careers—they will struggle to calculate things. But America's present wealth enables her to buy mathematicians from overseas.

As a businessperson employing others, you may have a distinct need to first test new employees as to their math skills and, second, to train them to overcome the deficiencies handed on to you by the school system. In today's business climate this is an unfortunate but necessary business expense.

The second factor affecting understanding of margin in business also stems from the school system. It is a philosophical problem loosely called socialism or Marxism. In colleges and universities across the United States, teachers influence students by running this country down, demeaning capitalism, stressing "oppression" against minorities and women, and denouncing anything different from their point of view. All too often the prevailing attitude is, "Do not confuse me with facts—my mind is made up." Many students graduate with a social conscience but weak math skills, resulting in employment difficulties.

American Enterprise magazine of Washington, D.C., in 2002 examined the political registrations of professors in 20 colleges and universities. The study divided the registrations into those belonging to a "party of the left"—either Democrat, Greens, or some other liberal political party—and a "party of the right," either Republican or Libertarian. Take, for example, UCLA. Of the 31 English professors with a registered political affiliation, 29 belonged to a party of the left. Of the 56 history professors, 53 belonged to a party of the left. Of 13 journalism professors with an affiliation, 12 belonged to a party of the left. Of 17 political science professors with a registration, 16 belonged to a party of the left. And of the 33 women's studies professors, 31 belonged to a party of the left.

Going to the east coast, what about Cornell University? Of the 12 anthropology professors, 11 were registered to a party of the left. Of 13 economics professors, 10 were with a party of the left. Also on the left were 35 out of 36 English professors. All 29 history professors were registered with a party of the left. Of the 17 political science professors, 16 were registered to the left. Psychology professors totaled 25 to the left, out of 26. Sociology managed all 7 professors registered to the left. In women's studies, 33 were to the left and zero to the right.

Stanford University? Anthropology, 15 of 16 to the left; economics, 21 of 28; English, 31 of 33; history, 22 of 24; political science, 26 of 30; psychology, 20 of 20; sociology, 11 of 12; and women's studies, 5 of 5.

And of Ivy League humanities professors, 57 percent called themselves Democrat, and only 3 percent Republican. When asked to identify the best United States president in the last 40 years, they named, by the largest plurality, Bill Clinton. So is it any wonder that fresh recruits from college are leaning heavily against capitalism from the philosophical viewpoint from day one? Many of the graduates leaving universities in this mental condition will be unsuitable for employment in the "evil world of business" without retraining.

To get your team solidly supporting free enterprise you will need to constantly have conferences where professional speakers hammer away at the "left brainwashed" college graduates. It takes time, but as they start to earn their own living and pay taxes, many of them get the message and realize that the idealism of Marx and Engels has no lasting place in the real world of measured results and performance. They learn that a distributive philosophy takes the cow's milk and only sells it, but the generative philosophy creates more cows. This is why the Soviet Union failed.

The third area of influence over the concept of margin in sales, marketing, and management is the type of advertising that is shown and published in the media, in particular via television and the Web. The television influence is a lot more insidious and actually reinforces the poor math skills picked up in the school system. These venues have such power over the mind because television and the computer screen provide the three attention-getting attributes of color, movement, and sound all at the same time.

You will be astonished when you look at the figures in Table 3.3 and consider the implications to your life.

Here is the scary part: There are 168 hours in a week, but only 112 hours that you can use productively—the remaining 56 hours are spent sleeping. Obviously there are other basic functions and necessities that consume part of our awake hours, but for the current discussion let's use 112 base hours.

In the United States, if you are that average TV/Web user at 27.8 hours, you will actually be donating a whopping 25 percent of your life, your time, and your mind to various media barons like Ted Turner (AOL/Time Warner), Sumner Redstone (CBS), or Rupert Murdoch (Fox). The Internet is changing people's habits and is steadily overhauling TV as it did in the United Kingdom. A study commissioned by Google and reported in the British newspaper *The Guardian* in March 2006 indicated that the average Briton spends 164 minutes a day on the Web and only 148 minutes watching television. Apart from sleeping and working, the Web and TV take most of their time.

Question: If a media baron stopped you on the street and asked you

TABLE 3.3   Weekly TV Viewing and Web Hours for Selected Countries

COUNTRY	AVERAGE WEEKLY TV	ON THE WEB (Not at Work)
United States	19 hours	8.8 hours
United Kingdom	18 hours	8.8 hours
Hong Kong	16.7 hours	10.7 hours
Japan	17.9 hours	6.9 hours
Australia	13.3 hours	7 hours

Source: National TV Auditing Associations, 2005.

to sign a contract requiring you to give him 25 percent of your brain or life or time, would you sign it?

Now for the next question: What is going into your mind from the 19 hours of TV input? Well, approximately 3.8 hours of that weekly TV contains advertisements, and what kind of advertisements are they? Many of the ads are retail or car ads that go something like this: "Lowest priced cars in town, nothing down, interest-free for three years, $5,000 off factory invoice, come and get them, sale ends Sunday!"

This kind of advertising insinuates that to be a successful business you have to sell great *volumes* of product, and the more you sell, the more successful you become. The constant ranting and yelling style ads in some industries are now accepted as the way to do business. Unfortunately, the constant brainwashing of this kind, with over a quarter of one's life given over to it, means that most of our adult familiarity is actually television hype. The underlying philosophy of this hype is the volume-selling argument or, put another way, the more you sell the better it is. It is worth noting that this volume-selling philosophy is part and parcel of strategic management and marketing taught in business programs at some elite universities.

The reason why so many companies yell discounts at us on TV is because mathematically a discount is designed to increase the volume of goods or services sold, and it can be very effective when the math is correct. Conversely, it is extremely damaging when the math does not work out. The risk with discounts is that the margin can be eroded to the point where the overhead cannot be paid and the business gets into trouble. Guess what—when people with weak math skills are propagandized for years with TV ads portraying discounts, the first business move they will make is to discount the product or service they sell because they do not know any different. This applies to managers, salespeople—in essence, anybody connected to customers and the price.

Math clearly demonstrates that if you want to make a profit from your sales volume, discounts done in isolation are *not* the most effective way. In our testing of employees around the world on this question, 60 percent erroneously say that increasing sales volume is the most effective way to lift margins and profits in a business.

Now I know you personally do not think this way, nor do you have any staff who are inclined this way. We are referring to your competitors here—they are the ones who start the discounting, aren't they?

Incidentally, from a personal time management viewpoint, one of the easiest ways to reclaim your life is to dramatically reduce the hours you watch TV or spend on the Web. The reclaimed time can be put back into productive activities like hugging your kids, reading a good book, learning to play a musical instrument, doing community service, and a myriad of other things that *you* do rather than have done *to* you. As life progresses, humans fall into three groups—there are those who make things happen, those who watch things happen, and finally there is the group who say "What happened?" Try and get yourself into that first group of people who make things happen.

Another issue affecting the ability to obtain effective margins is the software used to calculate prices or the price list. In a company requiring a 40 percent margin, the markup has to be 66.7 percent. However, if the algorithm used by the software program that calculates your prices runs on markup, as several of them do, it will mark up your pricing or price list by 40 percent, which yields a margin of only 28.6 percent. That means you have accidentally blown 11.4 percent of your gross profit—obviously not a good way to run a business that wants to generate positive bottom lines.

Not long ago I was speaking to a group of managers and salespeople at an air-conditioning company, and I asked them what software they used to price things. They replied "Pronto." I asked if they knew whether it used markup or margin when it calculated their prices. The sales and marketing director said he did not know. He left the room and walked down to the IT manager's office to ask, and found that it in their case the program used markup.

Unfortunately, the operation needed a 40 percent *margin* and not a 40 percent markup. But they learned this too late—they had lost money that year, and just before I got there they had written a big contract that was enough to sink them. They went broke and were sold off to a conglomerate for $2.00. The sales director was fired along with many more staff. There was absolutely nothing wrong with their software, but management and the sales staff did not fully appreciate the difference between margin and markup, nor did they know which one was being used in the program. If their math skills had been sharper or if they paid more attention to financial statements, as recommended in Chapter 2, they would have recognized the problem (after all, there is a significant difference between 40 percent and 28.6 percent gross profit) and might still be in business today.

At another company in South Africa, I asked the same question to both the sales director and the IT manager simultaneously. The sales director said markup and the IT manager said margin. I know there are problems when I hear those kinds of answers. Either they do not know or they are guessing. In either case it does not bode well for generating a positive profit. No guesses please—the lifeblood of the business is margins!

Table 3.4 shows the potential damage of markup/margin confusion. Notice that for those organizations needing 40, 50, or 60 percent gross profit margin, the error climbs beyond 10 percent. If your net profit goal was 10 percent you have wiped that out and gone into negative margin territory. Of course, the overall result depends on how many transactions fall into this category. Similarly, if you are in a retail business operating, say, in the 25 to 30 percent margin region and seeking a net profit of 5 percent, you have wiped out your net profit with this margin pricing error.

Again, this is math that is never going to change to suit rationalizations, excuses, or mistakes. We have to get it right to be happy puppies.

Another pitfall that I discovered from talking with a CEO (who was previously a CFO) is the "catch up" situation when margins start to fall short. His company was importing goods and the currency changed on them fairly quickly, necessitating a price rise across the board. The

Percent Margin Lost When Confused with Markup

Margin Required within Selling Price Calculation

Markup	10%	15%	20%	25%	30%	40%	50%	60%
10%	−0.9%							
15%		−2.0%						
20%			−3.3%					
25%				−5.0%				
30%					−6.9%			
40%						−11.4%		
50%							−16.7%	
60%								−22.8%

MoneyMath©

TABLE 3.4   Percent Margin Lost When Confused with Markup

CEO of this $200 million sales company, who is a really nice guy, needed a 7 percent increase in the margin to make up for the currency downturn that had suddenly hit them.

I asked him what he was going to do and he said, "Put my prices up by 7 percent!" I said "Bad luck, you're going lose a bunch of money that way!" He said, "How do you figure that out?" I replied, "If you put your prices up by 7 percent you do not get 7 percent margin out of it. You get 7 percent divided by 107, which equals 6.5 percent, exactly 0.5 percent short of what you need. Multiply 0.5 percent by $200 million in annual sales, and you have a $1 million mistake made by you, the CEO, in the privacy of your office, with only me as a witness." He went red in the face and asked me to show that to him on a calculator, which I did. He said thanks and then asked me not to tell any of his staff that he had not understood this important concept. I was glad I was there to help, but I went out of his office flabbergasted.

Have a look at the *MoneyMath* chart in Table 3.5, which shows the relationship between markup and margin. When you increase your prices by 10 percent it is a *markup* of 10 percent, and it does not yield an added 10 percent margin. The 10 percent markup in price gives you only a 9.1 percent increase in the margin. The math is 10 divided by 110, which equals 9.1.

A second example: If you increase price by 25 percent, what is the margin increase? The math is 25 divided by 125, which equals a 20 percent margin generated—a 5 percent mistake that will significantly damage the positive profit. And it's easy to make this mistake when you are in a hurry.

Salespeople are often railroaded by buyers who say they want a price on a special right away. It goes like this: "Come on, I'm in a hurry—what's your price? What's your price??" The sales representative gets flummoxed and, instead of achieving 40 percent margin, simply adds 40 percent on to the cost, and bingo, the buyer has an immediate bargain.

Margins for Given Markups

Markup	Margin	Markup	Margin	Markup	Margin	Markup	Margin
1%	0.99%	20%	16.6%	27%	21.3%	35%	25.9%
2.5%	2.43%	21%	17.4%	28%	21.9%	40%	28.6%
5.0%	4.76%	22%	18%	29%	22.5%	50%	33.3%
7.5%	6.98%	23%	18.7%	30%	23.1%	100%	50%
10%	9.1%	24%	19.4%	31%	23.7%	200%	66.7%
12.5%	11.1%	25%	20%	32%	24.2%	300%	75%
15%	13.0%	26%	20.6%	33%	24.8%	400%	80%

MoneyMath©

TABLE 3.5   Margins for Given Markups

The representative will have made only 28.6 percent margin when 40 percent was required. Most if not all of the profit on that transaction will have been lost.

Score: buyer 1, sales representative 0. No contest!

Do you think buyers are trained to watch for these errors and take advantage of them? Do you think a buyer is going to say, "Excuse me, but I don't think you got your full company margin in that calculation. Do you want to work it out again for me?" Pigs will fly before that will happen.

Application

☑ All pricing needs to be checked before it is passed over to the buyer.

☑ All price lists need to be proofread and double-checked by a senior manager before publication.

☑ Test your new employees on the math behind margin and markup.

☑ Check how your software works with regard to calculating prices and whether it uses margin or markup math.

LIST OF ACTIONS I CAN TAKE

_____

_____

_____

_____

_____

CHAPTER FOUR

The Weapon of Math Instruction

Probable impossibilities are to be preferred to improbable possibilities.
—Aristotle (384–322 B.C.)

Some time ago, I stumbled onto some amazing math that changed my sales approach, my management style, and my marketing strategies forever. Yes, forever! It changed them for the better, because it showed me how to achieve higher profitability and how to easily and quickly turn a company around. *MoneyMath.*

As you read this chapter, I hope you too will see the math clearly, and make some decisions about how you are involved with your own company's bottom line. Please accept my apology if you have a midlife business crisis after reading this chapter; it *has* been known to happen.

There are three basic ways to improve a company's bottom line. You can (1) sell more products or services (the volume approach); (2) cut the costs of doing business (popular with accountants); or (3) change your prices (last resort by many).

We have been asking audiences around the world this question: "Assuming everything else stayed the same in your business, which of those strategies would give you the biggest improvement on the bottom line (net profit)?" Before reading on, jot down your answer.

The voting result from our worldwide research comes out as follows: 60 percent vote for (1) sell more; 20 percent vote for (2) cut costs; and 20 percent vote for (3) raise prices. In fact, relative to (3), a small number usually say, "*Lower* the prices." We will have something to say about this later.

Keep in mind as you look at Figure 4.1 that it is only a *math* question. I am going to take this retail model and show some math that is awesome in its power and that will begin the process of upgrading your managing, marketing, and selling.

The base retail model, listed in the first column on the left, is sales volume of 100, variable costs of 70, fixed costs of 20, and net profit of 10. In order to demonstrate the impact on profits let's increase the sales volume by 10 percent in the second column; then, in the third one, let's re-

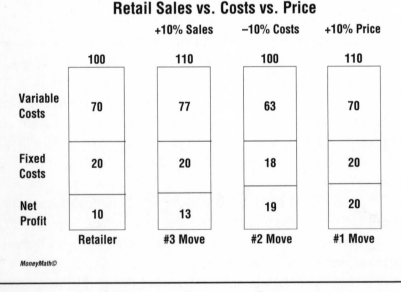

Retail Sales vs. Costs vs. Price

		+10% Sales	−10% Costs	+10% Price
	100	110	100	110
Variable Costs	70	77	63	70
Fixed Costs	20	20	18	20
Net Profit	10	13	19	20
	Retailer	#3 Move	#2 Move	#1 Move

MoneyMath©

FIGURE 4.1   Retail Sales versus Costs versus Price

duce all the costs, both variable and fixed, by 10 percent; and finally, in the fourth column, let's increase the price by 10 percent. In each case the underlying move is 10 percent.

As I said, this is purely a math exercise, set up to discover which move has the best impact on net profit. Do not worry about the effect it has on your market—we cover that aspect in a later chapter, and you will most likely be surprised with our findings. For now, we need to know which move has the greatest power in it. Follow the text while referring to Figure 4.1.

In the sales volume increase column, where sales have increased from 100 to 110, the variable costs also increase by 10 percent to create the additional sales, so that figure goes from 70 to 77. The fixed costs remain at 20, because you can absorb a 10 percent increase in sales volume with a negligible increase in fixed costs. Subtract 77 and 20 from 110 and your new net profit is 13, a gain of three, or a 3 percent increase from the 10 we started with.

This teaches us that it is a good thing to strive to increase sales because that *does* contribute to the growth of the bottom line. But is it the best improvement we can make here?

In the next column, instead of changing the sales value, we are reducing costs: the variable costs and the fixed costs by 10 percent. This is known as cost cutting, downsizing, or outsourcing, and is usually characterized by chopping off heads in an organization. As later charts show, cutting personnel is one of the crudest ways to fix an ailing company. However, in the meantime, let us look mathematically at our model.

The sales value remains 100, while the variable cost of 70 is reduced by 10 percent to 63 and the fixed cost of 20 is reduced by 10 percent to 18. Added together, the original costs of 90 now total 81, which, when subtracted from 100, gives us a new net profit of 19, a gain of nine points over our original 10 points. Clearly, 9 percent is greater than the 3 percent we gained from a 10 percent increase in sales volume. Additionally, note that even if we cut fixed costs alone by 10 percent, we have a gain of two points, nearly as much as the 3 percent from selling 10 percent more—and there is a lot less trauma inflicted on the organization.

In the last column, we increase the price by 10 percent, changing the top line from 100 to 110. The variable costs do not change, because we are only changing revenue, *not* volume, so it remains at 70. The fixed costs also stay the same, so the bottom line climbs from 10 to 20, a gain of 10 points to double our net profit.

What this math has just demonstrated is that raising prices is *the* most powerful strategy in any and every business on the planet. There is no more powerful option than *price*. Price change beats cost reductions and is easily superior to increased volume.

Now let's go back to the voting: 60 percent say sales volume is best; 20 percent say cost cutting is best; and only 20 percent opt for price increases. That means 80 percent of managers and employees do not know the most profitable and powerful strategy for your business. They could be pushing your business in a less profitable direction, when just a little math training would change their whole approach.

Think about those TV ads, the math results from school, the teachers who say *profit* is a dirty word, and the possible errors in calculation of price discussed back in Chapter 3. It all adds up to one thing: The forces for price erosion are lined up solidly against your business and will strike all the time, reducing your prices and margins. I call this the Gravitational Law of Pricing. If prices can accidentally or deliberately be altered, they will be—*downward!*

Some suggested business wisdom that follows from this math: Regarding the area of sales volume, when you write your budget for the next period, try to grow your volume at the market rate. For example, if the market for your goods or services is growing at 10 percent, then you can reasonably expect your sales to grow by 10 percent also.

However, if you adopt a budget that calls for 30 percent sales growth in a market that is growing by 10 percent, then you will have to steal sales from someone else in the market. Your competitors will not like having their sales reduced, so they will retaliate against you in the form of a price war, or by discounting your major accounts because you discounted some of their customers.

This is called "competition," but it is not really competition based on product quality or service quality; it is mostly price cutting based on grabbing someone else's sales volume, or motivated by the ego of a senior executive who wants to be able to claim "We're number one in the market," at any price. The price-cutting philosophy is also called competitive strategy.

In the United States in 2005, the major airlines were all losing money—$10.8 billion according to the International Air Transport Association (IATA), while Southwest, the seventh largest, was profitable. What is the point of being the biggest airline in the world if you are broke and bleeding to death financially? I would ask: Do you want to be big and broke, instead of smaller and profitable? If it is ego or the blind sales volume argument behind your business philosophy, you will not be able to say no, and you will write sales at any price, regardless of the margin obtained.

Regarding costs, I recommend you try to run your organization at last year's overhead level or lower. That means your fixed cost budget would be retained for this year. Implementing this strategy is difficult, but it is a worthy goal for the simple reason that it puts gentle pressure on your fixed costs when compared to inflation. If inflation is 3 percent in your marketplace, then sticking to last year's overhead will equal a reduction of those costs by 3 percent.

Let us recognize that eventually the utility supplier, the phone company, and the landlord are going to increase their charges, so you have to take that into account. Needless to say, there should be ongoing analysis of all major costs, variable and fixed, on a disciplined and monthly basis. When the trends are north, it's time to take action.

Regarding pricing, I recommend your prices be increased by a minimum amount, based on the inflation rate in your market, in order to keep your margin constant. So if inflation is 3 percent, your margins should go up by 3 percent, which requires a price increase of 3.09

percent. I would raise prices by 1.6 percent in the first six months and 1.6 percent in the second six months. That actually gets you a 3.227 percent increase, which is a tad more than 1.6 times 2. Remember, every little bit of margin helps, while Murphy ("If anything can go wrong, it will") is just around the corner, waiting to throw a monkey wrench into your margins.

If you have major quality or service advantages over your competitors, you should be able to command a higher price. If you have major technical advantages in your product, again you should be able to obtain a higher price. In both cases, your *quality* is why your customers are prepared to pay you a higher price and hence bring you a better profit.

Suggestions to Salespeople, Managers, and Marketing Staff

Now that you know, or have remembered, that price is *the* most powerful tool in the selling equation, it will be incumbent on you to become very good at explaining, defending, and increasing your prices. This is tougher than selling the features, benefits, and value of the products or services themselves, but it is an equally important skill to explain the value inside price.

This means becoming proficient at explaining value to your customers and helping them understand that they get what they pay for. It also means learning the discount and price increase charts presented later in this book. A certain amount of volume increase is necessary when any discount is offered to a customer. The volume increase has to make up for the revenue lost by the discount.

Conversely, a certain amount of volume can be sacrificed against a price increase while still maintaining a healthy bottom line. When this latitude becomes known, you and your sales, marketing and management people become bulletproof in defense of margins and net profit, because you know the amount of room you have to move. Most audiences I work with say they have never seen charts like this *MoneyMath* before.

Because of the absolute importance of managing price and revenue, as well as sales volume, I strongly recommend to management that a price committee be established, or that another topic, *price management*, be added to the regular sales meeting agenda, and that it be placed right at the top. I have developed a file of questions entitled "101 Price Management Questions," and included it towards the end of this book as Appendix C. These questions can form a great first agenda for your price committee. (A file explanation is also available by e-mailing me at GrahamHFoster@msn.com.)

It is a popular opinion that only a few people affect prices in a business. Usually the sales and marketing staff are the ones accused of diluting the price the most, through discounts. However, if it is everyone's job to improve profits, then a number of other departments get into the picture.

The accountant who extends payment terms from 30 days up to 60 or 90 days is, in fact, giving a customer another discount. That accounting manager would deny being a discounter like the sales team, but still it is a discount. The shipping manager who runs the warehouse might do an urgent delivery for a special client without charging extra for it, which is in effect a discount to that customer. Of course, the shipping manager will also deny being a discounter. In reality, anyone and everyone who comes into contact with customers can affect the margins of the company in some way.

How many leaks do you need to sink the *Titanic*? Just one! If it is a big hole, it will sink quickly, and if it is a small hole, it will sink slowly. Nevertheless, it will still sink.

Your company should be doing everything possible to improve its prices in good times and to hold them constant in bad times. Increases can be taken across the board, or selectively by product and by customer. If your competitor raises prices, follow them up as soon as possible. Holding off in the fond hope that the market will suddenly discover you are cheaper will only cost you margin. Get with it!

Application

☑ Reassess the underlying business strategy in your organization. Is it "Sell, sell, sell!" or "Cut, cut, cut"? Or is it to increase price?

☑ To increase profit, start figuring out how you can *balance* the strategic effort along the lines of leveraged selling with gentle cost control and price increase.

☑ Start a price committee to manage the quality of revenues generated.

☑ Use the "101 Price Management Questions" in Appendix C to get started.

LIST OF ACTIONS I CAN TAKE

_____

_____

_____

_____

_____

CHAPTER FIVE

Balancing Your Company's Selling and Management Efforts

It's unwise to pay too much, but it's unwise to pay too little. When you pay too much you lose a little money, that is all. When you pay too little, you sometimes lose everything, because the thing you bought was incapable of doing the thing you bought it to do. The common law of business balance prohibits paying a little and getting a lot. It can't be done. If you deal with the lowest bidder, it's as well to add something for the risk you run. And if you do that, you will have enough to pay for something better.
—John Ruskin, English Philosopher (1819–1900)

I n the world of business, there are many differing philosophies on how to run things. However, one thing is crystal clear: If the activities of the sales team do not yield margin-rich sales results, or the internal management group cannot keep the costs under control, the combined effect of these two facets will eventually cause heads to roll, initially at the bottom and eventually at the top. All too often the ones at the bottom are harmless and suffer, while the ones at the top receive nice packages to step down. At the top they should roll, because for directors and managers, the *results* are the boss, so why should they receive a "golden parachute"—for failure?

Because of the massive amount of brainwashing done to folks who watch TV and soak up the discount advertisements screened there, the majority of your untrained employees will first move to close a sale by offering a discount, just like they saw on TV. Because they have experienced heavy discounting in shops, at airlines, with auto dealers, and so on, they conclude that is the way to do business. You cannot blame, them either, because without training they will not know any better. Management has the responsibility to establish proper training along with policies and procedures to avoid this discounting trap.

I have watched it happen; they walk into the office and say, "Hey, Boss, I've almost got that big deal in the bag for you, but I need another five percent to lock it up!" If the boss is volume-driven, the answer will be: "Sure! Don't come back without the order!"

So off trots the salesperson, with discretion over price, or, in reality, the margin, and crucifies the price in order to get the deal. Everybody feels good until the end of the month when the P&L statement suddenly indicates falling margins or, in fact, that the sales department lost money.

The worst thing you can say to the sales team is, "Don't come back without the order!" That is the signal to go and get sales at any price, no matter what margin—*if* any margin is left in the deal. If you have an incentive program for the sales force based on the volume of sales they make, almost certainly they drive relentlessly toward volume. This type of reward structure creates an agency problem—namely, for whom does the sales force work, themselves or the company? Maximizing sales may maximize the income of the sales force but not the profits of the company. Therefore, we recommend that you switch your incentive plan to a margin basis, or at least a blend of volume and margin, to counter the discounters in the pack.

In fact, to discount-oriented salespeople, the best selling is done on the boss, in the boss's office, pleading for more discount latitude to give away to the hungry customers. Instead of the energy going into selling value to the customer, it goes into cajoling the boss for another favor.

Table 5.1 should scare your socks off, when it finally grips you. Let us assume your organization needs 40 percent gross profit margin to oper-ate. Look at the figures in the 40 percent Gross Profit Margin column and imagine that we want to run a discount of 10 percent. In fact, a 10 percent discount is the world's most popular discount, but I was never able to find out the scientific reason why. One day, a smart sales manager said, "Count the number of fingers you have." Of course, 10 fingers, 10 percent discount! Easy! Now you'll want to count the fingers of new sales recruits, because without 10 fingers, they may not be able to discount for you. And if they have lost a finger you are ahead, because they will only discount 9 percent!

Looking again at Table 5.1, find where the 10 percent price cut row intersects the 40 percent margin column. The 33.3 percent listed

Look Before You Cut Prices

Gross Profit Margin to Be Generated

Price Cut	5%	10%	15%	20%	25%	30%	35%	40%	50%	60%
−1%	25%	11.1%	7.1%	5.3%	4.2%	3.4%	2.9%	2.6%	2.04%	1.7%
−5%	—	100%	50%	33.3%	25%	20%	16.7%	14.3%	11.1%	9.1%
−10% (most popular)	—	—	200%	100%	66.7%	50%	40%	33.3%	25%	20%
−15%	—	—	—	300%	150%	100%	75%	60%	42.8%	33.3%
−20%	—	—	—	—	400%	200%	133%	100%	66.7%	50%

Sales Percent Increase Required to Maintain Same Gross Profit

MoneyMath©

TABLE 5.1   Look Before You Cut Prices

there is the amount of increased sales volume you have to do to make up for the discounting. In other words, you have to increases sales revenue by one-third to maintain the same 40 percent gross margin that you had before. Why would you want to work 33.3 percent harder for nothing?

Is 10 percent discounting common in your business? If so, it is okay, *if* your business increases by one-third because of it. In a $100 million sales company, that is an extra $33 million in sales. However, if you are not getting that growth, the discount is eroding your margins and your bottom line is suffering because of it.

Unlike sales volume increases and cost reductions, everything you do with price is *directly* connected to your net profit (see Figure 5.1). If you cut your price by 10 percent when there was 40 percent in the margin, you dragged the margin down to 30 percent. If the net profit had previously been only 10 percent, the discount just wiped it out. Ouch!

How to Generate Net Profit

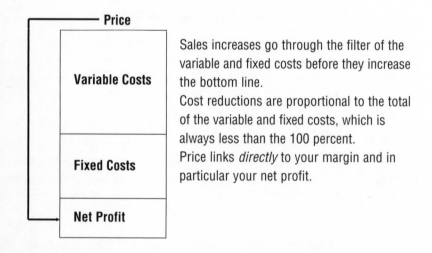

MoneyMath©

FIGURE 5.1   How to Generate Net Profit

Sales volume increases deliver profit improvement after passing through the twin filters of variable costs and fixed costs. Similarly, cost reductions deliver profit improvement proportionately to the total amount of the variable and fixed costs. So if your total cost is 90 percent of the selling price, a reduction of 10 percent in costs from the 90 percent will get you an additional 9 percent.

But with price, everything goes straight to the bottom line—100 percent of the discount impacts profits, as does 100 percent of the rise.

Because this is math, you simply cannot defy or ignore it to do something you feel is right. With the law of gravity, if you jump off a tall building you will not beat that law—you will confirm that it exists. Similarly, with *MoneyMath* you will not beat the math. Instead, it will turn around and bite you, and prove its validity, as Kmart found out in 2002, and GM and Ford have been finding out in 2005–2006.

If you thought there was something about discounting that did not quite jell, you were right. When you discount, you have to make up for it somewhere else, and the amount you have to make up is mathematically connected to the gross profit margin and the percentage discount. Of course, if you are selling a one-time capital item like a unique office building, with no repeat sales, then you have little chance to get back the margin given away in the discount exercise.

Notice I have not said, "Do not discount." There are occasions when it is an appropriate action. However, I am saying, be aware of the impact it has on your margins and net profit, and be prepared to make it up somewhere else in the deal or at some other time during the month. Do not discount just because you feel guilty making a reasonable profit. When the tough times return, you will be glad you made some extra hay in the good times.

Some markets become so discount-crazy that you have to first pad the prices with a buffer, only to lower them again at the time of the sale. That is okay, as long as your staff know the limits of the discounting and do not go below the set level. However, it is important to recognize that if you pad the price by 10 percent and then discount the padded price by

10 percent, the original target price is discounted by 1 percent. For example, $100 padded to $110 is then discounted by 10 percent (or $11), resulting in a new price of $99, or a 1 percent discount. This is okay as long as you make up the margin dollars by increased sales or cost reduction strategies.

In some mass markets, such as retail, where there is obvious and open competition, all sorts of damage can happen when employees make deals on the phone, without knowing the customer's needs, not accurately knowing the product benefits, and being unable to handle objections thrown at them.

We recently bought a screen over the phone to go with our data projection equipment. The first price we were quoted was $384. Then we phoned two other dealers and asked for details. They had similar products, and quoted $233 and $190, respectively. We asked about a discount for cash and one coughed up another 10 percent, so we pushed even harder. What about free delivery?

No problem! That saved us another $25. In the end, we paid only $185 for the unit, with every telephone salesperson offering us some sort of a deal. Finally, we paid with a credit card, so the dealer lost additional margin because of the merchant's fee. The discount was 55 percent in total.

With this lack of understanding of what they are doing, it is no wonder that hard times immediately put these types of traders to the wall. They are what I call fair-weather traders. They do okay in the good times, but they are out of their depth when tough times force them to manage. They don't make a profit; they only make a living.

In the balanced company, everybody knows why there are some sales you walk away from, recognizing that a sale with extremely low margin in it may not be needed because of the potential negative effect on profit. The staff in a well managed company knows why customers are divided into A, B, and C classes, and that it is mainly about margin and net profit, *not* volume and market share alone.

Your A-class customers are all large, and few in number. They get the best deals from you, but they also give you the most dollars to cover your fixed costs. We surround these clients with tender loving care and give them outstanding service. They are the bread and butter of the operation.

B-class customers are not big enough to get the top deal but they come close. They provide you with a lot of profit because their sales yield better margins than the As. Between the two you have about 80 percent of your margin.

C-class customers are small and they test the relationship. They do not buy much from you, demand top service from your staff, and want the high quality products or service at low prices. Then, finally, they do not want to pay on time, and want payment terms of 90 days or more. These customers should pay full list price and, if necessary, C.O.D. If you lose one of these customers it will not matter, and the bad debt risk will migrate to one of your competitors. In fact, in many cases, losing a C-class customer is a benefit to the bottom line and it frees up sales time to concentrate on the profit centers—A and B class customers.

I recall my time as a very young national marketing manager for TNT (the international transport group now run by the Dutch Post Office) back in the 1970s. We hired a sales guru, whose job it was to manage our sales force in a growth market. Let's give the guru a name: SalesSuperHero, or SSH for short. SalesSuperHero presented a plan to the TNT board about growing market share, because market leaders make more profit than others. He was awarded the job and immediately retained a PR firm to pursue corporate publicity, featuring himself in the communications. Out went a press statement about him joining the company.

Next, he started hiring bucket loads of salespeople. He dragged in the top-notch ones from IBM and Xerox, paid them handsomely, and started making star-quality presentations to major accounts. In fact, he doubled the size of the sales team, and had slogans posted everywhere: "TNT is our name, sales is our game." He was in touch with his team of hotshots daily, even phoning them at home.

The sales meetings, which were many, were held after hours and focused on recognizing salespeople who had achieved their goals and won an award. They all got commissions based on sales volume. SalesSuperHero broke all the previous sales records and beat the forecast by a country mile.

The PR firm sent out more success stories featuring SSH. Meanwhile, the profits were looking skinny, so our hero blamed operations, which didn't have enough trucks to keep up anymore. In fact, he cited that as a mark of his success.

The following year, SalesSuperHero got the extra vehicles, but now he needed payloads for them. So a giant nationwide advertising campaign stirred up hundreds of inquiries for the sales team. The effect of the advertising slowly wore off, so SSH decided to give his teams the authority to discount wherever they saw fit. Believing they were smart enough to do the right thing, he didn't lay down any rules about the discounting.

Now the trucks filled up quickly again, and SSH sent out his next success story to the industry. As profits faded further, operations was blamed again, but now SSH was getting flak from upper management.

Into his third and final year, SalesSuperHero decided to pull the rabbit out of the hat. The other transport companies had cut their prices and we were in a full-blown price war. So SSH announced the "We won't be beaten" campaign to get business away from competitors at any price. Sound familiar?

In the end, TNT had to let him go and start cleaning up the damage. Many of the employees had to be let go, but he got his payout—and guess what? Another transport company gave him a job, and it started all over again. Several industries are incestuous and keep recycling offloaded staff who bring their baggage, and their sales and management habits, to their new employer. For whatever reason, they focus on competitive advantage as measured by market share and fail to recognize the power of positive profit.

Later in life, as marketing director of a very large consumer goods retailer, I constantly saw managers and salespeople from competitors coming in looking for jobs. As soon as they arrived, they started discounting again. I recommend a rigorous training program for every new employee, spelling out the mission, vision, values, and profit objectives of the company as a necessary exercise, in order for them to be effective in generating profits.

If you do not, you will be like the driver who went out into the country and got lost. He stopped and asked a farmer, "Where am I?" The farmer replied, "Where did you want to go?" to which he responded, "I don't know." Said the farmer, "You just got there!"

Where indiscriminate discounting is allowed, you can expect human nature to take the easy way out. If you say to your salespeople, "You are allowed to discount up to 10 percent," how much of the 10 percent will they use? Of course, the whole 10 percent, and then the audacious ones will come into the sales manager's office and ask for 11 or 12 percent, or more! You know the story.

Combine an incentive scheme based on sales volume with the latitude to do discounting, and you have a powder keg as far as your profits are concerned. This is not to say that sales and marketing people are untrustworthy; they are human like the rest of us and will find the easy way. The balanced company combines a strong sales drive with price management and, at the same time, discipline and careful control.

In my experience, the balanced company will always outperform profitwise the company slanted toward sales volume or cost cutting. I have yet to find a successful firm predicated on price alone as a philosophy.

The Balanced Sales Effort and Balanced Company Approach

Most companies experience at one time or another a new leader or new sales manager who puts the whole emphasis onto selling, gaining market share at any cost, becoming number one in the market. This approach is generally represented by the catch cry, "We want you to get out there and sell! Sell! *Sell!*" In reality, it is fairly easy to balance the sales effort and the corporate emphasis using the *MoneyMath* illustrated in Figure 5.2. I call it the Golden 1 Percent, or the Platinum 2 Percent. (See Figure A.15 and Figure A.16 in Appendix A for the Platinum 2 Percent and the Awesome 5 Percent charts.) The math revolves around three basic strategies that, when combined, have an awesome effect on the sales outcomes and the bottom line.

Ask yourself three questions: (1) Could you grow your sales volume by just one percent this year? (2) At the same time, could you cut all your costs (variable and fixed) by 1 percent? And (3) could you at the same time increase your prices by just 1 percent? Do all three things together in a leveraged and balanced way and you have the math result shown in Figure 5.2.

Using the factory model of cost, as shown here, we have on a combined basis increased the sales by 1 percent, reduced all the costs by 1 percent, and at the same time increased the prices by 1 percent. The three actions are combined, leveraged, and balanced, and together they increase the net profit by a whopping 24.15 percent on this model.

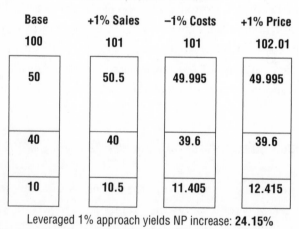

The Golden 1 Percent

Base	+1% Sales	−1% Costs	+1% Price
100	101	101	102.01
50	50.5	49.995	49.995
40	40	39.6	39.6
10	10.5	11.405	12.415

Leveraged 1% approach yields NP increase: **24.15%**

MoneyMath©

FIGURE 5.2   The Golden 1 Percent

The point here is that if the organization has this balance, you will not be so concerned with being number one (maybe number one in profitability) or taking market share at any price. Instead, your focus at every level becomes margins and net profit. The salespeople understand why they need to reach their sales volume targets *as well as* achieve gross profit margin targets. This is done through the proper selling at the prices applicable (i.e., low or no discounts). The rest of the organization has the role of keeping gentle pressure on the costs involved in their respective departments. Combine these three actions on a continuous, rolling basis and you have a formula for grinding out positive profits. It is not as exciting as "Sell, sell, sell!" or "Cut, cut, cut!" but it is more profitable in the long term, particularly if your team has been trained to understand why.

I remember counseling a young 22-year-old entrepreneur who told me he wanted to have the biggest detergent distributorship in the country. I asked him what his margins were and he said 15 percent gross and 2 percent net profit, to which I replied, "Wouldn't you rather have a slightly smaller operation that is very profitable than a big one with next to no bottom line? When you get older, do you want to sell your distributorship or maybe pass it on to your children?" The young entrepreneur answered yes to both questions. I said that the business would be worth a lot more to a prospective buyer if he could demonstrate years of steady profit in his books, rather than dramatic sales increases with no profit. He saw the power of positive profit immediately, increased his prices, and shaved his costs.

Application

☑ Check the discounting activities in your company or sales team and start educating today.

☑ Segment your customers and products/services into A, B, and C categories—20 percent of your customers generally provide you with 80 percent of your profit.

☑ Base your sales incentive schemes on bottom-line results, not only on top-line performance, or go half-and-half, if you must.

☑ Be wary of the flashy show business sales superstars who take just two years to drag your margins and your company down.

☑ Balance the company in regard to sales versus cost reduction versus price and revenue management.

LIST OF ACTIONS I CAN TAKE

_____

_____

_____

_____

_____

CHAPTER SIX

Now for Some
Real Bulletproofing

*It is to prevent this reduction of price, and consequently of wages
and profit, by restraining that free competition which would most
certainly occasion it, that all corporations, and the greater part of
corporation laws, have been established.*

—Adam Smith (1723–1790)

In Chapter 5 I examined the damage done by indiscriminate discounting. In this chapter, I want to show the opposite math and why this is
the foundation for powerful positive profit. Here is a bold statement:
Most managers, salespeople, and marketing people in the world have
never seen this math, let alone applied it! Wow! If that is true, then this
must really be something.

In most of the sales and management teams I have run, if you tell
them prices are going up, there is almost universal condemnation of the
move, expressed as: "Boss, we're going to lose a lot of customers doing
that!" This is in spite of the fact that a price rise may be necessary to
maintain margins. Some have said to me, "Okay, Boss, we'll go and sell
more for you!" rather than elevate the prices.

For some reason, there is a blind spot or mental block on the issue of raising prices. Personally, I think it has to do with all the reasons laid out in earlier chapters: poor math schooling, influence of TV commercials, confusion over terms, dislike of math, and so on.

Throughout its history, the United States has experienced and welcomed a steady flow of immigrants, as embodied in the famous Emma Lazarus poem, "The New Colossus," which is engraved on a plaque at the Statue of Liberty:

> Give me your tired, your poor,
> Your huddled masses yearning to breathe free,
> The wretched refuse of your teeming shore.
> Send these, the homeless, tempest-tost, to me,
> I lift my lamp beside the golden door.

Now, it is not without consequence that the continued growth of market in the United States is driven along by this incessant migration, and it can lead us into the following false security: If you miss a sale here today, you can go down the street and get another one to replace it.

This is a sales luxury that the rest of the world does not normally enjoy. In the United States it is not until a major catastrophe occurs, whether manmade like 9/11 or natural like Hurricane Katrina, that salespeople and managers actually have to knuckle down and get back to the basics. Most of the rest of the developed world is doing this on a daily basis.

Mind you, competition in the United States between suppliers and buyers is also fierce by comparison with other nations. Nevertheless, the concept of the volume market is easily understood when the population is growing substantially every year. It is not hard to make the next jump: "We can get all the sales we need, costs are under control, and the profits will take care of themselves." But I submit to you that even in burgeoning America today, more hidden profit is available to you, *if* the principles of this chapter are understood and used. The numbers in Table 6.1 will change the view of salespeople, managers, and marketers regarding

Look at What a Price Increase Does

Gross Profit Margin to Be Generated
(Providing Costs Remain the Same)

Price Increase	5%	10%	15%	20%	25%	30%	35%	40%	50%	60%
+1%	16.7%	9.1%	6.2%	4.8%	3.9%	3.2%	2.8%	2.4%	2.0%	1.6%
+5%	50%	33.3%	25%	20%	16.7%	14.3%	12.5%	11.1%	9.1%	7.7%
+10%	66.7%	50%	40%	33.3%	28.6%	25%	22.2%	20%	16.7%	14.3%
+15%	75%	60%	50%	42.9%	37.5%	33.3%	30%	27.3%	23.1%	20%
+20%	80%	66.7%	57.1%	50%	44.4%	40%	36.4%	33.3%	28.6%	25%

Sales Percent *Reduction* That Will Still Maintain Same Gross Profit

MoneyMath©

TABLE 6.1 Look at What a Price Increase Does

price and revenue management. The math is timeless and is not subjective because, after all, it is basic math.

Follow across the top line of the chart with your finger until you reach the 40 percent Gross Profit Margin column. Now follow down the left-hand price increase column until you hit 5 percent price increase, and follow that across to the 40 percent column. The figure at the intersection is 11.1 percent, which is the amount of business you can risk losing on that 5 percent price increase and still report the same or better bottom line. If the salespeople knew that, would they not react differently when you say the prices are going up? This *MoneyMath* chart empowers them to execute a price increase with little or no fear.

To put this into perspective, in a $500 million sales company operating on 40 percent gross profit margin, you go for a 5 percent price increase and you can afford to lose $55.5 million in sales and still show the same bottom line. To have an understanding of this latitude makes price increases less daunting for all concerned, and has them more willing to attempt an increase.

Many times, we are more sensitive about our prices than our customers are. There was a baker who made fabulous chocolate éclairs. His accountant told him to raise the prices of the éclairs from $0.99 to $1.50 each. The baker said, "I'll lose all my customers!" But the accountant insisted that the baker at least test a price increase for a day, to see what would happen. The next Monday, the baker displayed the éclairs with the new price. A customer asked, "Jack, weren't those éclairs 99 cents last week?" "Hmm, well, yes," he replied. The customer responded, "Well, it's about time, Jack. They're the best éclairs in the whole world!"

Murphy has a view of prices and profits as well (see Figure 6.1). It is like gravity: Raising prices is a devil of a job, but they tumble down naturally as unplanned events or costs enter into your results. Which busi-

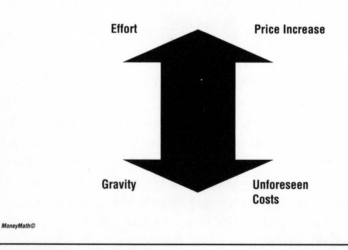

Murphy's Law on Profit

Effort   Price Increase

Gravity   Unforeseen
                          Costs

MoneyMath©

FIGURE 6.1   Murphy's Law on Profit

nesses planned for 9/11 in their budgets in 2001, or for the SARS virus in their 2003 budgets, or the tsunami in 2004, or Katrina in 2005, or the oil price hikes in 2006? Murphy is the first person in the door at work every morning and also has permanent residence inside every computer you use.

So now you have seen the awesome power of price increases, along with some reassurance about the amount of business you can afford to lose. In working recently with a division of a Fortune 500 major medical corporation, it became clear that a price increase was needed. Their managers had taken my profit and sales workshop and knew from their homework that they needed to increase the prices; however the sales force was initially resistant to it. So we ran the profit workshop for the salespeople. Guess what—they then went out and enthusiastically applied the increase.

Medical companies normally operate at about a 50 percent gross profit margin and, on a 5 percent price increase, can afford to lose 8.3 percent of their volume. This particular medical company has great products and awesome service and lost only 2 percent of its sales volume, putting it miles ahead with the price increase. This is an another example of *MoneyMath* resulting in positive profits.

We ran a profit workshop for a major international food company, one of the world's leading manufacturers and suppliers of food ingredients. I asked for its price list and was given one five years old. I said I needed the latest one, and was told, "That *is* the latest one."

I did not need to search any further. The company had world-class products and world-class service but had not increased prices in five years. Then came the standard reply from management that I get all around the world: "Graham, you don't know our industry. It's extremely competitive and it's not possible to increase our prices." If I have heard this once, I have heard it a thousand times: "Our industry is different!" In other words, "Math does not work in our industry," or "We do not understand the math," or both. Or "We are just plain scared to raise prices."

So we ran the profit workshop for their top 27 executives, with the

CEO present. Of the 27 participants, 23 failed the business math tests. After we showed them the right answers, the CEO announced that the prices were going up the following Monday by 3.5 percent. They actually needed more than that, but it was a good start. The staff were petrified of the outcome, visualizing dead customer relationships all over the marketplace.

The response from customers was an avalanche—of *silence*! Of the thousands of customers they had, not a single one phoned to complain. Why? Because they had had a free ride for five years on the great products and services and never received a price increase. So fantastic was the turnaround (millions of fresh dollars flooded onto the bottom line, putting them back in the black) that they did it again a month later.

This time, there were some minor complaints from 12 customers, while the remaining thousands of customers sucked it up like a baby. The whole company recovered, jobs were saved, shareholders were happy again. It was then sold as a going concern to another international food company in Europe. Mission accomplished!

When should you increase your prices? Several principles that have worked around the world include the following:

- Always increase prices when market demand is strong. Do not hang back in the market; if the opportunity arises, raise your prices. You can be sure Murphy is going to steal some of it back, so go for it.

- When competitors put their prices up, do the same and take cover with these others in the market. If you are the market leader, you have to take a risk, stick your neck out, and increase your prices first. It is not easy being a market leader.

- Always use a norm for your price increases, such as inflation, currency change, tax change, interest rate change, or fuel price increase. Generally everyone will agree that these are reasonable justifications for the increase.

- Increase your *real* prices to get margin. As shown in Chapter 3, if you increase prices by 10 percent, you get a 9.1 percent margin increase. If you want the full 10 percent margin to flow to your bottom line, you will need an 11.1 percent price increase. (See the Appendix A charts, which review margin concepts.)

- Increase prices more than once a year, but use small increases. The once-a-year regular price increase, preceded by a letter announcing the increase, is unwise. The buyers know exactly when you're coming, because you have made it all predictable. There is no law requiring you to advise customers of an increase; it is just habit or custom. Sometimes a contract will require you to send a letter. That is different, but do not send out letters if you're not contracted to do so.

- Fly some kites: Announce your price increases in advance. Send out a newsletter on the Web, telling customers of possible forthcoming increases. State a higher percentage than you need and, when your increase comes in at half that rate, you will be popular, instead of cannon fodder. Be aware that such signaling may currently be considered illegal in some European markets.

- Use computer programs to manage pricing and margins on a daily basis. Classify customers as A, B, or C and track their contributions. This is called segmenting.

- Use differential pricing. Do not just slap on a 5 percent price increase across the board once a year. Reserve the right to price up on different products at different times. Differentiate the prices to the A/B/C customers also.

- You can avoid losing business at price increase time. Think about the problems you are passing along to your customers. Some of them have production schedules that run, say, for six months (like the automotive companies). If you walk in wanting a price increase a week after the current schedule started, you are going to face a wall of stiff opposition. The key is to know your customers, both current and potential, so any potential difficulty from a price increase can be minimized.

- Give your customers solid and truthful reasons for the increase. Use the norms listed earlier plus any others you know. If you have some new investment that benefits them let them know this is part of the price rise.

As for the cherry pickers, the customers who are looking for the cheapest deal, avoid giving them the details of all of your costs even if they ask for it. All they will do is use the information you give them in a time-consuming argument about what is a legitimate increase and what is not. You can never win those arguments, so do not give them the ammunition in the first place.

Explain added value of service. This is the most powerful weapon of all price increase support mechanisms. In fact, Chapter 7 is devoted to this concept. However, before moving on, let's explore some more ideas dealing with pricing.

Price Increase Ideas

- Bundle and unbundle product/service packages. This is what Microsoft does so well. Their people are masters at making Windows obsolete, causing customers to require an upgrade or even a new computer altogether. When the old software is going to be phased out, you will often find another Microsoft program ready to replace the one being phased out. Clever! I believe Microsoft has added massive value to the human race, and Bill Gates is a great philanthropist.

- Offer the buyers some savings. For example, if they increase their volume of business with you from 60 percent to 80 percent, show them a savings for that increased loyalty and volume.

- Offer an options package with added value. If your customers commit to a long-term plan of purchases, provide some added benefits for them.

Maintaining Control of Your Pricing

How many employees does it take to set up a discount atmosphere in your business? It just takes one employee to set up loss-making deals, which quickly become precedents. Track the margins of all your sales representatives and find out which ones need training.

I believe few corporations know the amount of profit that is lost through unmonitored sales. The accountant, the shipping manager, the engineer—they all do little things that erode margin. Keep searching all the time for leaks in the *Titanic*.

Realistically, your sales representatives should be allowed to offer standard deals only. Any special deals are best controlled by senior managers. This is not popular but it is necessary, because human nature always gravitates to the easy way out—discounting. Plus, all too often, competitive advantage as measured by market share is the mantra of the firm.

When you lose control of sales prices, you lose control of profit, mainly through discounting. Tighten up the whole ship with computer monitoring. Put the *MoneyMath* discount chart "Look Before You Cut Prices" (Table 5.1) everywhere. If you give your sales representatives discounting authority, they could, and all too often will, apply discounts indiscriminately. Spell out very strict rules if you allow discounting.

Price and Management

If too many people influence prices in your company, they are influencing *net* price! That in turn influences net profit. So reduce or keep the number of your staff affecting prices to an absolute minimum.

It is management's role to ensure their people are highly trained with their power restricted within tight limits. Train and retrain all who interact with customers in handling price issues, even if they cannot alter prices or terms.

All your daily transactions must pass the average margin test and contribute to the bottom line. Manage by exception in this area. Require that any transaction priced below the budgeted company margin must be approved and signed off. Use a margin catch-up plan to recover losses.

Handling the Buyers from Hell

There are price-only buyers who are wheelers and dealers, always shopping for the best deals. In most industries, they are usually a small minority, but it feels like all customers behave this way at price explanation time or price increase time. As you know, they go ballistic when you tell them the price has to go up!

Then the histrionics start; they get coercive and nasty with you, with no understanding of value for money. In fact, you wonder if they are even listening. However, if they are small C-class customers who treat you this way, they should be dumped. Tell them they can have your product or service for full list price—no if, ands, or buts!

However, your larger (A-class), important, price-only clients should be handled by your negotiation-toughened and experienced salespeople. Get the sales manager or the CEO involved, if necessary, for this vital negotiation.

Build a price management strategy to which everyone in the business must adhere. Do not leave this issue to chance; if you do, human nature will take the easy way again and discounting will be rampant.

You have a sales strategy and a cost control strategy, why not a *pricing strategy*? Start tomorrow!

When customers request a "special deal," say no unless the deal is reciprocated (you scratch my back, and I'll scratch yours). Make absolutely no special deals for small C-class customers. Once you do a special deal for a tiny client, he or she will blab about it all over the place. Before you know it, a lot more of your customers will be asking for the same deal. Employees leave one place and go to work for another. They let the new employer know about your special deals and bingo! your lower prices spread far and wide while your profits decrease.

Who should control the pricing? I like to have the finance or commercial department set prices. The salespeople will often react negatively to this, but it brings balance. The salespeople usually side with the customers because they do not want to lose friends or the commissions they earn on sales volume, and that is natural. The accountants normally side with the company, and a balance between the two is useful to maximize margins.

But then a problem emerges when the accountants become head office–oriented and start to become arbitrary stand-over merchants wielding power. If that happens, send the accountants out with the salespeople into the marketplace to see how tough it is. They will soon become more empathetic with sales pricing requests.

Valuable Relationship Buyers

Usually your top customers are relationship buyers and they like the following: purchase ease, value, systems, and nothing to change. They are often the majority of important clients, and they need to be handled with kid gloves at price increase time.

Whether you are in retail, commercial, or industrial marketplaces, valuable buyers are the lifeblood of your business. In fact, they carry around your business reputation in the market, and to lose one is to take a direct hit amidships, where it hurts the most.

With your A-class buyers, price increases need to be negotiated in a win/win arrangement. I recommend a strategy meeting in your office to plan this before you commence negotiations. Negotiate on neutral territory. There are usually only a handful of these customers, so it is well worth the effort to please them when the pain of a price increase is necessary.

Remember that there is a lot of buying momentum with A-class customers, and these buyers like staying with proven suppliers. The last thing they want to have to do is change to a new supplier. Changing vendors messes up their comfortable lives. They huff and puff at price increase time, sounding like a nasty transaction buyer. However, if you carefully explain the reasons behind the increase (a consumer price index adjustment, the fuel price hikes, or better and more reliable service) they get over the resentment in a week or so and are soon back buying from you at the newer prices.

Next chapter: let's look at how you can use the quality of your customer service to differentiate your offerings and achieve higher prices.

Application

- ☑ All employees who come into contact with customers can influence prices, which in turn influence profits.

- ☑ *Price* impacts your net profit more than costs or sales!

- ☑ Train all your employees to increase, maintain, or defend your prices.

- ☑ For every business on this planet: Become absolutely expert at knowing when and how to increase your prices.

LIST OF ACTIONS I CAN TAKE

CHAPTER SEVEN

Why Your Perceived Value Beats Product Quality

A man who knows the price of everything and the value of nothing!
—Oscar Wilde (1854–1900)

Many salespeople could increase company profits by doing a better job of preparing their presentations for greater impact. They could do this first by investing more into homework, and second, by selling value, rather than just the features and benefits or price alone.

Let's attack the first issue of preparation. In Chapter 1 I mentioned that if your salesperson is the average TV watcher soaking up 19 hours a week in the United States, or 13.3 hours a week in Australia, there is little time left for preparing high-quality, powerful presentations. The centerpiece of selling is still presentation, and this is where the heavy-duty homework is needed in order for the sale to have ingredients that produce margin. These ingredients include a positive attitude, preparation, an appointment for the call, questions defining the customer's needs, and, in the case of regular customers, the history of the relationship. Customers buy value, which stems from benefits, which stem from the features.

Precise definitions of features and benefits are needed so the two factors do not get mixed up, as they often do. I remember attending the launch of a new range of major-brand white goods, and the executive who was speaking kept insisting all the way through his speech that the brand name was a benefit, when it is actually a feature. He was an example of the Peter Principle, someone who had been promoted up through the sales force to sales manager and then to CEO, but had never been precisely trained in marketing or selling. As he proceeded, I noticed that many features and benefits of these new models were mixed up in his mind.

So what are the definitions of features and benefits?

A feature of a product or service is a *permanent physical characteristic*. It is a tangible, quantifiable thing, identifiable from brochures, specification sheets, and the like. It is part of what the product or service includes.

By contrast, a benefit is the *intangible advantage in the mind of the customer*, and it flows from the feature(s). It is not what the product *is*, but what the customer perceives it will *do*. From the customer's viewpoint, it is "What's in it for me" (WIFM). It is the salesperson's job to reveal it and sell it.

To make the communication of benefits to customers a little easier, I have developed a simple formula that encapsulates the key things people are seeking in a product or service. I use the acronym *S-P-A-C-E-D*: Security, Performance, Appearance, Convenience, Economy, and Durability. To make these benefits work in the mind of the customer, use words that suggest the benefit concept:

Security: "Takes the worry out of . . ."

Performance: "You get more . . ."

Appearance: "Looks good . . ."

Convenience: "Makes it easy to . . ."

Economy: "You save XX dollars . . ."

Durability: "Lasts longer . . ."

What we are now looking for are some words to connect the benefit and feature with the value added. The best connector is: "(Mention feature) *which means* (mention benefit), *which is worth* (mention dollar amount)."

Here is an example of words to use in selling value: "This soft drink is *branded* Coke (the feature) and you cannot get that brand on any other soft drink. Being branded Coke *takes the worry out* (benefit) of the quality question, and it is *easy* to buy (benefit) wherever you see a Coke sign. Additionally we think the brand logo *looks good* (appearance), all of which makes it worth a *couple of cents more* per can (value statement)."

Value is the worth, utility, or desirability of the features and benefits in customers' minds. This is the amount of money that they think it is worth, based on the perception of the benefits that stem from the technical features of your product or service. Unless you communicate it, this value will be lost through default, discounting, or negotiation. It's never nothing.

To retain profitability, the price has to stand up as much as possible, which is done by assigning a monetary value to the benefits and features presented. In my experience, most salespeople in the world do not do this; in fact, many sales trainers do not teach it either. As a result, the sales team goes off chasing volume at any price, and the boss complains about the margins! It is a matter of perception.

As marketing director of a company that sold audio equipment (among other things), I asked some focus groups of customers what price they thought a stereo sound system was worth. The cost from Asia was $250, so we were hoping it would sell for about $750 by the time we added warranty, shipping, advertising, and merchandising to it.

Boy, were we wrong! The focus groups said it was worth from $600 up to $1,200. So we priced it at $950, and were able to increase its volume to dealers by using volume rebate incentives. The going price in the market averaged out to $850, so we saw an extra 12 percent margin! Had we followed our first instinct, we would have sold them at a lower price and made less margin.

So how is this value derived? We have developed an analytical *MoneyMath* tool (see Table 7.1) that has the effect of building up a value based on the differences between your product or service and that of a competitor.

To use this grid, in the "Features" column, list all the features from the brochure, specification sheets, and manuals. Next, in the "Major Selling Features" (MSF) column, compare the features to those of your competitors' products. Ask: Do only a few offer this feature in the market? If so, this partially differentiates your product or service from others. After identifying the MSFs, now identify the "Unique Selling Features" (USF) that you alone offer in the market. These USFs fully differentiate your product or service from all the rest. A product or ser-

How Perceived Value of Product Drives Up Margin

Feature	MSF	USF	Benefits (SPACED)	$ Value
1.				
2.				
3.				
4.				
5.				
6.				
7.				
8.				

Pacific Seminars International©

TABLE 7.1   Universal Benefits Analysis Tool

vice having no MSF or USF is a "me-too" product, which usually sells on price.

To determine benefits, using the SPACED formula presented earlier, ask questions about the features listed in the far left column. For example:

Security: Does it remove a worry or provide security in some way?

Performance: Does it give more (use units of measurement for this benefit, such as gallons/minute, horsepower, kilowatts, etc.)?

Appearance: Does that feature look good? Customers like things to look good. While it is a subjective benefit to some extent, it still applies and it includes the concept of image.

Convenience: Does it make something easier?

Economy: Does it save or make some money?

Durability: Will it last longer? For example, a metal bearing will usually outlast a plastic one.

One or all of these benefits could apply to any given feature. To make it easy to use this tool, simply write the initial of the applicable benefit in the box across from the feature.

The last column is the clincher, because it gets directly to value. I have taken about 20 sales training courses in my life and read at least 200 sales training books and manuals, but I have never seen *value* extrapolated from a product or service into dollars and loaded into a presentation. I know scores of sales trainers and experts, but none of them explain in detail how to actually sell *value*.

I submit to you that this is one of the main reasons so many of us in our selling and managing and marketing get caught on price. It is because we do not first have the *ammunition ready* to combat attacks on price. Perhaps we are also not game enough to put a value on something on behalf of someone else.

This concept of value is one of the key ways to defend the price of something. Better still, it is one of the best ways to get a higher price and margin. Let us use a can of Coca-Cola for an example of how to use this positive profit technique (see Table 7.2). Coke is well known around the world and, as the grid shows, is very well differentiated from its competitors. Sometimes a product will have up to 50 or so major features. Just imagine what it is like to have to list the features of a Boeing 747-400.

How are these values established? Some values come from scientific customer research. That is the kind where a research company goes out and spends $10,000 and presents you with a 400-page report that validates the worth of your quality or brand in the marketplace.

Every now and then your customer will readily acknowledge the value, saying something like, "Well, we really appreciate the quality of your product; it's second to none." Enough said! In addition, at other

Product Example of Coke

Feature	MSF	USF	Benefits (SPACED)	$ Value
1. Coca-Cola Brand	—	X	S, A, C	3% = $0.03/can
2. Soft Drink Leader	—	X	S, E, D	0.5% = $0.005/can
3. International Company	—	—	S, C, D	—
4. Publicly Owned Company	X	—	S, C, D	—
5. 25 Configurations	X	—	S, C	—
6. Regular/Diet/Caffeine-Free	X	—	S, A, C, D	0.5% = $0.005/can
7. Secret Recipe (Taste)	—	X	S, D	1% = $0.01/can
			Total Perceived Value	
			= **5% = $0.05/can**	

Pacific Seminars International©

TABLE 7.2   Product Example of Coke

times, it will be your own or your employees' subjective observation. Do not discount this just because it is an internal viewpoint; it *is* valid.

The best research is your competitors' viewpoint, which they will never give you, except maybe after a dozen beers at the bar. From working with a huge international hospital/medical company, I learned how good this company was with service. Some of its competitors shared with me how they use it as a benchmark for service quality in the medical industry.

When do most medical emergencies occur? Between 9 P.M. on Saturday and 3 A.M. on Sunday. If you are offering 24/7 service, how many of your staff want to be working in that six-hour weekend window of time? Professional people do, which is why it is so powerful in service quality.

However, no matter how you determine value, whether in dollars or as a percentage, it will never be *nothing*! This is how you add value when selling. Do the homework on the grid, work out what your differentials are, and then put a money value on the benefits, *before* the customer uses the price argument against you in negotiation. Now you have the advantage.

Continuing with the Coke example, it may sound something like this: "Sir/madam, you can go for the other soft drink with the slightly lower price. However, we believe the value of the Coke brand, our market leadership, and Coke's unique taste offer you a few cents per can added value which, when combined with our market share, will generate *more* net profit than the price saving on the other soft drink."

After this, you pop the trial close: "What do you think?" It is an open-ended question, which requires only the customer's opinion. The customer now has to prove your value statement and amount wrong. This will be hard for them to do if you have done your homework. I highly recommend that you listen carefully to the response so you can increase your knowledge of how and what customers think. Moreover, when you listen, you can reply in a positive manner to the customer.

This strategy can lead to an early close of the sale, or it can provoke an objection (question, condition, or excuse) to be dealt with. If the customer says, "Five cents more for Coke? I reckon it is half that," jump in and take it, because the customer just offered you an increase in margin.

The magic of this approach is to take the features on through the benefits all the way to an estimated value, forcing the customer to consider the ingredients engineered into your product in the first place. Using this grid, could each of the major products in your range be analyzed by the sales team and put into a manual for all to use? Could all your new products be analyzed this way before they come to market?

One international chemicals company I work with saw this and scheduled each sales representative to analyze one product per week and present it at the weekly sales meeting, until the company's entire lineup was done. Then each representative was given a photocopy to insert into the sales manual for use in the field. What a great idea!

Sometimes the grid process will reveal that a product has lots of me-too features, is poorly differentiated, and will tend to sell on price. In that case, the analysis will look like Line 3 in the Coke example above. Notice that the MSF and the USF columns are blank, which means Coke's competitors also have similar features. Pepsi, for example, like Coca-Cola, is also an international company.

In that case, we have the other shotgun barrel loaded and ready for you to use for those products requiring additional support to achieve their targeted price. In the case of poorly differentiated products/services, the MSF/USF columns are mostly empty, revealing that lack of differentiation. Products left on their own like that will often sell on price, because the customer says, "Well, it's the same as all the others."

Sometimes these products are termed *commodities*, because everybody has them and they get flogged to death in the marketplace. Do not despair; it is quite easy to differentiate a commodity once you've seen how to do it. I talk more about it later in this chapter

To keep the universal benefit grid going in the long term requires a commitment from management, marketing, and research to *continu-*

ous differentiation until the product reaches the end of its life cycle. Take the continuous innovation of Microsoft's Windows operating system. The Windows product has been around since 1990, but it is still Windows. It has been innovated, rebuilt, and reissued, and still it resides on 80 percent of the world's PCs. *Windows* is fast becoming a generic term for "operating system," just as *Kleenex* has come to mean "a tissue."

Continuous differentiation means getting back into the grid analysis and seeing what can be changed to revamp the product. Naturally, a cost/value analysis will accompany the revamping, to establish whether it is worth doing.

Do not be troubled if you think the product has run to the end of its life cycle. That second barrel is still available and this can extend the life of a commodity. The great thing about the second barrel is that it is relatively easy and inexpensive to set up differentials to complement a weak product. Hang in there!

Here is the solution: Using the grid again to analyze *service* gives you a second barrel to fire in your marketing, selling, and managing. It means you do not have to compete based solely on price. You add this second facet and help keep that price *up*, where it belongs.

This is how Lexus is whipping its opposition, by assuming the product is a given and working hard on service differentials to deflect the price argument. The example of service values analyzed in Table 7.3 is an assessment of a major Fortune 500 medical company. The analysis indicates that the service function is *so* strong that it could be worth anywhere up to 11 percent more than its competitors. When applied to a $3,000 piece of medical equipment, that is $330 built-in value based on the service that comes with it.

When the salespeople recognize this service benefit and the value it adds to the product, they are better able to defend the price and maintain the profits of the company. Customers appreciate service, even if they do not readily recognize (until it is pointed out to them) that good

How Perceived Value of Customer
Service Drives Margin Higher

Feature	MSF	USF	Benefits (SPACED)	$ Value
1. 73 Years Experience	X	—	S, D	2%
2. #1 Market Leader	—	X	S, E, D	0.5%
3. International (112 Countries)	—	—	S, P, C, E, D	0.5%
4. Technology Specialists	X	—	P, E	0.5%
5. NYSE-Listed Company	—	—	S	—
6. ISO9001 Manufacturer	—	—	S, C	0.5%
7. Web Site	X	—	P, A, C	—
8. 700 Offices Globally	—	—	C	—
9. Range 10,000 Products	X	—	S, C, E	1%
10. 6 Product Groups	—	—	S, C	—
11. E-Mail/Cell/Fax/Phone	—	—	C, E	—
12. Service 24 hours/7 days	X	—	S, C, D	2%
13. Highly Trained Staff	X	—	S, P, A, E	1%
14. G. Environmental Record	X	—	S, P, D	1%
15. 99% Inventory Level	X	—	S, C, E	1%
16. R&D = 7% Sales	X	—	S, D	1%

Total   **11%**
perceived value

Pacific Seminars International©

TABLE 7.3   How Perceived Value Can Increase Margin

service is a value that costs money to provide. Of the three facets of quality open for improvement—product quality, process quality, and service quality—the latter has the most legs to change your customers' perception of value.

Next, in Chapter 8 we look at the proposition that the sales team can use tools like this grid and actually make more margin while selling at higher prices.

Application

☑ If you are a salesperson, learn the S-P-A-C-E-D benefits formula and the statements that go with it.

☑ If you are a manager or sales manager, have the sales force start preparing a features/benefits value analysis for each of their upcoming sales.

☑ For all new products, get the marketing department to produce the grid analysis for the sales staff to use. It will help them work differentials into the product or service offering. In fact, in the product development stage, a grid analysis could help in the design of the product so value is maximized.

☑ Old products can be reinvigorated with the value of your excellent customer service, once you have analyzed what it is.

☑ Always put a monetary value on the outstanding features and benefits in your sales presentations to get in first in a positive way on the price issue.

☑ Use the grid to become proficient at price defense when you know you are under price pressure.

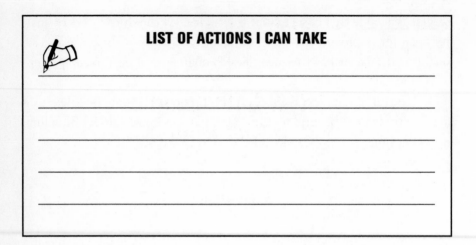

CHAPTER EIGHT

How Salespeople Can Sell Higher

The heights by great men reached and kept,
Were not attained by sudden flight,
But they, while their companions slept,
Were toiling upward in the night.
      —Henry Wadsworth Longfellow (1807–1882),
         "The Ladder of Saint Augustine"

Apparently the Marxist/socialist view of the customer has become prevalent in our time. In addition to giving conference keynote speeches, we get commissioned to run profit-based sales training courses, where we find that philosophy expressed like this:

- "All customers are equal."
- "All customers are equally important."
- "All customers deserve the same service."
- "It is not fair that some customers get better prices than others!"
- "All customers deserve the same price."

Strange as it may seem, many sales/service people have this view, particularly newer, younger recruits. When you hear that all customers deserve the same, you almost immediately know you have a Marxist/ socialist version of something or other. You also know that most likely the company is facing difficulties and is, at a minimum, struggling to be profitable.

Now it is true that customers are important, but you cannot give A-class resources to a C-class customer, unless you want to go broke. Customer differentiation is critical to companies that have to survive on margins (which includes all companies wanting to earn positive profits).

Controlling pricing to achieve differentiation is one of the great challenges in running a sales force. Try this one: Tell your salespeople prices are going up but differently for each class of customer and they will scream that it is the wrong move, that you are going to lose customers, that they will resign because of the "dumb management," and so on.

Most of us hate any controls; we avoid control freaks too. Announce price controls of any description to sales and marketing people, and the sky falls in! I had one employee tell me as CEO I needed to go back to square one and take another sales course, which would show me how to "get out there and write some decent sales again."

Other people inside companies come into contact with customers and they, too, can affect the prices obtained. This may not be face-to-face but, nevertheless, it affects the final price charged. Much of this is on the phone and, in my view, is relatively unsupervised by upper management.

Customers also phone warehouse staff, delivery personnel, and account staff, and there is a chance every time that a price alteration could occur. Now which way do you think it occurs? Is it upward in favor of the company, generating more margin? Or downward in favor of the customer, who achieves better savings? You got it, 99 percent downward! Once again this shows the drive for competitive advantage by increasing market share and the mentality of indiscriminate discounting that exists in society and business.

Sales staff, in particular, have to see some clients repeatedly and want the easy way out when under pressure—after all, these people are friends and there is a relationship. The last thing the sales team wants to have to sell is a price increase. They would rather have to go out and sell double the sales volume than negotiate a price increase. However, to achieve the profit your company needs, you must have them all on the same side, at the same time, and set some price controls. How?

Subjective research teaches us some interesting facets of price administration. Think about your total company sales value, or your total sales territory value, as 100 percent, and write it down. Now, pretend you are as white as the driven snow and do no discounting, but sell *everything* at list price—even to your own mother!

Then, being honest about the selling and marketing taking place in your market, take into account the fact that discounts do exist, and write down the new percentage that *would* be available to you if all the discounting were eliminated.

For example, let us say your company discounts, on average, 10 percent (that you know about). So, if you were discount free, your current 100 percent average price could be near 110 percent. Circle the percentage amount below that you think your company is currently foregoing through discounts:

100%   105%   110%   120%   125%   130%   140%   150%

Now multiply the percentage you selected by your total sales, and see what margin dollars you are potentially forfeiting! Let's say you circled 20 percent; a company on 40 percent margin doing $100 million sales should be doing $120 million, and 40 percent of the additional $20 million is an extra $8 million net profit. Only one thing can fix this for you: tighter controls on sales prices.

Have you noticed that some deals go on forever? I was working in a major medical company that had hospital contracts with specified expiration dates. But their business was so big and loosely controlled that many contracts expired unnoticed, so a customer would continue to receive contract pricing after the contract concluded rather than being quoted list price for new orders. Of course, the customer does not phone you to tell you this, but just laughs at your inefficiency and says, "Hey, that company is just like the government folks. What is this big deal about private industry being more efficient?" The result: more margin lost.

From the customer's perspective, real good deals give away the whole net profit and make them ecstatic. As shown earlier, if there is 10 percent net profit in the product and you empower the sales staff to discount up to 10 percent, how much will they use? The whole 10 percent, every time! There goes your net profit!

Many salespeople operate from their vehicles and are doing their selling "over the hills and far away"—out of sight, out of mind. I like the idea of electronic reporting, where sales are automatically reported daily and digitally, and where sales management checks the margins within 24 hours of the deal being done. It is normally not too late to correct errors, and most customers will listen to your story.

The world's most popular discounts are in the 10 to 20 percent range. In fact, 10 percent is the *most* popular discount level. Nobody knows why. I said earlier that we think it is because we have 10 fingers. However, there is no scientific explanation as to why the 10 percent discount is the most popular.

If your salespeople can discount up to 10 percent, how much will actually be used? Of course, the whole 10 percent, but they usually want more. They go to the boss and ask for an extra 1 or 2 percent above the 10. I have experienced some of the best selling in my life in my own office aimed at me, all the while wishing the sales effort was going into the customer! Senior executives have to say no. Give them the reason why when you say no.

What grand plans I have seen: The sales staff discount up to 5 percent; then the sales manager can go up to 10 percent, and the vice president of sales to 15 percent. Once customers find this out, they start a process that gets them into the vice president's office to get that 15 percent off. The smarter ones go even further and say, "Well, if I can get 15 percent from the vice president, let's see what the CEO will buckle at."

At a major chain of department stores, where I was a director, price shopping was done regularly by some of our customers. I remember one particular deal in a city where we had four stores, 10 miles apart along a major road. At the store that was furthest out from the city, the customer was quoted list price for carpet. At the next store, the price was the same, less a 5 percent discount. The store next closest to the city offered a 10 percent discount. Finally, at the inner city store, the customer received a 12.5 percent discount, all for the cost of 40 miles of driving.

Pressure is always on staff to do deals! It is an ever-present reality that buyers and purchasing agents are trained to use a myriad of traps to seduce a salesperson into discounting. Also, as discussed previously, we live in a discounting society, as demonstrated by TV advertising. This downward pressure on prices is a game we all play daily. Therefore it is necessary to establish proper pricing controls.

Setting Tighter Pricing Controls

The first step is to provide professional training to all staff who interact with customers over price. Make no exceptions. Repeat the training regularly to reinforce the skills that preserve margin.

Next, as noted in Chapter 6, cut down the number of people affecting prices to an absolute minimum. They will complain that it is an insult to their intelligence to have so many controls over their behavior. But they will also want their bonuses at the end of the year, so explain that controls are necessary to protect those bonuses. Their resentment will remain but their understanding will jump 200 percent at this point.

Finally, try and hold the sales force to doing only established, standard deals. This will draw a lot of resentment in some industries. Give them tight limits, with no discretion. It is okay to have an empathetic attitude, but do not waver or cave in.

What I do not recommend is that you remove responsibility from sales staff for the margins obtained by having chief finance officers signing off on their work. This demotivates the sales team and makes them order takers. Train them in how business, margins, and profits work from within the sale.

Customer service issues also come into the picture when discussing pricing controls. For example, in many companies, the orders come into a telemarketing area, or a customer service area, over the phone. In fact, the telephone is the front door to a lot of the world's business transactions and can have a major impact on the margins achieved.

It might go like this:

Customer: "I need Product X."

Salesperson: "No problem, we've got plenty in stock."

Customer: "And what's my discount?"

Salesperson: "11 percent."

Customer: "A competitor is offering 14 percent. If you don't match it, I'll give them the business!"

Salesperson: "Okay, no problem, 14 percent!"

If the gross margin was 35 percent and the net profit 15 percent, what just happened? The net profit on that transaction dropped to 1 percent (15 percent minus the 14 percent discount). Which manager monitored what happened? Most likely no one, because it was all done on the telephone. These days the same type of unsupervised sale can occur over the Internet via e-mail if a firm does not have the right pricing controls in place. If so, the same destruction of profit takes place, so it is necessary to establish policies and practices similar to those applicable to phone sales. Really clever Internet customers search all the web sites with similar products, find the lowest price, and then start negotiating to lower that!

Managing Phone Sales

Often the sales/service person feels bad that *only* 11 percent could be offered over the phone. Many staff actually feel good that they can help a customer in this way by discounting. If they are not aware of the margins but are aware of the prices to the larger customers, they could, without strong controls, be induced over the phone to make the better offer, in order to stay friends with the client or to increase sales volume and, accordingly, their commissions.

Now if it is an A-class customer, they will say they did the right thing. Maybe so, but if it is a B-class or C-class customer, they have just opened Pandora's box. As noted previously, customers sometimes talk with each other, and word will spread among the lower class customers that larger discounts are available to all who ask. In my experience, few managers do anything about this problem. It is out of sight, out of mind, and not at the top of anyone's thinking. Where possible (and legal), the manager should monitor both sides of sales order calls coming into the telemarketing or sales service area. Get a quality control program going on the kinds of answers and quotes your employees are giving out.

How should these calls be handled? It's not all that tricky. A little courteous skill and a strategy to do something about it in the first place can add significant margin points.

> *Customer:* "A competitor is offering 14 percent. If you don't match it, I'm giving them the business!"
>
> *Salesperson:* "I'd love to change your terms, and we'd be sorry to lose your business. Listen, I'm in good with my boss; if you can leave it with me, I can call you back with a solution. Is that okay?"
>
> *Customer:* "Yep, go for it."

Now this may not work every time, but it gives you a chance to make a comeback. You are stalling for a little bit of extra time to develop the right answer. Do not let your staff get bulldozed by clever buyers. Instead let them come back with a response that is based on the lessons covered in previous chapters, such as stressing quality of service and reliability, or allowing a larger discount if the order size is increased. Remember, losing a C-class customer who is asking for A-class preference is a benefit.

Some Other Solutions and Items that Kill Profits

Ask the customer what other business they do with your competitors. For the higher 14 percent discount, offer to rationalize the number of suppliers they have, and take a larger share of their business. Never give them a discount without getting something in return. Perhaps offer in-kind equivalents to the value of the extra amount of the requested discount— for example, shipping, goods in kind, or extended warranty—but only if they step up to the next sales segment (i.e., from C-class to B-class). The principle here is: No unreciprocated deals!

Some Freebies and Issues That Kill Profit
- Free delivery.
- No-charge invoice.
- Samples free of charge.
- Low-value small invoices.
- Urgent courier deliveries for free.
- Labor charges rounded down.
- Traveling time uncharged.
- Expired contract prices.
- Free-of-charge short service calls.
- Unenforced stock returns policy.
- Extended credit terms free of charge.

- Free training course and material.
- Premium levels for regular price.
- Buddies' rates.
- Outdated price lists.

Applications of Charging for Everything

Okay, so how do we have sales staff sell higher prices and enjoy it? If you have segmented your customers into classifications A, B, and C, based on their value to your organization, you will always have small C-class customers who creep in and demand top deals, suck the service out of your service department, pay their accounts at 90 days or more, and give your trusted sales staff a hard time.

Tell the sales force to inform these customers that from next Monday they are on full list price, with no discounts. The sales team will go bananas when they have to apply this to these customers. But do not worry about the consequences. If you lost most of those customers, your bottom line would improve.

The Pareto Principle (also known as the 80-20 rule) teaches us that 80 percent of your administrative costs are being burned up servicing these small customers who are probably only 20 percent of your sales volume.

The only warning here is that if there's a potentially large customer hiding among the C-class customers, make an exception. But also, be aware that some of your salespeople at this juncture will say that *all* the customers could be big ones later. For some reason, I find salespeople can take the customer's side at the most inopportune times.

I love salespeople—that's where I started in business myself. I speak at hundreds of sales conferences and run workshops for hungry leaders with hungry sales teams. I like watching the light bulb go on when they see the *MoneyMath* principles for the first time. The ANZ

Bank's national strategy manager in Auckland, New Zealand, said after exposure to *MoneyMath* at a public conference, "We changed our whole pricing strategy based on your presentation—we were blown away. We realized if we added 1 percent to our average sale ($2,500) we would never miss our monthly profit target again! The impact is seven figures on our bottom line. Pretty amazing!"

Salespeople are the lifeblood of the planet. Teach them *empathy*, not sympathy, regarding customers and pricing. Empathy is understanding the customer's viewpoint on price, but not holding that view. Sympathy is agreeing with the customer's viewpoint on price and discounting the company price list to accommodate the customer.

Another issue that affects price relates to things like returns, delivery charges, and so on. I was working with a company that markets technical instruments to the medical profession, each worth from $5,000 to $20,000. I asked, "How many of these are returned each year?" The estimate was about 120, so I asked to see the actual logbook figures, which showed 160 returns that year.

My next question: "Do you have a restocking fee policy on returns?" The answer: "Yes, we charge the customer 15 percent to sterilize it in an autoclave, repackage in sterile packaging, and put it back on the shelf in the warehouse."

Then I asked, "How many were actually invoiced for the restocking fee this year?" The figures showed that only three customers were charged! The CEO hit the roof.

I said, "Let's do the math. Assume you make no profit out of the restocking fee and that it is just there to recover costs and stop leakage of margin and profit. An average $1,800 restocking fee multiplied by 160 units equals $288,000 off your bottom line, *if* you don't recover the cost. You charged only three customers, so your potential bottom line loss is $282,600."

On that product, profitability of the firm was lowered because the sales team avoided selling the restocking fee as part of the deal. That is worse than a discount because no sale occurred in the first place and the company incurs costs, thus reducing the overall margin dollars. Typically this forces one of two things to happen: Either the salespeople are trained to sell the restocking fee and enforce it, or the prices have to go up by a small percentage to recover the extra cost involved and the restocking fee gets abandoned. If the compensation of the sales team is based on sales volume they will most likely push for the higher prices even if they dislike the notion of selling those higher prices.

Which way do you think the medical instruments company elected to go? It increased the price, dropped the restocking fee policy, and let the salespeople off the hook.

Delivery charges are another area of contention. If you do the customer a favor and provide a special delivery because something went wrong at their end, they should be invoiced for that special delivery, and at the full emergency delivery rate, which could be double the standard delivery fee.

When you make the mistake, it is the reverse. Emergency delivery is done free of charge, with apologies to the customer. You have to swallow all the costs for your own mistakes.

If you do little favors, like having a salesperson drop something off for a customer on the way home from work, these favors should be noted in some kind of service log book for future reference. This log book becomes the reference point the next time you want a price increase. Customers will conveniently forget all the good things you have done in the intervening time period and tell you the price increase is too much and they will not accept it! Then out comes the log book, which helps get your higher price to stick.

One company I work with, Foseco, is a world-class chemicals company that supplies major automakers with products that keep their engine foundry production lines running. One automaker received a memo from its headquarters, stating that it was to stop using Foseco products and to switch to another supplier. The reason had a little bit to do with price, and the competitor had similar products but vastly inferior service levels.

Late one Saturday evening, the automaker's production manager uncovered a problem: The foundry engine block production line was about to stop because the chemical binder that holds the sand mold together had run out. He phoned the new supplier, to no avail (Saturday night, out partying, with the company cell phone turned off?). In desperation, he ignored the corporate memo and phoned Foseco, whose manager got out of bed, opened the warehouse, and delivered two drums of chemical 100 miles away in the wee small hours of Sunday to keep that foundry running.

Guess what? Within a few months, Foseco had regained the automaker's business at its higher prices, based on its superior service. Since that time, it has logged these types of occurrences, which helps in the negotiation of the next price increase, as it should. Further, the competitor is almost out of business in this particular market, because Foseco's service is world-class.

This example proves again that value (value of service), not price, is what smart customers really want. That means that salespeople *can* sell higher! Of course, this implies that salespeople are professionally trained to do it and that proper policies and procedures are in place.

In the next chapter, I attack the issue of getting higher prices in the marketplace, which I think is a challenge to every CEO, sales manager, marketing director, and salesperson worldwide.

Application

☑ There will be unnecessary discounts happening inside your company—guaranteed! Track them down and establish policies to correct the problem(s).

☑ Move prices upward at every opportunity.

☑ Record all service favors in a service log book.

LIST OF ACTIONS I CAN TAKE

CHAPTER NINE

Getting Higher Market Prices

People of the same trade seldom meet together, even for merriment and diversion, but the conversation ends in a conspiracy against the public, or in some contrivance to raise prices.

—Adam Smith (1723–1790)

Growing up in Australia, one gets told as a school student the story of the world's biggest gold nugget. It was discovered in 1869, in the state of Victoria, at Moliagul, by John Deason and Richard Oates. The nugget weighed 2,284 ounces and would be worth way over $1.3 million U.S. dollars in today's values. It stood three feet tall and was named the "Welcome Stranger" nugget; it remains the world's largest nugget to this day.

Miners from all over the globe flocked to the 1851 gold rush in Australia. The news had traveled around the world about another gold rush, similar to the 1849 rush near San Francisco in California. The fledgling country Australia had changed from being a penal colony to the "Lucky Country." However, mining ceased in 1893 as a recession hit because of low prices for gold, and banks closed all over the place. Years later, in 1972, gold was only $35 per ounce because of regulated prices. Today, the gold mines are reprocessing the tailings in the old mines, because gold is now over $600 per ounce. My point: When demand is strong and supply is short, the price will go up. Notice that the cost of production has nothing to do with it. The opposite is also true: When demand is weak, the price will go down.

Current Supply/Demand Situation

Around the world today, we are operating in a mostly unstable supply/demand environment. Not only do we face the war on terrorism but we also have China and India, the two most populous nations on the planet, slowly recognizing the benefits of democracy and free markets. Furthermore, in the United States, some markets are very hard to reinvigorate, such as airlines and hotels. Throw in volatile oil prices to complete the cocktail. Because of this instability, price demand is hard to pinpoint accurately.

However, in a few other well-defined markets with stable demand, good history, and undifferentiated products and services, such as accounting, price demand can be accurately calculated because, for example, accounting is driven by law and the seasons. The audit is an annual event that has to done. It does not matter whether it rains or snows, the accountant still has his work to do *every year*. So the marketplace for those services is easily measured and supplied with professionals who, for the most part, do a great job.

Additionally, the U.S. government has added to the work load (and the costs) with the Sarbanes-Oxley (SOX) requirements. It provides more work for accountants, but SOX is at best a heavy-handed solution for the issues it is trying to fix, and my guess is that the cost of SOX conformance far outweighs the benefits.

Prices and Your Marketing Strategy

The critical role of pricing in affecting results and outcomes is illustrated in the Australian gold story. Once the price went back up, processing and mining started up again.

Most companies in industry and commerce regard their pricing as vitally important to their bottom line. Studies I have seen on pricing rated it in the 50 to 60 percent range of importance. Some industries vary a bit, but the overall trend is the same: Price is important but we must not talk about it! In fact, it would be foolish to suggest that no company considers its pricing policy as of no importance.

I have seen pricing set in manufacturing, retail, and service companies and, nearly always, the majority of the pricing decisions are made at several levels. Generally, very few pricing decisions are made solely by the CEO, CFO, or vice president of sales. Usually the field salespeople have the prerogative to give discounts and, nearly always, they are allowed to discount up to 10 percent. Once again, how much do you think they will use? The whole 10 percent! The total effect of your company's price strategy has a huge impact on the net profit, but it is generally put in the hands of folks who love discounting it. Once it is established that lots of people have authority to discount, do favors, make offers, give away freight costs, and so on, positive profits are hard to achieve.

My strong suggestion is that you severely limit the number of staff who can freely influence prices. Remember that Murphy, your number one employee, is lurking around the marketplace, taking every opportunity to drag prices downward. He works 24/7 and, like gravity, he never goes away. He is out there today, seeking ways and means to somehow get the customer a much better deal from you, especially if you follow the philosophy of providing buyer value and chasing market share.

I would limit the discounting discretion to only a handful of staff who are well trained on margin and profit, who know the market, and who can protect your higher-priced, quality products and services. Additionally, if you base compensation, reward, and/or evaluation systems on margin and profit (versus sales volume alone), positive profits are easier to achieve.

As a general rule, you should seek to price upward at every

opportunity the market allows you. I loved a sign I saw in a shop window in Los Angeles: "Staying in business sale: all prices UP 10 percent!"

The kinds of things that give you a chance to raise prices are distinct features you alone have. It might be a technology advantage, where you have a major technical breakthrough that customers will pay higher prices to get their hands on. Or it may be that you have a very strong market share, built on superior quality over many years, and customers will still want to deal with you at your premium price. Or it could be that you have high-quality products that are commodities, which you support with legendary customer service, to the point where your customers deal with you because of it.

Another commonsense idea is to make sure you are dealing with markets and customers who have some money in the first place, and preferably companies with high margins that appreciate quality. The key is to identify good quality customers who look beyond the lowest price, rather than just trading with anyone who walks in the door or phones you.

To that extent, you and your team are well advised to be on the lookout for signs of weakness among your corporate customers. Keep your radar running to pick up on any of the following signals (which assume ethical managers and directors, and trustworthy auditors):

- Organization: slow to change, poor accounting, inflexible management.
- Monetary controls: poor costing system and budgetary control, deficient cash flow plan.
- Exaggerated news reports being published by the CEO or chairman.
- Company accounts: over-leveraging, exaggerated trading, mega commitments (get a copy of the annual report).

Here are some signs of a dying company:

- Stage 1, sickness: Managers are mistake prone and sluggish, morale is declining.
- Stage 2, illness: Financial condition deteriorates, customer service slips, "creative accounting" arrives, regular maintenance is deferred.
- Stage 3, hospitalization (ICU): Desperation sets in, with sales, terms, capital at any price.

If you can identify these signs and ethically address them with your customer, it can be financially beneficial for both of you. And on the other side of the coin, if you see the signs and *don't* address them, you will be tagged with bad debt.

Of course, none of this probably applies to your company, but anyone in this situation who wants to reverse any downward spiral should immediately set challenging profit targets and then move straight to pricing policy. Their survival will depend on getting higher market prices. They may have to lose a bit of business, but getting back into the black is their goal. They can be *big* and broke, or smaller and profitable. Should American automakers in Detroit listen to this advice?

Commonsense Pricing Guidelines

Prices are a determinant of power in any marketplace. If you want customers to accept higher prices you have to operate from a position of advantage.

First, when demand for your product or service is strong, you can move your prices up. So keep monitoring total market demand as well as your customers' demand for your products and services. That is why it is good to have your customers segmented into A, B, and C classes.

When demand is weak, you cannot easily increase prices; in fact, you may even be forced to lower them. If you are forced to reduce prices you must keep margins and profits in mind. If you have healthy margins and profits, you have the option to lower prices, because you can afford it. That is why you always need margins to achieve anything constructive in the long term.

This law of supply and demand is not new, but it gets refined as it moves through your sales and management teams' activities. You must keep some value in the firm and pass it on to the shareholders, the employees, and the customers.

Key Market Scenarios and Pricing Strategies

Several pricing strategies are available to you, depending on the type of market you are operating in. The common theme among most of these strategies is that they help produce positive profits.

Top-End Strategy Market Position.   Objective: short term, with extremely high prices and very high margins and profit. This is the approach used in high-fashion clothing companies. In good seasons, they make really handsome profits but, if the season or the market backfires, they have to sell their merchandise at close to cost to avoid being badly burned.

Up-Market Strategy Market Position.   Objective: good volume at above average prices. This is the approach of Lexus, BMW, and Mercedes. They price at a premium above other makes and seek to have exceptional service. By definition, not everyone can afford this market, but it will always exist.

Competitive Strategy Market Position.   Objective: Compete at market prices. This is the approach of Ford and GM, which control huge sections of the middle market. They seek the trade-off between higher volume, medium prices, and lower margins. The mathematical connection between volume and price discounts is important to players in this market.

Down-Market Strategy Market Position.　Objective: Enter market, hold share, entrench. This is for professional market players who know the risks and have some capital and a bit of margin to fight with in a very competitive market. The McDonald's business model works well in this market. The mathematical connection between volume and price discounts is also critical to players in this market (see Figure A.8 on page 231 in Appendix A).

Low-End Strategy Market Position.　Objective: Remove and block some competition. This is for the brave (or the foolish) who want to buy their way in on price and find it necessary to do so. Eventually these prices will have to go up. This is the approach used by Virgin Airlines. If this strategy does not work, any firm using it will most likely be on the rocks before long.

Getting Higher Prices

Educate all your staff on the *MoneyMath* discount chart (Figure A.8 in Appendix A) to eliminate the "sell more, make more" syndrome. Some companies have placed a copy of this diagram alongside every workstation to remind staff of the consequences of their actions. It is particularly useful in telemarketing departments, where there is price latitude over the phone. As discussed previously, pull back from the position of allowing numerous members of the staff to adjust discounts, terms, and so on.

My recommendation is to shift the internal emphasis from sales volume to service domination and move over to margin and balanced pricing. Maybe even consider giving one person the title of "Vice President of Pricing." Most customers would be astonished if you actually had the nerve to hit the nail right on the head and manage prices!

If you use an old-fashioned, standard cost approach to pricing your goods or services, consider switching over to a market-related pricing system, where the price the market is prepared to pay is the principle. Here you can discover the highest price, and use it in your price list accordingly. (This pricing strategy assumes that the market price is high enough to provide a healthy margin in the first place.)

I have a simple test to challenge you: How many letters of complaint have you received in the last year about your exorbitantly high prices? In most cases, I find it is next to none. Isn't it entirely possible that you are actually underpricing, and that you have not had complaints because your prices are too low in the marketplace?

The only way you can truly test a higher margin product with a higher price is to price it at what you think is the maximum the market will pay. If the complaints are thunderous and customers threaten to leave you, back down and apologize. However, if most accept it, and only a handful complain, consider a slightly lower-quality offering for the complainers, and enjoy the full margin from the majority. Never persuade yourself that it is a success, just because you landed a piece of business at any price.

This leads me to suggest you pay an expert to study the price aberrations caused by product quality, promotions, sales pressures, and supply chains. Perhaps your product or service is too high a quality for the market, and the market would be happy to support a lower quality one at less cost. Perhaps your salespeople trade in myths that sound like "We are way overpriced and we cannot sell anything." This needs researching as to accuracy, and you also need to determine how your product or service is portrayed and viewed in the marketplace.

How effective is your advertising? It is a good idea to scientifically determine its effectiveness. For example, are you selling the quality aspects as presented in Chapters 6 and 7, and is the market recognizing and accepting your message?

What if your delivery system is in the hands of a third party and you are getting complaints about it? With research, you can confront the delivery company and discuss changes that are mutually beneficial. Then tie them into your own quality system, and ask them to contract with you (say for 12 months) regarding the quality of their delivery on your behalf. It is very hard to get top prices in the market if the perception of your service is poor, especially if it is handled by a third-party contractor. If they do not agree to provide quality service, it is time to consider a new contractor.

In retailing, the practice of "price pointing" is popular in stores that sell volume goods that are widely distributed and sold as commodities. Products like washing machines, refrigerators, and middle-market cars fall into this category. The price that local area competitors charge is copied or very nearly matched, for no other reason than that they are competitors. We think the customer perception of price is paramount, so we do not want to be seen as noncompetitive on price. However, keep in mind the margin concept discussed earlier. Having sales volume with no profit is not a good strategy.

This price pointing approach is generally pushed by those folks who believe that everything sells on price and nothing else matters. However, no two businesses have the same model of cost, so this surely has to be nonsense. To have the same TV set priced identically as the people down the road also sends a signal to the customers. The smart ones figure it out and start to get quotes and threaten to buy elsewhere unless they receive a discount.

Maybe it is okay to have some price leader products to attract customers, but to have too many of these products at prices pitched low for the sake of competition or market share reasons will make you a low-ball operator. There are lots of retail products that, in my opinion, are sold too low because the store owners have not drawn up a model of cost for their store to establish the average margin required.

Once the required margin is established, products can be segmented into A, B, and C classes to further differentiate the pricing and still maintain the average margin throughout. The ideal retail store is one where the computer shows the margin on every product before and after the sale. Only then will margins be managed, preferably on a daily basis, by the responsible manager.

Another way to achieve higher prices in the market is to educate the customers. In some markets, suppliers publish newsletters or Web e-zines in which they discuss industry social issues, people movements, and industry pricing issues. Here the customers come looking to see what to expect in the next round of increases. For example, if the raw material going into a product is increasing in price, it is fair to point this out as a precursor to a product price increase in your newsletter. In this way, the market comes to expect a round of information and negotiations over the new, higher prices.

The invincible way to get reasonable and fair price increases without a hitch is to dominate and control the market, as Microsoft, for example, dominates the software market. Under these circumstances, no one is seriously going to get in the way when the prices are elevated, except perhaps a government watchdog who is against the free market, or against monopolies. The French government is trying under the guise of cost cutting.

To learn how the free world works, the first board game kids should get is Monopoly. I am so glad my parents gave us this game as a Christmas present one year. In Monopoly, you do not get to decide whether to accept a price, as if you had a choice in the matter—you *receive* a price as an outcome. See how much easier it is.

All attempts to achieve higher prices in markets where price is a sensitive issue will need justification. Everyone will want to discuss it and negotiate, and try to get a lower price out of you. Among the things you can use in the discussion is inflation. Inflation is with us most of the time; it creeps into the cost of our goods and services and must be recovered. So it is a good perennial that can be rolled out to justify small increases in price. Currency fluctuation can also be an issue, particularly if the goods for sale are imported or contain imported parts. Where applicable, use this to justify a higher price. If interest rates go up, they become another bargaining issue to increase prices. In fact, any and all increases in your costs of doing business represent sufficient justification to raise your prices.

Right now, because of the large increase in the price of a barrel of oil you should have applied a fuel levy to your invoices or an overall price increase to recover the additional costs in your business.

If you introduce some dramatic new technology no one else has yet, you will be justified in raising your price, in order to recover the research and development costs that went into it. You may decide you need a new factory to provide improved goods and services, which will benefit your customers. Or you invest heavily in a series of new services that will make life easier for them, and you provide better service.

All the expenditures noted here justify price increases, and if you provide the appropriate PR in advance, you may find little or no objections when the higher prices go into effect. If you educate your customers, both current and potential, you can achieve positive profits. Additionally, keep in mind that you are more concerned with your A- and B-class customers; do not focus your justifications on C-class customers.

Application

- ☑ Follow supply and demand information in your industry and, when demand increases, move your prices upward.

- ☑ Consider limiting the power of those who push prices downward.

- ☑ Monitor all incidental costs—freight, emergency deliveries, extended terms, returns, and so on—and their effect on pricing.

- ☑ Analyze your own customers' financial health.

- ☑ Set and sell at prices based on what the market will pay, rather than on a standard cost-plus system, assuming you are maintaining margins.

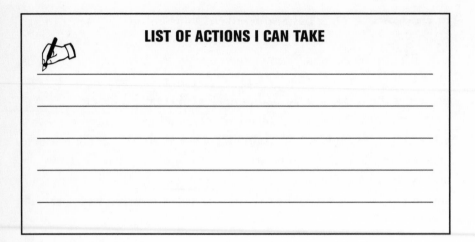

CHAPTER TEN

Price Wars and Profit

Nervos belli—pecuniam infinitum:
The sinews of war—unlimited money.
—Cicero (106–43 B.C.)

Nothing damages the bottom line or the positive momentum in a company quite so much as a price war. Some price wars start and then quickly finish; others seem to go on forever, and almost characterize the industry. In this chapter we look at the effect a price war has on profit, and what sales, marketing, and management people can do about it.

In a price war your prices get cut by your competitor rather than by the customer. While the bottom-line effect is similar, a price war is different than a market downturn because the latter affects everybody in the marketplace equally, while a price war is normally between two or only a few competitors.

Let's say a few of your competitors have decided to cut their prices in an attempt to increase sales volume because they are struggling, or because they want more market share and plan to steal it from you under the guise of competition. Keep in mind that numbers in Table 10.1 apply mathematically to your competitors as well as to you. If they cut their prices, they will need a corresponding increase in volume to cover their

Look Before You Cut Prices

Gross Profit Margin to Be Generated

Price Cut	5%	10%	15%	20%	25%	30%	35%	40%	50%	60%
−1%	25%	11%	7.1%	5.3%	4.2%	3.4%	2.9%	2.6%	2.04%	1.7%
−5%	—	100%	50%	33.3%	25%	20%	16.7%	14.3%	11.1%	9.1%
−10% (most popular)	—	—	200%	100%	66.7%	50%	40%	33.3%	25%	20%
−15%	—	—	—	300%	150%	100%	75%	60%	42.8%	33.3%
−20%	—	—	—	—	400%	200%	133%	100%	66.7%	50%

Sales Percent Increase Required to Maintain Same Gross Profit

MoneyMath©

TABLE 10.1   Price Cutting and Sales Volumes

market behavior, and many times this will not happen, leaving them with reduced margins.

Another approach for a price war is to buy as much market share as possible, in the hope the competition will fail. Often, this kind of competition is not a result of the free enterprise system at work, but rather the ego of an aggressive CEO or marketing director wanting to make a mark in an industry from sheer unbridled ambition. No thought is given to the industry or market itself; it is war for war's sake.

In 2005 when GM and Ford conducted their employee discount sales promotion it filtered down to their subsidiaries and inflicted pain on the automotive industry worldwide. One Volvo (part of Ford) dealer told me that his dealership made only $700 profit for the whole month of August.

Your business objective is flawed when you think your aim in life is to beat your rival to pieces. You *attract* customers based on the quality of your product, service, and process; that is what generates long-term profit. Everything else is short-term, fast-buck sales volume and, if lucky, increased market share.

The best example of this price market is the continuing war in the gasoline industry. Worldwide, the gasoline market has service stations opening and going broke everywhere. You see them closed down and boarded up along roads in every major Western nation. Why? You also see new stations being built just 50 yards from one another. These outlets are in a state of continuous war, with price signs out front that, at times, change hourly.

I saw one service station in Australia where the owner left a ladder permanently installed on a manual sign, because the prices changed so frequently it was too much trouble to lug the ladder back and forth for the next change, so he just left it there. Most stations now have electronic signs that are changeable as soon as a shift is detected down the road, or changed from the home office of the refining company, or changed on the latest news from the Middle East.

The pricing war by gas stations has become a fine art. The buying patterns of the public have become known to the petroleum marketing industry, and the prices are regulated by day of the week, which side of the road the outlet is on, and what the competitor is doing nearby. This is all in an endeavor to salvage what little retail margin is left in the world's most widely sold commodity—petroleum gasoline.

We often complain about the price of fuel, but it really is a good value. Compare the price of a gallon of bottled drinking water with a gallon of fuel and you will see what I mean. We do not question the price of the refined water, but you will find it is two or three times the price of unleaded fuel, especially if the water is purchased at the service station. In reality, the margins are so low that fuel sales have to be supplemented with the sale of other items, such as candies, food, and drinks of all types in order to get the service station's overall margins up.

Another factor that makes us competitive is that, to a greater or lesser degree, Western nations are sports crazy. Sports are included in most school curricula, and the interest carries over into young adult-hood. Sports are now widespread in some countries, having become an industry, despite the fact that it is an elite few enjoying their pastime at the expense of the many.

The sports industry has become so powerful that it dominates television watching in many homes (e.g., the "March Madness" of NCAA basketball), but it *is* only entertainment. Next time you go to a football or baseball game, or any national sports event, ask yourself at the end how it added value to your life. Better still, next time you spend a couple of hours watching it on TV, ask the same question: How did this add value to my life as compared to other activities such as being a member of a club team, or just taking a walk with or without the dog?

While we are discussing TV, we should recognize that the time spent in front of the box exposes us to the advertising shown there. In the United States, where TV sets are turned on 57 hours a week and the average American watches 31 of those hours (of about 112 hours when they are awake), the commercials with discounts dominate the airways. Many automobile commercials proclaim, "Lowest priced cars in town, no deposit, and $3,000 for your old trade, in any condition." Some people are watching less TV—instead, they spend time in front of their computer screens and see pop-up ads showing discounts.

Is it any wonder kids grow up believing it is sales volume that make a business successful? The TV brainwashing via the ads, plus their poor math skills, renders them ineffective in the business world without training. Now if you have an MBA, it is fine, but the majority of em-ployees I meet and work with at conferences and in training workshops do not have much of a clue about how a business works. All too often MBA programs teach market share theory as the ultimate competitive advantage and fail to stress the absolute need for positive profits. So when the boss announces we are going to neutralize Competitor X in an exciting campaign, with lots of promotion and discounts and prizes and holidays overseas for those who do the best (do the most damage!), we are then motivated by a hype merchant, and it is all systems go! The war is on: Go get 'em!

In the 1990s especially, we saw erosion of value concepts in business and society. Corporate executives blatantly stole from their own companies, which my parents called "biting the hand that feeds you." Where did ethics go? These issues, when tolerated, slowly break down the moral tone and make it okay to do wrong as long as you do not get caught. I believe it is still *not* okay to carry on in this manner. Fortunately, more and more MBA programs are including an ethical component in their offerings.

In terms of price wars, as noted previously, sometimes it is simply the ego of the CEO or marketing director at work. There are no qualms at all; he or she wants to smash the competition, no matter what! None of it is based on quality improvement or profit, just sheer bloody-minded price cutting to teach somebody else a lesson.

Price Wars and Market Types

The three main types of markets where fights are likely to start include dominated, fragmented, and dangerous.

Dominated Markets

The first type is the market dominated by one large player that controls in excess of 51 percent of the market. An example of this dynamic is shown in Figure 10.1. This kind of market can usually survive a price fight quite well because it is rare to have a full-blown war. The large dominating players have no strong interest in attacking the smaller ones, unless their goal is outright monopoly. Most governments have laws limiting the amount of business one player can have. The large player usually lets the rest play among themselves with what's left. If the large player is a professional organization, the margins will be healthy, and the

Types of Markets—Dominated

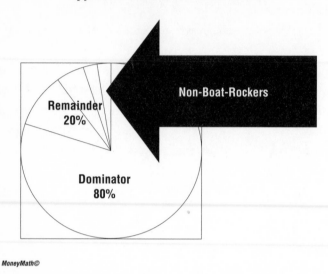

MoneyMath©

FIGURE 10.1   Dominated Market—Concentrated and Safe

smaller players, even though they are getting the crumbs, are still okay because the margins in the market are good.

Of course, if those smaller players decide to have a price war among themselves, it is exceedingly risky because a stray shot may hit the large player, who will most likely retaliate without mercy. It is like a flea biting the elephant; the elephant will turn around and stomp on that annoying flea. It is not wise to punch the big schoolyard bully on the nose, not even accidentally, because you are going to get it back double! Whatever you do, if you are in this kind of market, leave the big guy alone, to avoid being taught a lesson. On reflection, the dominated market is pretty safe from price wars, as long as each company is relatively content with its market share and position and does not rock the boat.

A good example of a company that dominates its market is Microsoft. It has the lion's share of operating systems worldwide, and a galaxy of software lines complementing Windows. I am a Microsoft supporter; this book was written using Microsoft Word. It should be noted that Microsoft does not do monopolistic pricing; instead, it has a reasonable package price based on what the market will pay. The problems come about because the package tends to eliminate or reduce the effectiveness of competitors. As a result Microsoft is facing lawsuits in several countries around the world. I believe Bill Gates has added substantial value to the human race and deserved his award as businessman of the last century, along with Henry Ford. What is particularly pleasing is that he has set up the Bill and Melinda Gates Foundation for philanthropic purposes and he gives something back!

Fragmented or Splintered Markets

The second type of market, the fragmented or splintered one, is quite scary because of the prevailing behavior. This is a market that has a lot of small players and a very low barrier to entry. This kind of fragmentation leads to the point where nobody has the power to outdo another participant on price. There is insufficient muscle available (see Figure 10.2).

This kind of broken-up market is often mistakenly viewed as safe because everybody *says* they are profit oriented and most survive. However, in reality, most of these entrepreneurs are just making a living, working 6.5 days and 80 hours a week in their own business. The types of businesses normally in this type of market are small retailers, franchises, small manufacturers, agents, mom-and-pops and some self-employed professionals. With few or no barriers to entry, the marketplace gets crowded with opportunists who hop in for their buck. A lot of small, independent retailers frequent this type of market and they discount like crazy to attract customers with the hope of achieving some level of market share.

A pharmacy manager once said to me, "If you make a profit, you just got lucky." He indicated that he made some margin on prescription items but discounted all the other products to build traffic into his pharmacy. Business wisdom requires that you produce a business plan that deliberately

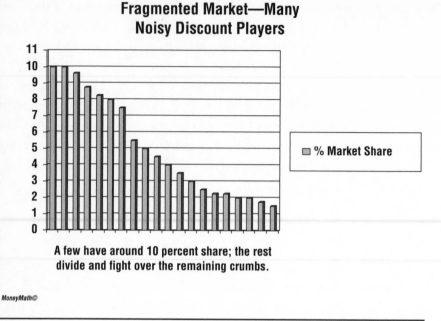

Fragmented Market—Many Noisy Discount Players

A few have around 10 percent share; the rest divide and fight over the remaining crumbs.

MoneyMath©

FIGURE 10.2   Fragmented Market—Many Noisy Discount Players

targets profit as a goal—it is, or should be, deliberate, not luck! A pilot does not say he will give the landing of the plane his best shot—he deliberately lands as planned, on the white dot on the chosen runway.

There are many fragmented markets, typically involving businesses like service stations, shops, pharmacies, small franchises, and car retailers. Most of them have one thing in common: They discount publicly to attract customers. As a result, they study each other's prices in the local area and use that as their marketing guide. If a service station on one corner has fuel at $2.65 a gallon, the one across the street will be at $2.64. Gasoline is the world's most produced chemical, and is now classed as a commodity with little or no differentiation. The clever franchisors make their franchisees stick with the head office price book, which causes the franchisees to preserve margin and run a model business with profit already planned.

Commodities generally have little brand loyalty, so the customer just drives in where the sign shows a low price. In 2002 in the United States, the average service station operator made 8 cents per gallon net profit on prices that ranged between $1.40 and $1.80. That is a net profit of only about 4.5 to 5.7 percent. In 2005 in the United States, the average service station operator made 12.7 cents per gallon net profit, on prices that ranged between $2.00 and $2.95. That is a net profit of only about 4.7 to 6.3 percent. Most of the margin (27 percent) is gobbled up by state and federal taxes and levies, and by local government laws requiring special blends to be made.

Did you know there are around 400 blends of gasoline in the United States, all with varying degrees of cost to manufacture? Maricopa County, Arizona, for example (where Phoenix is located), requires different blends of fuel, one in winter and the other in summer. The cost to close down a refinery in California or Texas just to make each blend adds another 20 cents to a gallon of fuel. There are only three grades of gasoline: regular, medium, and high octane. However, the bureaucracy requires 400 different blends across the United States. The cost of all this duplication is paid for by customers at the pump. With the higher price of fuel, something is going to have to give.

Is it any wonder the large oil companies and local distributors are in a day-to-day dogfight over what is left in the margin? Compared to the government, they get the smallest share, and then the government runs inquiries into the oil companies! The irony of it all? The war goes on!

The nature of businesses in these markets is they tend to have price wars in which there is a lot of flak. The discounting can be ferocious. In reality, it is more like a *continuous* price war from so many suppliers chasing the same customers.

In this kind of market you should play the game of matching fire with fire *only* if you have margin to waste. If it is driving you crazy, seek to acquire someone else. Draw up a business plan to buy one of the smaller competitors and get your bank to fund it. Consolidate and/or merge to form a bigger, more powerful company that can defend itself.

At a minimum you want to be one of the 10 percent players, but do not try to achieve market share by discounting and eliminating your margin.

Under no circumstances should you cut your prices across the board to buy sales. Show long-term commitment to your industry with wise leadership via your marketing sanity. In this kind of market, there is enough to feed everyone, keeping in mind that no one is going to get rich, unless they buy out a huge number of other players. Figure 10.3 shows how to survive this continuous type of price war by merging.

Companies A and B are in the same business and have similar cultures. Company A merges with Company B, thus achieving higher sales volumes. The fixed costs of Company B are trimmed down in the merging process, producing a lower fixed cost percentage. The effect

How to Merge to Survive

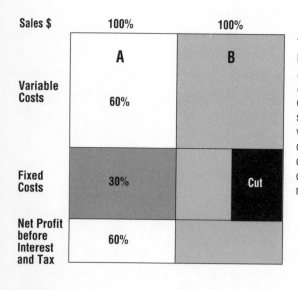

MoneyMath©

FIGURE 10.3   How to Merge to Survive

is increased sales volume and a higher margin, yielding a stronger bottom line.

The extra margin obtained through a merger will help you fight off your predators in a price war. This has been the conventional business wisdom down through the ages. The unwise business approach is to cut prices, thinking that will give you a gigantic increase in sales, giving you a great lift in profits to get you through the war. If you cut prices, refer back to the discount chart (Table 10.1) and determine how much extra volume of sales you need to pay for the price cut. When you do that you will probably need to throw in some additional sales to pay for the psychological counseling you will need as you slowly go crazy! The popular notion that you cut price to get business from a competitor to build a bigger company is, in the long term, mathematically flawed.

Dangerous Markets

There is another marketplace, like a swamp filled with crocodiles, that is dangerous, and price wars there can be terminal. This market is different from the other two in that it has just a few competitors who control about 80 percent of the market, with the remaining 20 percent left to the sitting ducks, the also-rans who get wiped out in the crossfire.

It is that 80-20 rule again. Each major business has 20 to 30 percent of the market and they are all very territorial about their share. The 80 percent is generally limited to two, three, or four players. It can look like Figure 10.4. For the sake of the discussion, let's say there are three major players in this market, all with similar market shares and competing strongly to hold their place. Then there are all the leftover players, who are too small to have any impact on the three major ones. I have called them the sitting ducks. Notice the two large barrels of a 12-gauge shotgun aimed right at them.

Now imagine a price war where you get an egotistical leader of Company A who wants to "put the other guys out of business." The idea is "We are going after market share at all cost!" So, believing the sales

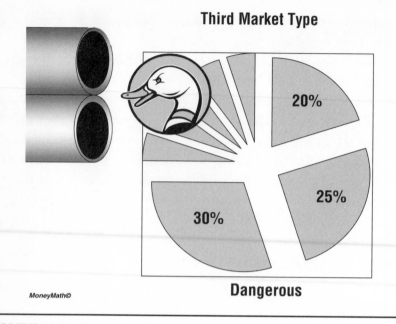

FIGURE 10.4   Dangerous Market Type

volume argument, they start strategic warfare by sending in the sales force with dramatic discounts to the major accounts, some of whom buy the deal—and the war is on!

To retaliate, Company B attacks Company A in the same way. Discounts are flying all over the place and the customer has never had it so good. Then a stray shot hits Company C and it is on for young and old alike: collateral damage! Two or three major suppliers carve each other's profit to bits, along with their own profit.

The first price war I witnessed was in the trucking industry in Australia. It started one weekend when the third biggest supplier somehow got hold of all our computer printouts with customers' prices on them, and started undercutting each one systematically.

Well, it took us a few days to find out what was happening. Our loyal customers phoned and told us they had been offered a better deal and asked what we were going to do about it. We retaliated, using the boss's "EFAE" technique: "eye for an eye." We could not get our hands on their customers' details, so we had our representatives follow every one of their vehicles picking up loads, and wrote down the name and address of the clients. We noted the big ones and attacked them with huge discounts the following week.

It was a nightmare. One of my own sales representatives won the prize for the largest discount—92 percent off the rate (price) schedule! Imagine, 92 percent! What on earth was he thinking? I was embarrassed.

We developed the policy that if a competitor stole one of our accounts, we would knock off two of theirs of the same value. It was total mayhem. Over 40 percent of the accounts in the industry changed hands inside of a month. After that stage, people started to see the lunacy and it stopped. They had run out of stuff to give away—*margin*! Stability returned.

A more recent price war of notice is in the medical industry, where three major equipment suppliers dove into an almost worldwide price war on dialysis equipment. It is not a huge market, but it is a lucrative one and the equipment is high-tech.

This war involved a U.S. company, a German company, and a Swedish company. These people *did* have the margins to engage in a long-drawn-out war. Not only that, all three also had other medical products with high margins, enabling them to fight for an extended period. After a few years of warfare, the market shares, by 2004, in a $30 billion market for dialysis equipment, had settled down to the following:

German company	25 percent
U.S. company	23 percent
Swedish company	16 percent
All others	36 percent

There are approximately 1.6 million end-stage renal disease patients in key global dialysis markets:

North America	26 percent
Europe	31 percent
Asia Pacific	32 percent
Latin America	11 percent

This market is growing at 6 percent per annum, so you can expect more heavy-duty competition. It is still in a "dangerous" state, because the three major suppliers control 64 percent of the market and price wars can break out again at any time. The biggest market, Asia Pacific, is where a lot of the flak keeps flying. It includes discounting, legal cases, movements of staff, contracts changing hands within the hospitals, and so on. In a way it is a testament to the free enterprise system, but there is always an end to discounting isn't there?

Another war is running between Intel and Advanced Micro Devices (AMD) over chipsets for computers and PDAs. Intel is feeling the pain of a slight market share loss and weaker chip demand. Just as AMD moves up to some better technology, they get hit by the price war and will be forced to either respond with their own pricing cuts and maybe lose some profit, or lose some market share and stick with their current prices. Tough call! The 2006 inventory of Intel chips in the supply chain is higher than the industry thought, so it is slash and burn on price. Profits at both Intel and AMD have suffered from this fierce price competition between the companies. The CEO of Intel plans to cut 10 percent of the workforce to try to regain profits. The inventory glut at Intel grew in the second quarter of 2006 partly because the price war caused customers to wait for further price cuts. Intel's situation at a time when a growing share of the world's economy is driven by the microprocessor flows largely from a series of strategy bungles in the past decade.

Warfare Philosophies

Make all your staff aware of the consequences of panic price cutting. Assess the war costs before you start retaliating against your competitors or before you start a price war. One of the amazing features of the first Gulf War in 1990 was that Saddam Hussein had not been outside of Iraq or seen the rest of the world, and had no idea of what he was up against. How can you fight a battle based on bravado alone, without a proper assessment of the firepower confronting you? The same thing occurred again in the second Iraq war—the Iraqi ministers went on TV and declared "We are winning" while outside the TV studio the coalition tanks were rolling by.

In a price war started by the competition, where your sales have already been cut by your competitor, do not take it personally. If you do, you will drain your sales team of adrenalin. Just stay focused on margin, rather than on market share. This last comment assumes that critical mass is maintained in your company; that is, you have enough overall business to survive.

If you do not already do it, start tracking margin via computer as a percentage and in dollars, with a view to reducing costs. In a price war, you need to quickly reduce your costs and not necessarily your prices.

From the management viewpoint, plan to reduce your variable costs and your fixed costs. Generally it is not a good idea to just reduce fixed costs by cutting staff. If you do, you reduce the morale of the remaining staff who have to deliver your awesome service, and they are left looking over their shoulders saying, "Who's next to go?" or worse, "I am the next to go."

Cutting staff sends a message to the market and your competitors, and you could find yourself trying to pull your company out of a death dive. Make staff the last cost you want to trim. It depends on what proportion of your total cost structure is people. If the staff is a 20 percent component of the 25 percent fixed costs inside your operating margin, then to cut the staff by half will only add 2.5 percent to the bottom line, and you need more than that. If the employees make up 30 percent of your variable costs and you retrench 15 percent of them, you will add 4.5 percent to the bottom line less the costs of doing it (termination costs).

Start with all the extraneous costs: newspaper subscriptions, daily donuts in the canteen, staff parties, lights left on all night, country club memberships, corporate jets, and so on. Cut the "nice to have, but unnecessary" items. If you do have to reduce staff costs, start by substantially lowering the salaries and perks of all the highest-paid people, including yourself if you are CEO. This is moral leadership, but all too often you do not see this type of leadership unless the firm is close to bankruptcy.

One of the great examples of salary leadership in a price war was Lee Iacocca when Chrysler was in trouble and he engineered a loan guaranty for $1.5 billion from the government, but the reason people got behind him was sacrifice. Iacocca reduced his pay to $1.00 a year, to show he was prepared to make the sacrifice and was morally able to ask staff if they were prepared to join him. What followed is history. A couple of years later, when profits reached $2.4 billion, Iacocca was a national hero and then entitled morally to collect on the Chrysler shares and options he held. That is the power of positive profit at work, even in a price war.

Application

☑ Consider having a permanent but annually adjustable contingency plan to fight a price war.

☑ Distinguish between a price war and a market downturn, which affects everyone equally.

☑ Decide to compete on quality—quality of product, process, and customer service—*not price*.

☑ Establish whether you are competing in a dominated, fragmented, or dangerous market.

☑ When you are attacked, selectively discount your attacker's key accounts.

☑ In a dangerous or fragmented market, you can survive the damage by merging with another company with a similar culture.

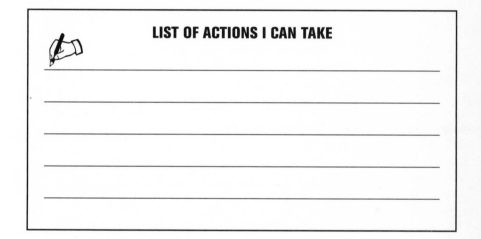

LIST OF ACTIONS I CAN TAKE

CHAPTER ELEVEN

Price War Recuperation

Without health all persons are poor.

—Anonymous

There is no doubt that a price war can upset the balance in even the best companies. When this happens, it is a good idea to reassess your position. This is a job for the company as a whole and, in particular, for senior management, sales, and marketing. Reestablish in your mind the nature of the market you are in. The famous Revlon quote is worth repeating. When the late cosmetics genius Charles Revson was asked what business he was in, he said, "In the factory we manufacture cosmetics; in the drugstore we sell hope in a jar!" What is your position in the market? When the air clears from the warfare, that is the time to clarify again your vision, mission, values, and objectives in the marketplace.

Having analyzed and classified your market as dominated, fragmented, or dangerous, you can then step back and decide what position you hold or would like to hold in that market.

Markets are broken down into five fundamental segments in Figure 11.1: low, middle (market leader), and then the top-end segment comprising segment leader, market specialist, and niche.

It does not really matter which position you are in, as long as you can *make a margin there*. In some markets, having a positive margin is

Market Position in the Egg?

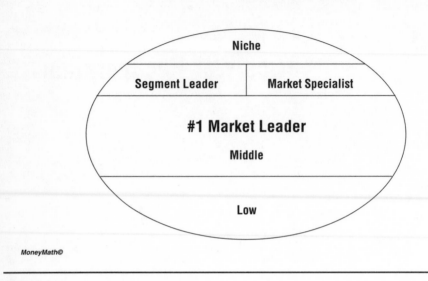

FIGURE 11.1   The Market Egg

intrinsically harder to do than in others. Let's examine this, starting at the bottom of the marketing egg and moving up.

The low end of the market is the budget price end. Margins are usually skinny in this segment and the customers are envious of the better quality goods in the middle or the top end, so they ask for that better quality, along with a low price and the option not to pay for 90 days. A lot of refined skills are needed to make acceptable profit in the low section of any market.

The middle part of the market is where the mass of goods or services are transacted. A general rule of thumb is that the market leader in this segment is the most profitable company in the market because they have the chance to spread their costs over a larger volume of goods or services and achieve economies of scale.

The top end is not as large as the middle but it can be very profitable. A segment leader is a firm that doesn't lead the whole market in volume terms but it leads a valuable segment of it. A specialist is a company that is prepared to do things that no one else wants to do and is able to get a premium price for this work. The niche firm is one that has developed something totally on its own and no one else has it. Top prices are enjoyed by companies in this segment as long as they keep their mouth shut.

Price Wars in the Low-End Market

Now to the wars. If you have survived a price war in the *low end* of a market, you can put a giant feather in your cap. This is one of the toughest parts of any market to survive a war or a downturn. It is that part of most markets where price dominates the transactions. If it is the retail low end, most of your trading will be on price alone. The battle to have a decent margin and maintain quality service will be a tall order. A good example of a business that concentrates on the low end is McDonald's restaurants. Its average meal price around the world varies, but it is in the range of $5 to $10 per person. McDonald's is highly systematized, and when that system is ignored or goes slack, there are major consequences, as we saw in 2002. The company started to recover in 2003–2004, and in 2006 it is still making adjustments to its new menu and shifting stores from being company operated to being franchisee operated, but there was severe pain for a while.

There is little room for error in something as tight as a low-end fast-food operation, for several reasons. Such a company's costs, although spread over a large revenue base, are tight. For example, when McDonald's saw its profit in the European company stores drop from 15.4 percent down to 14.9 percent, it decided to sell off hundreds of them to franchisee operators who run more efficiently. Because of the characteristics of the customer in these businesses, a number of pervasive market elements affect the transactions. However the key to be successful in this market is to get customer service quality up, get fixed costs down, and inch the prices back up to the optimal margin levels existing before the price war. Then perhaps introduce some new product in your price range, in order to re-establish your supremacy and brand image, such as the new deli selection and coffee shop in McDonald's.

Low-end operator Wal-Mart is moving into new markets and having a major impact on them. Its recent entry into the UK grocery market through a takeover of Asda generated a lot of headlines, with some predictions that this move would dramatically change UK retailing, bringing in a low price regime that will transform the whole market. However, it is important to note that this media spin hides the fact that the British supermarket price wars are indicative of a whole series of issues in the marketplace. Without the action of Wal-Mart, there would still be pressure on store prices, although changes may have happened at a slower rate.

The UK situation is a good model to show the impact of Wal-Mart in an already highly competitive market. Safeway, Sainsbury's, and Tesco keep announcing substantial reductions, reacting to Asda's claim that it was bringing U.S.–style pricing to the UK grocery industry. At the beginning of this war, Asda had stated it would cut the prices on 10,000 lines by the end of 2000, only a matter of weeks after the takeover, although Asda claims it planned it beforehand! Tesco then promised to cut 20 percent off 1,000 branded lines. Part of Tesco's strategy is aimed at developing long-term low prices by moving away from single promotions. And Tesco is a self-appointed "consumer watchdog," with newspaper advertising pointing customers to competitive price comparisons announced on the company's web site.

The Sainsbury's approach was more subtle. The company provided shoppers with a personal letter from the chief executive that was also printed in daily newspapers. This message promised to continue to provide its customers with "the highest quality food at the most competitive prices." Sainsbury's also promised to match its competitors' prices.

Now in 2006 we see that Asda (Wal-Mart) intends to "invest" £102 million in price cuts against Tesco, Safeway, and Sainsbury, fueling the price war to white-hot heat. Wal-Mart deserves no respect for its continuous destruction of quality, pay packets, and margin wherever it goes.

I have found the predominant characteristic of customers in the low end of the market is that they want the good products and services that are available in the middle part of the market, where the market leader operates, but they do not want to pay for the quality offered there. So they first argue over the quality. Second, they want the good-quality product or service at a low, low price. They can become quite irritating and nasty when pushed by the salesperson on this issue, as if they have a right to a low price. Third, they want 90 days to pay the account.

Now, the industrial salespeople love these low-end customers because they are generally soft sales targets, always wanting to buy and to argue a bit over the quality, but nevertheless buy! The trouble is most of them should be cash-only customers on full price, and that is what is difficult to establish.

So once the price war is over, put all these types of customers on full price and, if necessary, require cash in advance. In reality, they comprise a small part of your net profit, and you should be able to afford to lose them if they scream at your post–price war terms and conditions. But do what you have to do.

Price Wars in the Middle Market

In the vast middle part of most markets, there are several players, and the one with the biggest market share generally makes the most money. The number one market leader has the greatest profit because they are able to spread fixed costs over a larger volume than anyone else. The market leader usually gets a better return on investment than the others—in well-run companies, the difference is generally a few percentage points.

A price war in this section can be costly. One such war running hot now is the price of pharmaceuticals sold in Canada, versus the same or similar drugs sold in the United States. Pfizer, a manufacturer of best-selling drugs, including Lipitor and Viagra, has announced it will no longer supply drug wholesalers with its products in Canada, and will restrict sales to pharmacists who export its products to U.S. customers at Canadian prices. A recent international study showed that while senior citizens in the United States were paying $1 for a drug, that same drug sold for 65 cents in the United Kingdom, 64 cents in Canada, 71 cents in Germany, and 68 cents in Sweden.

With pharmaceuticals, there is a lot of research and development (R&D) cost and a long development timeline. Generic drugs have lower prices because they avoid the R&D costs, which can lead to diminishing research for future drugs and medicines. This is a tough question because of the moral issues and legal questions. It seems that everyone wants drugs provided at low prices because the cost of manufacturing is low; new drugs developed—magically, since they do not want to pay for R&D; and the right to sue for millions if they get sick or if a loved one dies. While the jury is still out on this situation, there is no doubt that the vast group of baby boomers will test the whole world's view of help for the elderly over the next 25 years.

Recovery and Regrouping after a Price War

Here are some clues to price warfare recovery after the war and preparation for the next one:

- Put customer service at the top of your list.
- Keep your product competitive in quality.
- Make your staff aware of the margin damage.
- Look after your loyal customers as if they were gold nuggets.
- Concentrate on the positive aspects of your brand image.
- Let the others yell about prices.

Reset your radar; it is reconnaissance time. What market knowledge do you have of your competitors? Do you have all their public information? Do you have a copy of your competitors' manuals and price lists? Any public documents they have are lawful for you to possess. Get on the Internet and see what they are doing and saying. When price wars start hitting your bottom line, the last thing you need is guesswork by your staff; you need actual details, concrete facts on which you can base strategy.

It will also be critical to check your margins of bread-and-butter products (20-80), and the yield from your A-class (80-20) customers on a daily basis.

How close a shave can you get? You will get one if you occupy any of several nearly impossible positions. For example, when the costs of your product or service are much higher than your competitor's and you do not have the quality or service levels to justify higher prices, you face an uphill recovery. Just when you need to use margin in a fight, you have little ammunition. This needs to be reviewed, so your costs don't blow out again.

If most of your business is in the low end of the market with low margins, you are going to have a tough job facing any more warfare. Look to change the mix as soon as possible, and get some high-margin product or service into your top line. This is what McDonald's did as part of its turnaround in 2003–2004, introducing new salads, new breakfast sandwiches, and the coffee shop.

For a quick injection of enthusiasm, services are usually the easiest to add. Customers quickly notice improvements in service, and the news spreads fast.

If your main technology is old or has been surpassed and is incapable of rapid further refinement, you stand a chance of being consigned to the scrap heap by the war, even though you survived it.

If your cash flow for a quarter is negative, and you have reached your borrowing limit, do not count on any further assistance from lenders. In the United States, you're heading for Chapter 11 and, in

many other countries, you are close to liquidation or a takeover if someone wants to acquire you.

It is also important to know when to stand your ground in a price
war. Some time ago, I was involved with major companies that sold
agricultural chemicals. It was the mid-1990s and the patent for the
world-famous herbicide Roundup, manufactured by Monsanto, was expiring first in Australia, one of their major markets. Monsanto had li-
censed the Roundup product to the Chemicals Division of Nufarm,
which distributed the product under the name Glyphosate (also its
chemical name).

At the time the patent was expiring, a small player, Davison Industries, entered the market with some imported glyphosate from Asia at a
lower price than Monsanto or Nufarm. That is fine; it is a free-market
economy and players are welcome. (In a twist of fate, Davison later fell
on hard times and was purchased by Nufarm in 2001.) The prices quoted
on the imported product were so much lower that the Monsanto field
sales representatives claimed they could not compete with them. They
asked me to be the keynote speaker at their national conference and I
was invited to deal with this issue.

In preparing for my presentation, I did all the homework a sales
representative might do in selling to a distributor. My homework revealed a hole in the arguments that were being used with the distributors. MoneyMath came to the rescue! If you sell through distributors,
this math will be helpful in defending against lower prices and surviv-
ing wars.

Many of the Monsanto sales force wanted to lower the price against
Davison and "teach them a lesson." Monsanto had about 60 percent of
the market, Nufarm had about 30 percent, and the cloned imported
product had taken 10 percent by the time of the conference. I think this
quick growth to 10 percent scared the Monsanto people a bit. They had
done years of hard work building up loyalty with their clients; they had
invested a lot in fixed costs such as satellite farming ideas and drum recycling; and they had a large and professional field force. These quality ser-

vices basically meant their price had to be higher than a small import/wholesale operation with lower costs.

Carefully study Figure 11.2, which is a math exercise to show the principle of bankable dollars. Let us say Product A is Monsanto, Product B is Nufarm, and Product C is Davison's Glyphosate. The first piece of homework is the comparison in market shares across the top: 60, 30, and 10 percent. Next is the amount of gross profit margin the distributors could expect to make: 20, 20, and 25 percent.

Notice the first advantage of the cheaper product. Davison's reps would say: "Our product offers you a better margin," and that was true, as a percentage. Price was the next issue: $200, $200, and $180 for the same amount of product in a similar drum. So the second argument the Davison reps could use was: "See, we have a better price, too!" And, to the un-

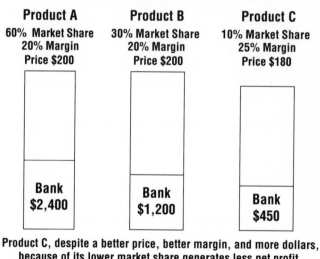

Bankable Dollars & Market Share

Product A	Product B	Product C
60% Market Share 20% Margin Price $200	30% Market Share 20% Margin Price $200	10% Market Share 25% Margin Price $180
Bank $2,400	Bank $1,200	Bank $450

Product C, despite a better price, better margin, and more dollars, because of its lower market share generates less net profit.

MoneyMath©

FIGURE 11.2   Bankable Dollars and Market Share

trained mind, it would seem to be a better deal. With a lower price and higher margin, how could the distributor lose?

However, the market shares are the secret here. If Monsanto had 60 percent of the market versus 10 percent for the imported clone (market share meaning units of volume sold in a given time period), this means six times as much of the Monsanto product was sold in the same time period. This is because Monsanto (and Nufarm) had massive advertising, a large field sales force, satellite farming assistance, drum recycling schemes, and professional labeling of the herbicide. The other product could not match this firepower, except for a lower price, which they had.

Follow the *MoneyMath*. Let us use the 60-10 comparison: 60 drums of product at 20 percent margin ($40) yields $2,400 of gross profit margin, while 10 drums of product at $45 yields $450. In other words, because of the greater market share (demand) for the Monsanto product, even though its price was higher and its margin lower than the other product, its market share multiplied by its margin yielded *more net bankable dollars to the dealer*.

When the Monsanto reps saw this math, they realized they did not need to match the lower price. All they had to do was demonstrate the profit likely to be generated by the dealer, reinforce all the great market support their higher price reflected, and then explain this economic value to the customer. They did this and held their market share comfortably. In 2006, Monsanto and Nufarm cooperate happily with a number of glyphosate herbicide agreements that have expanded their geographic coverage globally and profitably.

There are some valuable math lessons in this herbicide example. Do not panic when a small competitor undercuts you with cheaper, cloned products. Do your homework before reacting. Note that sometimes the seemingly less attractive scenario is still the most profitable, *if properly explained*.

Work out your competitor's sales story in terms of benefit and value of product and service, and quantify it in dollars and cents as best you can. Sell the benefits and value of your product quality versus theirs, *not* price. If that is not enough for some of your more demanding customers, also sell the benefits and value of your *service* that accompanies the product, instead of cutting your price. See Chapter 7 and the Universal Benefits Analysis grid in Table 7.1 to assist you in these tasks.

So you can be sure that *service* will actually swing the argument your way, learn this great lesson from Microsoft. When a customer contacts many of its departments by phone, what does Microsoft ask? They ask for your credit card number, because you need their intellectual property and assistance, and they are going to charge for that service!

During a price war, keep prices intact and move on costs first, both variable and fixed costs. Perhaps take less sales volume and keep your margins up, while your next option is cutting costs. Only as a *last* option should you lower your prices.

Protect Your Customers

Before, during, and after a price war you need to protect your A-class and B-class customers. During the war, selectively protect your A-class client base with discounts only after severe attack. After the war you need to judiciously increase the prices and regain your margin. Surround them with TLC to ensure full healing from any damage of the war. And re-rank them as to loyalty to you during the war, and hence vulnerability if it happens again. Immediately surround them with support, value adding, service, and good public relations.

Protect Your Product Line

It is also very important to protect your key products in core markets. These are the A and B products, where you enjoy leadership and strength. To reassure your client base, repeat and emphasize your value stories.

If you took a lot of damage, compare each product's vulnerability on price, and the new low margins. Educate your staff, and tell them not to panic and cut prices. Recall the lessons learned in previous chapters about pricing, margins, and valuing service and quality.

Application

☑ In wholesale markets, it is important to calculate the market share you offer dealers, because that, multiplied by the net profit per sale, is what they really get, not just price alone.

☑ Understand where you are in the market egg (Figure 11.1), and constantly reset your prices to suit your market segment.

☑ When you are undercut, do not drop into panic price-cutting; reassess, and protect your product and A-class customers with awesome service.

LIST OF ACTIONS I CAN TAKE

_____

_____

_____

_____

_____

CHAPTER TWELVE

Pricing for Profit in the Market

When we mean to build, we first survey the plot, then draw the model; and when we see the figure of the house, then we must rate the cost of the erection; which if it outweighs ability, what do we do then but draw anew the model in fewer offices, or at last desist to build at all?
—William Shakespeare (1564–1616), *Henry IV, Part III*

Price has absolutely nothing to do with cost!

If your pricing approach is tied by percentage or philosophy to your costs, generally you will be underpricing because your price is based on a formula rather than on what the market will pay you. If pricing is the dominant factor in the profit mix, many organizations appear to use inappropriate main pricing systems. They use a standard cost system rather than a market-based pricing system.

Most companies I know add a fixed percentage to their last cost each time they newly price something. Standard costing divides the fixed costs by the number of items produced, and treats the result as if it were a variable cost. This enables managers to effectively ignore the fixed costs.

If they do not use a percent, they normally calculate a fixed amount of the selling price. In either case it is much the same thing as far as the approach is concerned. Our anecdotal research shows little difference across all sections of business—80 percent of companies use cost-based systems for pricing! I submit to you that many customers would pay you more for your product or service based on its value in the market rather than last year's price plus 5 percent. Happy days for customers!

The prices you set *must* generate a margin. Notice in Figure 12.1 that both sales generate a 50 percent gross margin. However, one sale is at $90 and makes a $5 profit while the other sale is at $100 and makes $10 in profit—but *both* generate 50 percent gross margin. It is the dollars at the end that matter, not the percentage margin. A margin percentage is only a useful ratio, and not necessarily a profitable way to price a product or service. Most companies use this system even though it does not work well; the pricing system always amounts to total costs (variable and fixed) added up and taken off the sales price as a fixed percentage.

This assumes that costs cause people to buy and that you always want 10 percent on everything you do. The pricing principle that works in the long term is what will the market bear, not last year's price plus 5 percent as a formula.

Notice that in the *MoneyMath* chart in Figure 12.1, as your selling price goes down, so will your profit per unit, but not your magic percentage. In that diagram there is a constant 50 percent gross margin.

Because the gross margin percentage is still 50 percent you can be tempted to say, "We are doing okay, our margin is 50 percent." However, as shown in this example, your profit has nosedived in dollar terms despite still making 50 percent margin. In the chart it has dropped from $10 to $5, a 50 percent drop. You cannot bank percentages—you bank dollars, euros, or the currency of the market in which you are selling. To price something accurately you should check both the margin percentage and the actual dollars generated. If you want to use cost-based pricing methods, the resulting price would have to represent the *minimum* price you will accept in the marketplace. The reality is that many cus-

Why You Bank $ Not Percentages

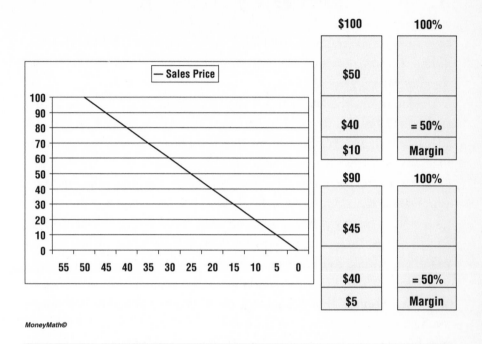

MoneyMath©

FIGURE 12.1 Banking Dollars, Not Percentages

tomers would actually pay you more for your product or service. The problem with cost-based methods is that they do not tell us the maximum that the customer is happy to pay.

It's not until we try a higher price that we discover the joys of higher profitability. And if you think you have pushed the market just a little bit too hard on the new pricing, you can always come back down a bit with a discount and appear empathetic to your customer's price demands.

As first presented in Chapter 9, here is one of my tests: How many letters of severe complaint about your high prices did you get last year? None? Then there is a distinct possibility that many of your prices are too low and the market would actually give you more if you asked for it. This is why I recommend market-based pricing where possible. Where your product is widely known and popularly priced, you most likely will have heavy-duty competition. However, you can always include value-adding services alongside the product and uplift the margins. The world does not run on price alone!

Market-based pricing means that you price according to what the market will bear, as opposed to using the same percentage cost formula on every product. When you use the formula approach, many of your goods and services could end up being priced at rates unnecessarily lower than the market would pay. By imagining that the price must first fit a formula and then that it must be so low that absolutely no one would complain about it, you have inadvertently squandered margin and profit. Price your products and services individually according to the market and not according to a formula.

When you follow a marked-based pricing system, you also need to be sure to monitor performance and sales. When you accidentally price too high, the market will inform you by not buying the product or service. Okay, so you have to make a correction. Do not feel bad about pricing upward. It is a necessary facet of keeping pace with inflation. It is essential to have margin-rich elements in the profit mix to cover the "lemons" that your predecessors manufactured or introduced!

In 1982, I went into partnership with a lawyer friend and we imported range hoods from Italy. They were good quality, the prices were competitive, and we sought to give good service. It was a handy little business that suited both of us at the time. One day my curiosity got the better of me and I asked my partner about the fees he charged in his legal practice. I asked how he worked out his prices. His answer was instructive: "I charge the maximum that the market will bear."

This is a very important principle because there will come days and months when you cannot achieve your best prices and therefore your best margins. In those leaner times, you will wish you had sold at higher prices in the good times so that the good and the bad times will balance out a bit. There is wisdom in the old saying, "Make hay while the sun shines!"

Try my baker's dozen questions about your price competitiveness:

1. What are your clients' buying habits and buying motivations?
2. Does your product or service fill a real need, and for how many market prospects?
3. How much are your customers willing to pay?
4. Have they got the money to pay you?
5. What is their past and current price behavior?
6. What is the availability of alternative products and services at similar prices to yours?
7. Have your competitors' prices dramatically cut your sales volume?
8. What quantities of product or service do the customers need?
9. What is the benefit and value to your buyers?
10. What is the degree of price sensitivity? (price on volume)
11. How will your competitors react to your price? Are there any historical patterns?
12. Do your customers shop around in your marketplace?
13. What is the degree of price awareness among your customers?

Based on your answers to these questions, you may be in a position to better know your market and how to price your products and services within it.

Personalized pricing is a great way to price for profit. If you advertise throughout your marketplace, your competitors will immediately know exactly what you are doing. Find ways and means to keep your pricing strategies more private and secure. Keep your pricing cards close to your chest, as they say.

Sell to each user if possible at a different price by having another version—alter the product just enough to make it a different version at a higher price. Do you think your current version of the Windows operating system will be the same in 18 months time? Bill Gates knows better.

Offer a product line and let users choose group pricing based on group membership and identity. This is a successful method used by Costco in the United States.

Nielsen research studies in consumer markets show that price offers of less than 10 percent discount bring hardly any consumer response, but offers of between 10 and 12 percent have an impact on just more than 50 percent of the customers. Discounts of 13 percent or more have distinct sales effect; however, the higher the offer the less likely it is that the brand will maintain its market share afterward.

So we can confirm Murphy's law on pricing! It's the same as Murphy's law on profit: 99 percent of the outcomes are like gravity, always dragging the price south, and only occasionally does something go up and stay up like a space shot—and we know it takes a lot of energy to get something up there into space where gravity loses its effect!

In the United States, 60 percent of all special offers are bought by only 22 percent of households. That means a lot of people still opt for a quality story. One American company charged 97 cents for latex gloves, but when the price went up to 99 cents, they sold more. Don't ignore price pointing as a strategy in retail. It is all about customer perception. Men's shirts in one department store were sold at $14.29 each, but when they were priced at two for $29, sales increased by 40 percent! Who can figure out the consumer's buying behavior? A survey of consumers defining *bargain* indicated that it means 25 percent off freshly frozen goods, but only 15 percent off the list price of washing machines.

Some products and services are seen as "begrudging purchases." High on this list are fire extinguishers, electricity, car tires and batteries, soda pop, briefcases, and airline tickets. Low on this same index are things such as milk, bread, butter, ketchup, and many other everyday items. A Nielsen study from Sweden shows that high price is associated in consumers' minds with high quality. The survey showed an even stronger relationship between price and quality in fashion, items of taste, and sophistication. Low prices are of less importance for most shoppers when selecting a store, but that does not mean price is of no importance. It is more important to avoid being recognized for having high prices, than to be the cheapest.

Marketplace Applications and a Moral Aspect

Your business plan must start first with the market, not the product or service. Since so few companies keep records of price effects, there will seldom be enough market data on which to base your pricing. Additionally, the information you do have is often unreliable because it will be subjective, anecdotal, and hearsay. Comparisons of similar products and services are rarely available unless you are a retailer and you can walk in and survey the competition.

Because there is no guaranteed method to determine "what the market will bear," pricing is never a mathematical formula, but rather it is an art that is learned from experience. The *MoneyMath* charts in Appendix A can help determine the limits of your selling and managing to a certain degree.

Regarding pricing philosophy, often the idea of what is "morally" right enters into the price discussion. Different people have different limits, and when staff members feel profit goals are too high, they throw in extras for free. This can occur when they see extraordinary percentages that they may not understand. It can also stem from employee resentment that the company is making too much profit and "I'm getting only a miserable wage out of it."

Staff members need to be comfortable with the profit aspiration in their workplace. If they understand it, they are more likely to be circumspect when the discounting temptation arrives, and certainly they will be more open to execute a price increase when it is explained as necessary.

A key to having positive profits is to be sure everyone is educated in pricing, margins, and profit. Too often we ignore the free market principle when our own pocket is affected, such as by prices for gasoline at the pump, and then we complain bitterly. Sitting back and complaining and agreeing with the media stirrers solve nothing. We support the supply and demand principle when it suits us and cry foul against it when it works the other way. In truth, there are several options available to us all:

- We can use less of it by walking more.
- We can waste less of it.
- We can move to a more fuel efficient vehicle.
- We can economize somewhere else in our budget.
- We can discover service stations that offer lower prices.
- We can buy on the cheaper days.
- We can ensure correct inflation in our tires.
- We can drive more conservatively.

Some market segments are bigger in percentage profits but not as big in dollar profit terms as the market leadership position.

Market-Based Pricing Systems in Egg-Shaped Markets

Figure 12.2 reveals some factors relative to price leadership in the market. Here are several research findings:

- Market leaders make the most money!
- On average, their price is higher, volumes greater, and unit costs lower. This does not mean you have to be the biggest to be profitable.

- Price premiums for market leaders can range 5 to 7 percent above the market average.
- There are other very profitable sections of markets that are not as big.

In just about every market that exists in the world, price pressure is *south*—exactly as Murphy designed it! It does not matter what section of the market you are trading in, the forces in the market want your prices to go down.

In Figure 12.2, the market egg has three sections. The first section is the low price area (scrambled eggs), where people use the penetration price model to gain market share. This is the trickiest part of any market to participate in because the latitude for pricing errors is nearly nil.

Pricing Egg-Shaped Markets

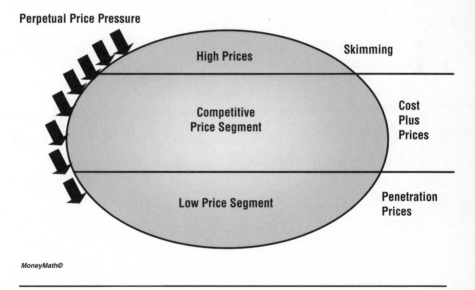

MoneyMath©

FIGURE 12.2   Market Pricing Strategies

An example of a good player in this low end of a market is McDonald's Inc. They offer a basic meal for under $10 USD worldwide, which would have to be one of the lowest price meals around. To compete with them, you need the systems, the promotional power, the supplier agreements, the training, and the real estate dollars. Penetration pricing is rock-bottom pricing from the first day into the market—it is usually lower than other competitors' so that a foothold amount of market share is obtained. Business wisdom is that the price is increased later (to make profit) once the market entry is deemed secure. Of course, this is a high-risk game, from staying power to customer loyalty, which is hard to maintain when they are looking for the lowest price (or maximum buyer value).

The competitive middle sector of the market (boiled eggs) is where most participants compete. This is usually the biggest volume sector, and cost-plus prices are the norm in this arena. The middle sector of the market is probably best represented by Ford, General Motors, and Toyota. They have some luxury vehicles but their goal is volume.

The high-priced end of the market (Eggs Benedict) is smaller than the volume-dominated middle but often has higher margins and often uses the skimming strategy in pricing to its customers. *Skimming* means going in on a high price and reducing the price later. Fashion clothing is a good example of the top end. Luxury items sell even though there is price pressure there, too. The market for quality is always there in the good times and the bad.

No matter where you think your business operates in the market, the never-ending pressure from customers is to try and reduce your prices. It is a game the whole human race enjoys. As you engage in the game, do not forget Murphy's law on pricing, presented earlier in this chapter, and Murphy's law on profit, discussed in Chapter 6.

Here are 18 things you can do to be the market price leader:

1. Be totally dedicated to and persuaded of the success of your upward-pricing strategies.

2. Develop totally unique (differentiated) products and services.

3. As a company, be the early entrant with new products.

4. Plan for long-term profits, as opposed to fast bucks.

5. Keep your competitors under subtle price/promotion pressure.

6. Constantly improve your production efficiencies.

7. Heavily concentrate on awesome customer service quality.

8. Introduce one new customer service initiative annually.

9. Compete on quality and service, not price and volume.

10. Be very aware of the changes in your marketplace.

11. Keep costs under gentle but constant pressure.

12. Run meetings and conferences that feature business learning, not just hype.

13. Use the Internet as your next channel.

14. Price lower on the Web because of its lower overhead.

15. Train your people in *MoneyMath*; remove the naysayers.

16. Ensure that your employees are all confident and positive with their price explanations.

17. Purge out products, customers, and staff who make insufficient margin contribution.

18. Be consistent and fair with your clients in your pricing.

Application

☑ Be careful not to manage and sell based on percentages; you can only bank dollars (or whatever currency you sell in).

☑ Conduct a regular check of how many letters of complaint you get about your exorbitantly high prices.

☑ Set out to be the price leader based on quality of product, process, and service, particularly customer service.

☑ Check whether your price pressure comes from customers, sales-people, or leader/bosses.

LIST OF ACTIONS I CAN TAKE

_____

_____

_____

_____

_____

CHAPTER THIRTEEN

For Hard Times Have a Plan B

To be or not to be: that is the question:
Whether 'tis nobler in the mind to suffer
The slings and arrows of outrageous fortune,
Or to take arms against a sea of troubles. . . .
　　　　　　—William Shakespeare (1564–1616), *Hamlet*

If you were given three options to improve your business performance—increase the sales volume (advocated by sales trainers), cut costs (advocated by accountants), or raise your prices or fees (rarely advocated)—which one of the three would you say is the most effective?

The scientific answer is raising your price.

Let's look at an example from an actual operating business (small) that ran into hard times between 2000 and 2003, which included the last U.S. recession. (See Figure 13.1.) We will compare the effect on the bottom line when we

- Increase sales by 10 percent.
- Decrease costs by 10 percent.
- Increase price by 10 percent.

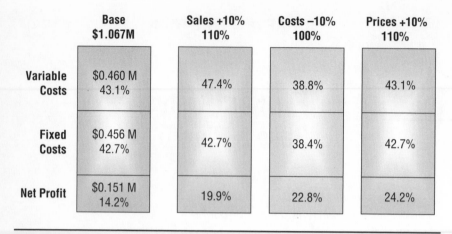

	Base $1.067M	Sales +10% 110%	Costs −10% 100%	Prices +10% 110%
Variable Costs	$0.460 M 43.1%	47.4%	38.8%	43.1%
Fixed Costs	$0.456 M 42.7%	42.7%	38.4%	42.7%
Net Profit	$0.151 M 14.2%	19.9%	22.8%	24.2%

FIGURE 13.1   Sample Business with 10 Percent Changes Applied

The base model of cost of this business is shown in the first column. The business is a nice small service business showing just over a million dollars in sales and a handy $151,000 net profit in 2000. It could be any small business in your neighborhood.

Now refer to the mathematical remodeling on the base figures in 2000. Notice that the increase in price contributes more to net profit than do either the sales increase or cost cutting. This math never changes, as we saw earlier in the book.

Unfortunately, raising your price is not always an option in a tight economy such as in a recession. For many businesses, the temptation is to *cut* prices to revive sagging sales. However, when you cut prices, it comes straight off your net profit.

For example, if your business operates at a 60 percent gross profit margin and you give a 10 percent price cut, your sales will need to increase by 20 percent to make up the margin you gave away (see Table A.4 in Appendix A on page 233). And in tight times, who can get a 20 percent increase in sales?

Panic price cutting is the way to join those broken companies making the headlines daily, except you won't make the headlines doing it.

When you take this path, the way back to a healthy bottom line is made so much more difficult.

Of course, if you are at subsistence levels, you may have to take sales at any price you can get. But if you have suffered the average percentage downturn that the industry has suffered as a whole, there is something you can do to revive your numbers. Let's call it plan B.

Plan B

In tough times, the math says to reduce your fixed costs and retain as many sales as possible at the best price to maintain the right margin. So first, you need to know your costs and model them so that your margin covers your overhead and leaves some net profit.

Second, you must be able to calculate gross profit margin, both as a percentage and in dollars. I have come across business managers who do not—cannot—determine the margins they generate in their own businesses. The easiest way to calculate gross profit margin is to subtract your variable costs (or cost of goods) from your revenues. To figure the percentage, it's the revenues minus all costs, divided by the revenues.

Let's use our previous example of a small company with a few employees. A typical service industry company operates with approximately one-third variable costs, one-third fixed costs, and one-third net profit before tax. That puts the gross profit margin at around 67 percent. Our next figure, Figure 13.2, gives us the last three years real P&L of our example company.

What observations can we make? The *sales* downturn was 4 percent from 2000 to 2001, then down 22 percent from 2001 to 2002, for a total 26 percent downturn. This was close to the industry average downturn. *Variable costs* declined 27 percent over the same period, in proportion to sales. That's why they are called variable costs, because they generally go up and down with the increase or decrease in sales volume.

Fixed costs in 2001 actually increased over 2000 by $55K, or 12.1

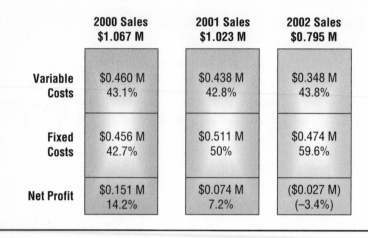

	2000 Sales $1.067 M	2001 Sales $1.023 M	2002 Sales $0.795 M
Variable Costs	$0.460 M 43.1%	$0.438 M 42.8%	$0.348 M 43.8%
Fixed Costs	$0.456 M 42.7%	$0.511 M 50%	$0.474 M 59.6%
Net Profit	$0.151 M 14.2%	$0.074 M 7.2%	($0.027 M) (−3.4%)

FIGURE 13.2   The Profit and Loss Figures Modeled for Analysis

percent. In 2002 fixed costs were reduced by $37K (7.2 percent). In 2003, just to return to breakeven annually, this business now needs $28K pulled out of its fixed costs. To return to only 10 percent net profit it needs to reduce its fixed costs by $107K, or 13.4 percent. On checking further into 2001 expenses, it was noted that an extra $22K was spent on advertising expenditure to drive sales up in the recession. That was surely a waste of money and helped commence the death spiral as far as profit was concerned. You cannot get blood out of a rock.

Margins are down, down, down. Margins in any business must always be sufficient to cover your fixed costs plus net profit—or else! In this case study company, gross profit margin was 57.9 percent in 2000, 57.2 percent in 2001, and 56.2 percent in 2002. So margins for this company were below average to begin with, and declined each successive year—a sure sign of trouble.

The *net profit* fell from $151K to $74K between 2000 and 2001, a drop of $77K, or 49 percent down. Alarms should have been ringing in the profit and loss reports toward the end of that trading period. The sales were down a bit, but the fixed costs were up dramatically. The experience would have been equivalent to being in the cockpit of an airborne plane and not knowing which control button or lever to touch next.

Between 2001 and 2002 the sales plummeted, and the variable costs came down with sales proportionately. There was a belated attempt to reduce the fixed costs but it wasn't enough and the net profit tumbled down below zero to a loss of $27K. That's a year-on-year reversal of $101K.

How does your business compare? It really doesn't matter whether your turnover is huge, medium, or small, the mathematics remains the same. The only difference is there may be a few more zeros at the end of the line.

If your margins are below average or declining in tough times, all it means is that you'd better make cuts in your fixed cost structure to regain profitability. When the market recovers you can start spending that money again if you need to, or pocket the savings. Preferably, leave your prices where they are and take less business. With less business, you will have lower variable costs of doing business.

In Table 13.1, we have represented the proportion that the fixed costs (overhead) in a business are as part of the whole. In most meaningful companies the fixed costs are going to run between 20 and 40 percent. Included in the fixed costs are a lot of wages, which are often the target for heavy cuts. But when you reduce staff, your customer service quality will diminish, your staff will be demotivated, and insecurity will set in among the remaining staff, no matter how clever the explanation.

The reason why the staff cutting approach is inefficient is that huge cuts are required before substantial contributions flow through to the bottom line. Now I know there are thousands of different models of cost for the millions of companies that are out there, and it's going to be different for each company. Bear with me and follow this principle using this *MoneyMath* chart (Table 13.1) as a guide.

Say, for example, that your company is running with 30 percent fixed costs, and 20 percent of that 30 is staff wages and salaries. If you cut 10 percent of your workforce you are going claw back approximately 2

Percent Margin Gained When Fixed Costs Are Reduced

Fixed Costs Percentage

Reduction	15%	20%	25%	30%	35%	40%	50%	60%
1%	.15%	0.2%	.25%	0.3%	.35%	0.4%	0.5%	0.6%
2%	0.3%	0.4%	0.5%	0.6%	0.7%	0.8%	1.0%	1.2%
3%	.45%	0.6%	.75%	0.9%	1.05%	1.2%	1.5%	1.8%
4%	0.6%	0.8%	1%	1.2%	1.4%	1.6%	2%	2.4%
5%	0.75%	1%	1.25%	1.5%	1.65%	2%	2.5%	3%
10%	1.5%	2%	2.5%	3%	3.5%	4%	5%	6%
15%	2.25%	3%	3.75%	4.5%	5.25%	6%	7.5%	9%
20%	3%	4%	5%	6%	7%	8%	10%	12%

Margin Gained with Fixed Cost Reduction Only

MoneyMath©

TABLE 13.1   Margin Gained by Cutting the Fixed Costs Only

percent in margin points, 20 divided by 10 equals 2. If you had a 5 percent slide in your profits, the cut of 10 percent of the people won't be enough. In other words, when the cost of your people is such a small proportion of the overall cost structure, and you hack into it, it will be small gain for a lot of pain. The reason managers in large companies hack into the employees is that it is a quick fix, and if they are reporting to Wall Street every 12 weeks then they had better be able to show that some action has been taken.

What really great leaders do in hard times is to start at the top of the ladder, not the bottom. The chief leads by example by taking a savage cut, and so on down the echelons. Next come the miscellaneous costs like the administrative expenses and all the little luxuries, extras, and marginal expenses; these are all trimmed. Fewer newspapers, magazine subscriptions, club memberships, corporate jets, company cars, free medical, free school fees, free food at work, free travel, free credit cards for executives, frequent flyer points for staff, coffee with chocolate cookies, cream doughnuts on the company, and so on. Now when all that has been excised, then and only then do you start cutting staff—as a last resort, and after all the other cuts have been taken first.

Profit is a *thing*, and *people* matter more than things.

I remember speaking to Les de Celis, the CEO of Tyres 4U, a Sydney, Australia–based tire wholesaler for whom we have done a lot of customer service and profit work since 1990. His words were, "No, I don't believe in cutting the staff; if I need to, I will cut everything else before that. I will cut my pay before I cut theirs."

That's leadership. If you are a CEO, I suggest you read his words again. The leaders who follow this approach support families, children, communities, shareholders, customers, and local infrastructure.

The Long Term: Plan A

To run a continuously successful operating business, I believe you must run a balanced company. If all your emphasis is on "Sell, sell, sell" (volume), the balance will be distorted. If the emphasis is all on "Cut, cut, cut" (costs), again, it will be distorted. If you jack your prices up so high that you lose a lot of customers, you have another aberration. Any of these three strategies in simple isolation produces a new set of problems.

The long-term secret is to do all three together on a leveraged basis; *balance* your selling and management efforts.

Do this math: Hike your sales by 1 percent, gently lower your total costs (that's the variable and the fixed costs together) by 1 percent, and

FIGURE 13.3   Simultaneously Increasing Sales 1 Percent, Decreasing Costs 1 Percent, and Raising Prices 1 Percent Leveraged and Balanced for This Firm

raise your prices by 1 percent. Doing this with our case study company results in a 24.6 percent increase in profitability! (See Figure 13.3.) Our original 10 percent net profit in this mathematical model has climbed to 12.46 percent, showing a 24.6 percent increase in profitability in three easy moves.

This is the balanced, leveraged approach of all three strategies working together at the same time, and it's the opposite of the Ivy League/GM/Ford strategies.

Application

☑ In easier times, grow your sales at the market rate. If the market is up 5 percent then your sales volume should be up 5 percent also.

☑ If you want more market share, buy a second company and merge the two for bigger sales. If you try to grow by discounting, you almost certainly will have much lower or no profit.

☑ Try to run your business at last year's fixed costs structure. That will effectively put gentle pressure on the fixed costs to the level of inflation.

☑ Your price structure should climb each year at the level of inflation. If the market is tight, then you may not get this increase. If you have new features, new products, new skills, or a new reputation, then you may get a higher price as well as sell more products.

☑ Inflation rates 2006: United States, 3.2 percent; Canada, 2.2 percent; United Kingdom, 2.2 percent; Australia, 2.7 percent; New Zealand, 3.0 percent.

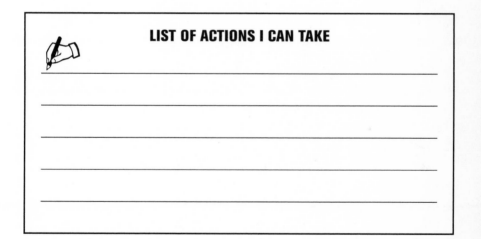

LIST OF ACTIONS I CAN TAKE

CHAPTER FOURTEEN

Cash Flow: Indicator of Financial Health

Money, like flowing water, when it becomes stagnant, is less useful.
—Anonymous

In the early part of this book, I referred to the importance of cash flow. On the surface this looks like a boring topic, of interest only to accountants and bookkeepers. To the contrary, this topic is vital to sales and marketing people, and absolutely critical to CEOs and CFOs.

As with margin, you *cannot* survive without cash flow. One of the *most* important indicators of financial health of a business is the amount of net cash used or provided by operating activities. To use a time-honored sales cliché, "The sale isn't closed till the money is in the bank." Yet so many sales staff complain when asked to collect some money or its equivalent. Chronic inability to generate positive cash flow is a sure sign of financial instability. Profit diminishes as cash flow decreases, so let's look at cash flow concepts and how they can help build positive profits. So far, we've looked at the profits generated by operating activities, such as manufacturing, selling, wholesaling, retailing, and service activities, but further profit can be generated from financing and investing cash flows.

The Significance of Cash Flow

Why is cash flow so important?

- It controls working capital levels.
- It generates cash for acquisitions and payments.
- It raises capital for plant and equipment. This could be done through borrowing, but loans must be repaid; or through the issuance of stock, but dividends have to be paid.
- It ensures profits are generated into usable funds.

The purpose of a cash flow statement is to provide information about the cash inflows and outflows of an entity during a given period, and to summarize the operating, investing, and financing activities of the business. The cash flow statement helps us to assess a company's liquidity, financial flexibility, operating capabilities, and risk.

The statement of cash flow is useful because it provides answers to the following important questions:

- Where did the cash come from?
- What was the cash used for?
- What was the change in the cash balance?

Specifically, the information in a statement of cash flow, if used with information in the other external financial statements, helps us to assess:

- A company's ability to generate positive future net cash flow.
- A company's ability to pay dividends and meet its obligations.
- A company's need for external financing.

- The reasons for differences between a company's net income and associated cash receipts and payments.
- Both the cash and noncash aspects of a company's financing and investing transactions.

Can't we just look at the balance sheet for this information? The balance sheet is like a snapshot in time that equates to what the company's net asset value would be today. The change in cash could be determined from this, but the statement of cash flow provides *detailed information about a company's cash receipts and payments during the period.* A lot of things you want to know about a company are summarized in this one statement. It's also an excellent forecasting tool.

Net income doesn't always tell the whole story about operating performance, because net income also includes gains and losses from investing and financing activities. It must be adjusted for these items to determine the cash provided by operations. The operations of any business—the manufacturing and selling, or the buying and selling, or the provision of services—generate cash flow. Let's use an example of ABC Company, whose figures show it reported a handy net profit of $800,000 on sales of $9 million. Its results are shown in Figure 14.1.

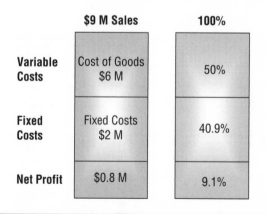

FIGURE 14.1   ABC Company—Costs and Net Profit

Let's look next at the cash flow from investing and financing activities, shown in Table 14.1, and then put them all together with operating activities.

In terms of accurate and timely information, this is a critical area. This is where the auditors have to earn their pay. This is also where fraud and deception can flourish, as we saw in the late twentieth century and into this new millennium. It's harder for senior executives to play around with the operating activity numbers, because many of them are tied to manufactured items and traceable transactions. However, once a CEO recruits "flexible" accounting and financial staff, lots of things can be manipulated within the areas of finance and investments. It's at this point where a company needs to set the highest standards of accounting and ethics for all its employees.

When you are dedicated to your company, you will be less likely to

TABLE 14.1   ABC Company—Cash Generated from Operations

ABC COMPANY
CASH GENERATED FROM OPERATIONS
FOR YEAR ENDED DECEMBER 31, 2006

INCOME STATEMENT		ADDITIONS	DEDUCTIONS	CASH FLOW
Sales	$9,000,000			
Cost of Goods Sold	6,000,000			
Gross Profit	$3,000,000			
Operating Expenses	2,200,000			
Net Income	$ 800,000			

bite the hand that feeds you. Dipping into your own company's cash flow stems from the "greed is good" philosophy, and an attitude of "I don't care about the rest of them, I just care about *myself*." This is both unethical and abhorrent!

Statement of Cash Flow

The purpose of a cash flow statement is to provide information about how cash was generated and used during a given period. It divides cash-related activities into three categories:

1. Operating activities.
2. Investing activities.
3. Financing activities.

Cash Inflow and Outflow from Investments

Examples of cash inflow are proceeds from such things as:

- Collection of principal on loans made.
- Sale of property, plant, and equipment.
- Intangibles and other productive assets.
- Sale of investments in debt and equity securities.
- Discounting notes receivable.

Examples of cash outflow include such things as:

- Loans made to other parties.
- Payments to acquire property, plant, and equipment.

- Intangibles and other productive assets.
- Payments to acquire investments in debt and equity securities.

Cash Inflow and Outflow from Financing Activities

These are transactions dealing with the exchange of cash between the company and its owners and creditors. Examples of cash inflow include:

- Proceeds from borrowing money through signing a mortgage, issuing a bond or any loans.
- Proceeds from extra investments by owners, or the issuance of stock.

Examples of cash outflow include:

- Repayment of principal on loans.
- Dividend payments to stockholders or withdrawals by the owners.
- Payments to purchase treasury stock.

Let's use our imaginary ABC Company, to understand this. By referring to the balance sheet in Table 14.2, which includes the assets and liabilities of ABC Company over a two-year period, we can spot the changes and make a judgment. The investing activities recorded in this table involve ABC's purchase of a new building and equipment, totaling $2,400,000 within the trading period. This new information will reflect in the final cash flow statement, which rolls all operating, investing, and financial activities together.

Now let's look at financing activities and start with the liabilities, by analyzing the notes payable account differences between 2005 and 2006 in the next section of the balance sheet (see Table 14.3). The "Notes payable" entry shows that a note for $100,000 was issued and the account grew from $500,000 to $600,000 in the year.

TABLE 14.2   ABC Company—Balance Sheet

ABC COMPANY
BALANCE SHEET
DECEMBER 31, 2006 AND 2005

ASSETS	2006	2005	INCREASE (DECREASE)
Current Assets:			
Cash	$ 900,000	$2,000,000	(1,100,000)
Accounts receivable	1,600,000	1,900,000	(300,000)
Merchandise inventory	1,800,000	2,000,000	(200,000)
Total current assets	$4,300,000	$5,900,000	(1,600,000)
Property, Plant, and Equipment:			
Land	$ 400,000	$ 400,000	0
Building	**1,400,000**	**0**	**1,400,000**
Equipment	**1,000,000**	**0**	**1,000,000**
Total property, plant, and equipment	$2,800,000	$ 400,000	2,400,000
Total assets	$7,100,000	$6,300,000	$ 800,000

TABLE 14.3   ABC Company—Liabilities and Stockholders' Equity

LIABILITIES	2006	2005	CHANGE
Current liabilities:			
Notes payable	**$ 600,000**	**$ 500,000**	**100,000**
Accounts payable	1,200,000	1,800,000	(600,000)
Total liabilities	$1,800,000	$2,300,000	(500,000)
Stockholders' Equity			
Common stock $5 par, 100,000 shares authorized; issued 580,000 in 2006, 500,000 in 2005	**$2,900,000**	**$2,500,000**	**400,000**
Paid-in-capital in excess of par-common stock	**1,300,000**	**1,000,000**	**300,000**
Retained earnings	**1,100,000**	**500,000**	**600,000**
Total stockholders' equity	$5,300,000	$4,000,000	1,300,000
Total liabilities and stockholders' equity	$7,100,000	$6,300,000	$ 800,000

Also look at the investing activities in capital accounts. The stock increased by an issue of 580,000 shares at $5 each, or $2,900,000. But in the previous year an issue of 500,000 shares was made. The only sorts of transactions that increase or decrease the capital stock account involve the issuance of new stock or the retiring of stock.

Paid-up capital in excess of par common stock increased in 2006, and stock was issued for $300,000. Retained earnings came in at $1,100,000, reflecting growth of $600,000.

These figures are rolled together with the operating results to form the annual balance sheet, and to establish the monthly trial balance. As we see in Table 14.4, for ABC Company, the largest amount of cash flowed from the operating activities, rather than from investing and financing activities.

When you hear of *asset stripping* inside a company, it means some-

TABLE 14.4   ABC Company—Cash Flows Summary

ABC COMPANY SUMMARY OF CASH FLOW STATEMENTS FOR YEAR ENDED DECEMBER 31, 2006		
Cash Flow from Operating Activities		
Cash received from customers		**$9,300,000**
Cash paid for merchandise	**$(6,400,000)**	
Cash paid for operating expenses	($2,200,000)	
Total cash disbursed for operating activities		**$8,600,000**
Net cash from operating activities		$ 700,000
Cash Flows from Investing Activities		
Purchased building	$(1,400,000)	
Purchased equipment	$(1,000,000)	
Net cash used by investing activities		($2,400,000)
Cash Flows from Financing Activities		
Issued notes payable	$ 100,000	
Issued notes payable	$ 700,000	

one has purchased the company and typically sells off its buildings, valuable land, and other disposables, and leases premises instead. You need to follow the trail of the cash received for those kinds of sales to see that it's all legitimate.

Okay, we roll all these figures together at the end of the year and get a final result. For ABC, it would look like Table 14.5. Bring forward the figures from the investing and finance activities cash flow to build the final picture.

Looking at these figures, you can almost hear the conversation in the board meeting about the "enormous cost of the investment in the

TABLE 14.5   ABC Company—Cash Flow Generated from All Activities

ABC COMPANY
SCHEDULE FOR THE CALCULATION OF CASH GENERATED FROM ALL ACTIVITIES
FOR YEAR ENDED DECEMBER 31, 2006

INCOME STATEMENT		ADDITIONS	DEDUCTIONS	CASH FLOW
Sales	$9,000,000	$300,000*		$9,300,000
Cost of Goods Sold	6,000,000	600,000***	(200,000)**	$6,400,000
Gross Profit	$3,000,000			
Operating Expenses	2,200,000			$2,200,000
Net Income	$ 800,000			
Total Cash Disbursed for Operating Activities				$8,600,000
Net Cash from Operating Activities				$ 700,000
Net Cash from Investing Activities				(2,400,000)
Net Cash from Finance Activities				$ 600,000
Net Cash Flow from All Activities				($1,100,000)

Adjustments are made to the operating cash flow as follows:
*Cash received from customers = sales + decrease in accounts receivable.
**Decrease in merchandise inventory.
***Decrease in accounts payable.

new building and equipment," which severely decreased cash flow. Several things could happen:

- The CEO reiterates the board's prior approval of the investment.
- The board demands an explanation of it "running over budget."
- Shareholders call board members and the CEO to account, and ask for a detailed explanation.
- The board and the CEO are content that the investment will pay for itself with improved productivity over the next three years, and everything is fine.

Never turn your financial radar off, no matter what position you have in your company.

Next up, we look at the damage that can be done when all this is messed up and becomes profit failure.

Application

☑ If you are an executive, remember that "The boss is the *results*!"

☑ Constantly check these seven basic company measures from reports and take particular note of the cash flow:

1. Collection period (accounts receivable divided by credit sales per day).

2. Sales to inventory ratio.

3. Sales to net worth ratio.

4. Return on sales (ROS).

5. Miscellaneous assets to net worth ratio.

6. Assets employed.

7. Return on investment (ROI).

LIST OF ACTIONS I CAN TAKE

CHAPTER FIFTEEN

The Social Damage of Profit Failure

Sack the lot!
—Lord Fisher (1841–1920), September 2, 1919,
in London, England

When you think through the positive effects of good profits on a company and on an economy, it's not hard to see the key fact that a truly profitable company is a secure place to work. Employees in profitable companies are proud of their organization and appreciate their employment there. They tell others. Shareholders are happy, too. In the end, people are more important than things, and profit is merely a thing, but it's an index.

All sorts of politically correct terms have been dreamed up for firing staff: downsizing, letting go, outsourcing, retrenchment, dismissal, job redundancy, restructuring. All too often, it adds up to one thing: "We're going to fire you because we mismanaged the whole show."

For the big failures of the late 1990s and the first decade of the new millennium, the main blame belongs to the CEOs who had the final authority and responsibility for management and financial reporting. They dare not claim to be doing their jobs and to be ignorant of accounting fraud. The CEO may not personally make the bad accounting numbers but definitely shouldn't tolerate those who do. Accounting is the direct responsibility of the accountants, but they report ultimately to the CEO. It seems to me the only reason poor CEOs hang around while the company burns, is greed. They still had the duty to produce timely and accurate financial reports. Accountants should not be swayed by personal greed or by the need to produce the desired result. If the public is improperly informed, the corporate CPA is squarely responsible.

A similar blame accrues to the external auditors (appointed by the board and/or the CEO) who review the accounting and the financial reports. Any external auditing company's responsibility is to ensure that burns is the inordinate pay packets they are sitting on—in other words continuing their personal greed at the expense of workers, shareholders, and customers.

Corporate accountants understand both the company and accounting. Corporate accounting follows Generally Accepted Accounting Principles (GAAP). They are the trusted watchdogs, charged with giving independent, unbiased, and meaningful opinions. There's no excuse for overlooking abuses in the billions of dollars.

To me, the saddest corporate moment of the past decade was the demise of Arthur Andersen. This firm was supposedly a trusted watchdog providing truthful, timely, and accurate audits, accounts, and services for companies of all sizes. When the virus has already claimed the doctor, we can never know the danger we the patient are in or the risks we have taken.

The discipline and enforcement arm of the American Institute of Certified Public Accountants (AICPA) has accomplished little and, through inaction, has encouraged creative accounting and other misdeeds. Self-regulation and self-discipline are preferred, but only if they have teeth and will. Regulators and Congress have failed their charters also. The Sarbanes-Oxley laws seek to regulate where ethics and morality have broken down, but the new laws will add nearly one trillion dollars in overhead to the U.S. economy, offsetting any benefit gained from their application.

Stockholders must accept some of the blame. Greed and exuberance, particularly surrounding the rise of the dot-coms before 9/11, rocketed prices to unsustainable levels. Management was often forced to live up to unachievable capital market expectations. The spin followed, with "reported results" like Enron's inexplicable figures, while the impeached Bill Clinton stood in the background playing games.

Many employees have seen their savings and retirement funds disappear in just a decade. Boards of directors and their audit committees have generally been rubber stamps and not true overseers. Involvement, courage, independence, stewardship, and public duty have not been their hallmarks.

The social damage caused by all this incompetence, greed, dishonesty, self-interest, and corporate fraud is transparent to anyone with a conscience. If you are a director of a board reading this book, do something about honesty around the board table and the rules governing those who bring you the numbers month by month.

Let's take a look at some statistics. In 2002, United Airlines lost $1.74 billion and let another 9,000 staff members go from its 83,000 employees. It had already let 20,000 go following the 9/11 tragedy. On top of all this, the ailing airline asked its employees to take pay cuts.

The social damage there is at least 30,000 jobs gone. That's 30,000 breadwinners who came home to the dinner table and said, "Guess what, I lost my job today." To those families that had only one income, that was an absolute nightmare of a day—no more income, no more health care, nothing. That's real social damage. Now I admit that 9/11 didn't help the U.S. airline industry one bit, it was in dire straits before that happened, and it was in that condition because of poor management and weak boards. United has since emerged from Chapter 11 in late 2005, but the damage has been done.

WorldCom, with over 60,000 employees, admitted in 2002 to "overstating" its books by $3.8 billion. Other folks call that "cooking the books." WorldCom managers and directors started their social damage campaign in April 2002 by laying off 3,700 employees. Then in June 2002, they laid off another 17,000. That's nearly 20,000 folks who came home from WorldCom for the last time, with a bad taste in their mouths and tears in their eyes. Bernie Ebbers, the ex-CEO, has been sentenced to years in jail, but the damage is done. Remember it's *always* bad management and boards that wreck companies, not the employees!

In 2001, to cut costs, Global Crossing said it would lay off 1,200 of its 9,200 workers worldwide. In 2002, the federal government committee reviewing Global Crossing's demise said, "The fourth largest bankruptcy in American history resulted in the loss of 9,000 jobs, closed 71 offices and resulted in a meltdown in the value of the employees' 401(k) plans, as the stock fell from a high of $64 a share to 30 cents before the company filed for bankruptcy. The company also moved up its last payday by a week, so executives and others still employed could get paid before the company declared bankruptcy, while severance checks to employees already laid off either weren't written or bounced." (House Financial Services Subcommittee, March 2002; chair, Rep. Sue Kelly, R-NY) The top brass made off with $15 million while employees didn't even get their severance pay! How utterly irresponsible, greedy, and anti-American— probably legal but absolutely immoral.

Such dishonesty and malfeasance were by no means limited to U.S. companies. The collapse of HIH Insurance, Australia's second largest insurance company, at the beginning of March 2001, with debts of between $4 and $5 billion, is still reverberating, with thousands of small and large-scale builders left without insurance coverage. HIH was placed into provisional liquidation with estimated losses of $2.7 billion to $4 billion. More than two million insurance policy holders were affected.

As of 2001, Britain's biggest corporate failure in its history was high-tech telecommunications group Marconi. The company lost £5 billion! The CEO was fired but received a £1 million payoff, despite being one of the main architects of Marconi's failure. Overall, 8,000 employees lost their jobs, and in addition, 2,000 more jobs were outsourced to another company. Marconi, now owned by Ericsson, has shrunk to a medium-sized group employing 29,000, but the social damage is complete.

Ansett Airlines also went belly-up in Australia. The cost of the collapse to Australia was 17,000 jobs directly, with another 61,000 jobs lost in businesses that supplied Ansett. The fallout: loss of an Australian icon; a transport system in chaos; a levy on future air travel tickets. And there's no Chapter 11 protection in Australia.

There's no doubt that 99 percent of profit failure is the work of top management and boards worldwide. The business press is filled daily with the *excuses* of management and directors, blaming outside issues for their bad results. It's clear that boards and shareholders have to take a much bigger role in controlling the greed of senior executives that has emerged lately. If not, governments should, sadly, regulate honesty. Shareholders should design executive contracts that have clauses limiting total compensation and basing it squarely on positive results.

If a CEO dramatically rescues an ailing major company, fine; something extra should be provided by way of options, bonuses, and so on. Executives who wreck a major company should get *nothing* for their poor efforts. And further, if corruption, bad ethics, immorality, or illegality is involved, the full force of the law should be invoked against them. They will have destroyed the household income of hundreds, maybe thousands, of families, while they themselves lived well. If possible, future laws should enable governments to commandeer the ill-gotten gains of these corporate leeches and require them to repay the company any debt or losses they caused illegally.

In 2005–2006, General Motors in Detroit ran its "employee discount" sale. This was a classic example of the Ivy League/GM business model at work: Increase sales, maximize market share, and kill any competitor who gets in the way! This was all approved and therefore perpetrated by the CEO and the GM board. Well, the campaign was run (I predicted a disaster) and GM got a 14 percent increase in sales, a small 1 to 2 percent increase in market share, and sought any means available to take sales from competitors on price rather than quality. Result? They lost nearly $11 billion doing it!

The CEO and board of directors of GM in 2005–2006 have absolutely no idea how to run a balanced business. To say they have pricing incontinence is an understatement! Now if that wasn't a perfect example of the Ivy League market share model at work, here is the salt going into the wound: Just prior to Christmas 2005, General Motors (CEO plus the board) announced they were firing 30,000 employees to save the sinking ship. Merry Christmas!! What did the workers do wrong? It was the unwise actions of the CEO and board of GM that did it, and they kept their jobs while the workers got fired. The final result for GM in 2005: $190 billion income, $10.6 billion loss.

In its despair in the 1990s, GM decided to switch emphasis to SUVs and trucks because the competition on cars was too hot. Murphy was waiting for them—the price of fuel skyrocketed, sales of SUVs stalled, and GM is left holding straws. Sadly, they have dragged everyone down with them.

So guess what—GM started the year in 2006 announcing "deep discounts" on their Cadillac products and other cars. Their U.S. sales rose 6 percent in January, and the automaker credited the latest price cuts with drawing more traffic. General Motors resorted to the drastic price cuts in large part to win back consumers who increasingly started on the Web when shopping for a new car. The latest 2006 incentives average $2,702 per GM vehicle. The math explanation goes like this. The average discount across all of the GM range is 10.5 percent. The average price paid for GM vehicles early in 2006 was $25,643. Working on a 40 percent gross profit margin for the company, GM needs to sell 33.3 percent more volume (see Table 15.1) to make their strategy work. Their sales declined in February 2006. On production of 11 million vehicles they need to sell an extra 3.67 million vehicles! Fat chance!

General Motors in Australia (Holden) has been forced in 2006 to offer full refunds to customers who bought cars in the "You pay what we pay" promotion after the Australian Competition and Con-

GM—Look Before You Cut Prices
Gross Profit Margin to Be Generated

Price Cut	5%	10%	15%	20%	25%	30%	35%	40%	50%	60%
–1%	25%	11.1%	7.1%	5.3%	4.2%	3.4%	2.9%	2.6%	2.04%	1.7%
–5%	—	100%	50%	33.3%	25%	20%	16.7%	14.3%	11.1%	9.1%
–10% (most popular)	—	—	200%	100%	66.7%	50%	40%	33.3%	25%	20%
–15%	—	—	—	300%	150%	100%	75%	60%	42.8%	33.3%
–20%	—	—	—	—	400%	200%	133%	100%	66.7%	50%

Sales Percent Increase to Maintain Same Gross Profit

MoneyMath©

TABLE 15.1   Look Before You Cut Prices

sumer Commission (ACCC) found them guilty of misleading advertising. An investigation revealed that GM employees received discounts that were not available to the general public, which included discounts on factory-fitted options and accessories as well as a discounted dealer delivery fee. At the beginning of the advertising GM employees enjoyed 25 to 29 percent discount but the general public didn't, with the result that the consumer paid $4,729 more than the GM employee. Holden believed that the inclusion of fine-print qualifications regarding options, accessories, and dealer delivery fee would limit the offer to the base price only, but the ACCC disagreed and made them cough up.

So GM is bleeding to death, and still the executives don't see this. It's because they are preoccupied with market share and volume sales, and are prepared to put the whole auto industry of America and the world at risk to hang on to the title of number one biggest producer, even though they lose money doing it. Their shares have been downgraded and it is only a matter of time before the once mighty General Motors goes broke, unless dramatic changes arrive soon! Unfortunately, Ford has followed GM into the same abyss and is in bad shape also. All this will have drastic repercussions in Detroit, for the U.S. economy as a whole, and for the car industry worldwide.

Toyota in the meantime has moved up to number two in volume and has long since been the most profitable automotive company in the world. Its secrets: Put the customer first; value every employee; compete on quality of product and service, not on price; practice *kaizen* (Japanese for "continuous improvement"); and use *ichiban* (Japanese for "number 1") to describe the company's goals.

If you run a small company and you are forced through bad results to terminate employees, you will have sent breadwinners home to their family with a sad message and possibly a sour taste in their mouths. Try and run the company keeping the staff on lower pay after giving them a full explanation of the difficulties being faced. Many employees would rather keep their job on lower pay than lose it altogether.

If you run a large firm and you "retrench" a lot of people due to bad results, and the top brass keep their fancy pay packets at the same time, you will have built a quantity of anti-the-company customers who will actively speak against the company and seek to reduce your sales as pay-back. In the same way that an unhappy customer does not shop with you again, so also the ex-employees will each tell up to 20 others of their experience. Justice is such that if the whole company is hurting, why doesn't it affect the CEO and top echelon, too? Of course, the bad times should be shared across all levels of a company. The treatment of employees and staff as no more than a cost in the financial structure demeans them to the point where they lose pride in the company and simply work 9 to 5 without passion. You see it everywhere. This social damage that has been done, often by nothing other than poor management, becomes part of the slide into even worse results and is a devil of a problem to arrest.

Radical Executive Compensation Suggestion

This is something completely off the wall, now that I have retired as a CEO! Many reports have appeared and continue appearing on the subject of lavish executive pay. Basically, the average pay of the top 500 Standard & Poor's companies' CEOs is around $4 million, which seems about right for running a major public company in times of great uncertainty.

I believe a CEO is worth about the same hourly rate as that of a top-qualified, world-class management consultant at say $1,000 to $2,000 per hour. That establishes a base salary at $4 million. If more is needed to attract greater talent, then link it to performance tied to the bottom-line results and shareholder value, which makes it open-ended but still based on results.

If a CEO dramatically rescues a major company in trouble, fantastic—something extra should be provided, such as options, bonuses, and so on. But if executives wreck a major company they should get *nothing* for poor effort, and if it went belly-up, they should be obliged to repay performance bonuses, shares, and remunerative items they received during the reporting period of the poor performance. You must have it both ways, in my opinion. And further, if corruption, bad ethics, immorality, or illegality is involved in the failed effort, jail them. They will have destroyed the household income of hundreds, maybe thousands of families with children, while they themselves lived in the lap of luxury.

Let's change that.

Next up, we will look at the opposite of failure: success stories of positive profit.

Application

☑ Focus on results, positive results—the boss is the results.

☑ Treat people the way you would like to be treated.

☑ Share any corporate pain evenly with truthful explanations.

☑ As a leader, lead by example, one that will motivate and inspire your team to work with you through the tough periods.

☑ Reward all the loyalty that your employees have shown with all the job security that is available.

☑ Make sacking staff and employees the last resort through good management.

LIST OF ACTIONS I CAN TAKE

_____

_____

_____

_____

_____

CHAPTER SIXTEEN

The Delight
of Positive Profit

You cannot strengthen the weak by weakening the strong. You cannot help small men by tearing down big men. You cannot help the poor by destroying the rich. You cannot lift the wage earner by pulling down the wage payer. You cannot keep out of trouble by spending more than your income. You cannot further the brotherhood of man by inciting class hatreds. You cannot establish security on borrowed money. You cannot build character and courage by taking away a man's initiative. You cannot help men permanently by doing for them what they could and should do for themselves.
—President Abraham Lincoln (1809–1865)

So much for some of the bad news. Now let's look at the power of positive profit. Fortunately, there are other companies that shine their results like a lighthouse. There was and remains no absolute guarantee that they will all hold their positions. My view is that the results of a firm are only as good as the leadership—if it appoints weak, corrupt, greedy, or incompetent leaders, then the results turn sour within a year to 18 months.

Keep in mind also that the majority of workers are not employed in these large companies but work for small to medium enterprises. It's a worldwide fact that most employees work in mom-and-pop businesses. So the publicity pumped out by many larger companies is either to inform the shareholders of progress or to justify to them some really dumb move that is going lose them money, but in the meantime the CEO wants to keep his job and inordinate pay packet. The mom-and-pop businesses don't usually get the publicity that the giant firms do.

The top 50 profit earners in the world in 2005 in dollars earned are listed in Table 16.1. The firms listed in boldface type are the leaders in dollar profit terms and percentage profit terms. ExxonMobil makes more dollars than anyone else, and Qwest (the telecom) just edges out Microsoft for the percentage profit position. The two lowest earners in this year were Mercedes and Wal-Mart, both making a paltry 3 percent.

What follows next is a selection of companies from around the world and their results over the last few years or so. Of course, I am looking at companies with good profits both at the net profit percentage and the dollar level. To me, if you have huge sales but make less than 5 percent net profit from your operations, you would do better to park your money in the bank and earn the same amount. So my opinion of corporations who end up with those kinds of results is that they need a drastic overhaul, starting with a new CEO and a new board of directors whose goal is profitability, not just sales at any price. That's why Wal-Mart is not in my short list. Take a look at those companies in my table of 50 who have a net profit of 5 percent or less and ask yourself what they are doing.

If you own or work in a small business, keep in mind that you are the salt of the country you work in and the majority of people derive their livelihood in places just like yours, despite the fact that you don't get anywhere near the publicity that the big boys (and girls) do. I wish I could publish a similar list of small and medium companies whose profits are outstanding like yours.

Also, a CEO or board is only as good as their last audited result, so it is entirely possible that some of the companies I have selected could

TABLE 16.1   Top 50 Profit-Earning Businesses in the World, 2005

2005 RANK	NAME	COUNTRY	ACTIVITY	SALES ($ BILLION)	PROFITS ($ BILLION)	PROFITS PERCENTAGE
1	**ExxonMobil**	**USA**	**Oil and gas operations**	**222.88**	**20.96**	**9.4%**
2	Citigroup	USA	Banking	94.71	17.85	18.8
3	General Electric	USA	Conglomerates	134.19	15.59	11.6
4	Bank of America	USA	Banking	49.01	10.81	22.0
5	British Petroleum	UK	Oil and gas operations	232.57	10.27	4.4
6	Freddie Mac	USA	Diversified financials	46.26	10.09	21.8
7	Altria Group	USA	Food, drink, and tobacco	60.70	9.20	15.2
8	Wal-Mart Stores	USA	Retailing	256.33	9.05	3.5
9	Microsoft	USA	Software and services	34.27	8.88	25.9
10	Total	France	Oil and gas operations	131.64	8.84	6.7
11	Royal Dutch/ Shell Group	Netherlands/ UK	Oil and gas operations	133.50	8.40	6.4
12	Toyota Motor	Japan	Consumer durables	135.82	7.99	5.9
13	IBM	USA	Technology hardware	89.13	7.58	8.5
14	ChevronTexaco	USA	Oil & gas operations	112.94	7.43	6.6
15	Merck & Co.	USA	Drugs and biotechnology	30.78	7.33	23.8
16	Berkshire Hathaway	USA	Insurance	56.22	6.95	12.4
17	Johnson & Johnson	USA	Drugs and biotechnology	40.01	6.74	16.8
18	HSBC Group	UK	Banking	44.33	6.66	15.0
19	Fannie Mae	USA	Diversified financials	53.13	6.48	12.2
20	American International	USA	Insurance	76.66	6.46	8.4
21	GlaxoSmithKline	UK	Drugs and biotechnology	34.16	6.34	18.6
22	Pfizer	USA	Drugs and biotechnology	40.36	6.20	15.4
23	Wells Fargo	USA	Banking	31.80	6.20	19.5
24	SBC Communications	USA	Telecommunications services	39.16	5.97	15.2
25	Samsung	South Korea	Semiconductors	50.22	5.95	11.8
26	Procter & Gamble	USA	Household and personal products	46.99	5.81	12.4

(Continued)

TABLE 16.1   (*Continued*)

2005 RANK	NAME	COUNTRY	ACTIVITY	SALES ($ BILLION)	PROFITS ($ BILLION)	PROFITS PERCENTAGE
27	PetroChina	China	Oil & gas operations	29.53	5.67	19.2
28	Intel	USA	Semiconductors	30.14	5.64	18.7
29	Nestlé	Switzerland	Food, drink, and tobacco	64.56	5.48	8.5
30	Novartis Group	Switzerland	Drugs and biotechnology	26.77	5.40	20.2
31	UBS	Switzerland	Finance	48.95	5.15	10.5
32	DaimlerChrysler	Germany	Vehicles	157.13	5.12	3.3
33	Royal Bank of Scotland	UK	Banking	35.65	4.95	13.9
34	Barclays	UK	Banking	33.69	4.90	14.5
35	ConocoPhillips	USA	Oil and gas operations	90.49	4.83	5.3
36	ENI	Italy	Oil and gas operations	53.29	4.82	9.0
37	BNP Paribas	France	Banking	47.74	4.73	9.9
38	ING Group	Netherlands	Diversified finance	94.72	4.73	5.0
39	Nokia	Finland	Technology hardware	37.05	4.52	12.2
40	JPMorgan Chase	USA	Banking	44.39	4.47	10.1
41	**Qwest**	**USA**	**Telecommunications**	**14.51**	**4.45**	**30.7**
42	Cisco Systems	USA	Technology	19.82	4.35	21.9
43	Coca-Cola	USA	Food, drink, and tobacco	21.03	4.35	20.7
44	Wachovia	USA	Banking	24.47	4.25	17.4
45	BT Group	UK	Telecommunications	29.58	4.24	14.3
46	Nissan Motor	Japan	Vehicles	57.77	4.19	7.3
47	Home Depot	USA	Retailing hardware	62.90	4.04	6.4
48	ABN-Amro	Netherlands	Banking	23.64	3.98	16.8
49	China Mobile (HK)	Hong Kong/ China	Telecommunications services	15.53	3.96	25.5
50	Washington Mutual	USA	Banking	18.01	3.88	21.5

Source: www.forbes.com.

see a reversal due to the appointment of a CEO or board that takes their eye off the ball. The *MoneyMath* in this book, however, will never change because math is permanent. It will never change to suit a business fad, strategy based in poor mathematics, or some notion that defies the laws of mathematics.

All the following data is from the public published results of the firms.

Microsoft (United States)

I start the list with Microsoft and its results because Bill Gates, via his Bill & Melinda Gates Foundation, has decided to invest a lot of his earnings back into the human race that has made his fortune possible. He is becoming with time a philanthropic icon like Andrew Carnegie. Figure 16.1 shows Microsoft from 1997 to 2002.

Table 16.2 shows five years of Microsoft's annual results and I have summarized the net profit margin into percentages as follows. Its profit records continue: in 2001, 29.0 percent; in 2002, 18.9 percent; in 2003, 30.8 percent; in 2004, 22.2 percent; in 2005, 25.9 percent.

Microsoft has over 50,000 employees worldwide, and is listed as the seventh most admired company in the United States. It is clearly a

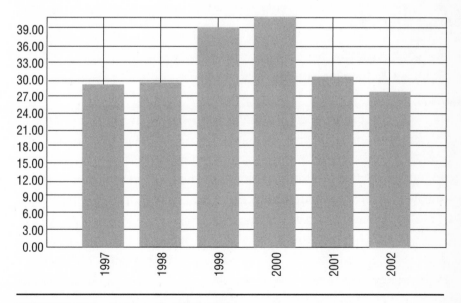

FIGURE 16.1   Microsoft, 1997–2002

TABLE 16.2   Microsoft Financial Highlights, 2001 to 2005
(Dollars in Millions Except Per-Share Data)

FISCAL YEAR ENDED JUNE 30	2001	2002	2003	2004	2005
Revenue	$25,296	$28,365	$32,187	$36,835	$39,788
Operating income	11,720	8,272	9,545	9,034	14,561
Income before accounting change	7,721	5,355	7,531	8,168	12,254
Net income	7,346	5,355	7,531	8,168	12,254
Diluted earnings per share before accounting change	0.69	0.48	0.69	0.75	1.12
Diluted earnings per share	0.66	0.48	0.69	0.75	1.12
Cash dividends declared per share	—	—	0.08	0.16	3.40
Cash and short-term investments	31,600	38,652	49,048	60,592	37,751
Total assets	58,830	69,910	81,732	94,368	70,815
Long-term obligations	2,287	2,722	2,846	4,574	5,823
Stockholders' equity	47,289	54,842	64,912	74,825	48,115

secure place to be. Look at Microsoft in 2005: Globally it ranked number two in market value worldwide behind GE, but not number one in sales worldwide. Which title would you rather have—biggest sales or most profitable?

Johnson & Johnson (United States)

Johnson & Johnson (J&J) is listed as number 17 in worldwide profitability rankings and number 6 among America's top 10 most admired companies. Its results in recent years are shown in Table 16.3.

Note J&J's continuing profitability and sales growth, coupled with steady growth in employment. Do you think staff like working there? They're paid well and have job security.

To grasp the outstanding success of Johnson & Johnson, have a look at their model of cost diagram (Figure 16.2) applied to their 2005 result. They made a gross profit margin of 72.4 percent ($36.56 billion) and a net profit of 20.6 percent ($10.411 billion).

TABLE 16.3 Johnson & Johnson Five-Year Results in Brief—Worldwide (Dollars in Millions Except Per-Share Figures)

	2005	2004	2003	2002	2001
Sales to customers	$50,514	$47,348	41,862	36,298	32,317
Net earnings	10,411	8,509	7,197	6,597	5,668
Percent return on average shareholders' equity	28.1	25.4	29.0	26.5	25.4
Net earnings/share					
Basic	3.50	2.87	2.42	1.65	1.87
Diluted	3.46	2.84	2.40	1.61	1.84
Cash dividends paid	1.275	1.095	0.925	0.795	0.70
Shareholders' equity	12.73	10.71	9.05	7.64	7.95
Market price (year-end close)	60.10	63.42	50.62	52.53	59.86
Average shares outstanding (millions)					
Basic	2,973.9	2,968.4	2,968.1	2,998.3	3,033.8
Diluted	3,012.5	3,003.5	3,008.1	3,054.1	3,099.3
Number employees (thousands)	115.6	109.9	110.6	108.3	101.8

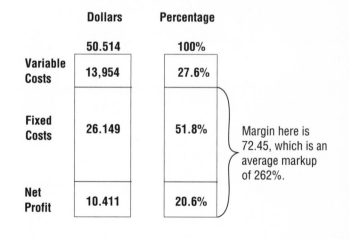

Johnson & Johnson 2005 Model

	Dollars	Percentage	
	50.514	100%	
Variable Costs	13,954	27.6%	
Fixed Costs	26.149	51.8%	Margin here is 72.45, which is an average markup of 262%.
Net Profit	10.411	20.6%	

MoneyMath©

FIGURE 16.2 Johnson & Johnson 2005 Model

TABLE 16.4 GE's Statement of Earnings for the Years ended December 31, 2003–2005 (In Millions; Per-Share Amounts in $)

	2005	2004	2003
Revenues			
Sales of goods	$59,837	55,005	49,963
Sales of services	32,752	29,700	22,391
Other income	1,683	1,064	602
GECS earnings from continuing operations before accounting changes	—	—	—
GECS revenues from services	55,430	48,712	39,930
Total revenues	149,702	134,481	112,886
Costs and Expenses			
Cost of goods sold	46,169	42,645	37,189
Cost of services sold	20,645	19,114	14,017
Interest and other financial charges	15,187	11,656	10,460
Investment contracts, insurance losses, and insurance annuity benefits	5,474	3,583	3,069
Provision for losses on financing receivables	3,841	3,888	3,752
Other costs and expenses	35,271	33,096	26,480
Minority interest in net earnings of consolidated affiliates	986	728	308
Total costs and expenses	127,573	114,710	95,275
Earnings from Continuing Operations before Income Taxes and Accounting Changes	22,129	19,771	17,611
Provision for income taxes	(3,854)	(3,486)	(3,845)
Earnings from Continuing Operations before Accounting Changes	18,275	16,285	13,766
Earnings (loss) from discontinued operations, net of taxes	(1,922)	534	2,057
Earnings before Accounting Changes	16,353	16,819	15,823
Cumulative effect of accounting changes	—	—	(587)
Net Earnings	16,353	16,819	15,236
Per-share amounts			
Per-share amounts—earnings from continuing operations before accounting changes			
Diluted earnings per share	1.72	1.56	1.37
Basic earnings per share	1.73	1.57	1.37
Per-share amounts—earnings before accounting changes			
Diluted earnings per share	1.54	1.61	1.57
Basic earnings per share	1.55	1.62	1.58
Per-share amounts—net earnings			
Diluted earnings per share	1.54	1.61	1.51
Basic earnings per share	1.55	1.62	1.52
Dividends Declared per Share	0.91	$0.82	$0.77

General Electric (United States)

General Electric (GE) traces its history back to Thomas Edison, who was America's greatest inventor. Edison executed the first of his 1,093 successful U.S. patent applications in October 1868, at the age of 21.

General Electric Company was incorporated on April 15, 1892, in a merger of the Edison General Electric Company and the Thomson-Houston Electric Company. GE is the only company listed in the Dow Jones Industrial Average today that was also included in the original index in 1896. Edison's company has gone through transformation after transformation, and has survived the first World War, the Great Depression, World War II, and every other obstacle that got in its way.

Today GE is a diversified technology and services company dedicated to creating products that make life better, from aircraft engines and power generation to financial services, medical imaging, television programming, and plastics. Operating in more than 100 countries, GE employs more than 300,000 people worldwide. Table 16.4 displays GE's Statement of Earnings for 2003–2005. Interestingly, GE has paid dividends *every quarter since 1899*, and it has increased dividends every year since 1975.

Southwest Airlines (United States)

This company started in 1971 and has had consecutive years of profit ever since. It is headed by the 71-year-old Herb Kelleher, whose pay in 2002 right after 9/11 was $652,000 and is still less than $1million. Is he a legend or what?

Southwest Airlines has provided short-haul, high-frequency, point-to-point, low-fare air transportation services since 1972. At the end of 2005 it had 445 Boeing 737 aircraft flying between 61 cities in 31 states throughout the United States. In 2005 Southwest reported that

TABLE 16.5   Southwest Airlines Year-End Figures, 2004 and 2005

SOUTHWEST RESULTS	2005	2004	% CHANGE
Operating revenues	$7,584 M	$6,530 M	16.1%
Operating expenses	$6,764 M	$5,976 M	3.2%
Operating income	$820 M	$554 M	48%
Operating margin	10.8%	8.5%	2.3 points
Net income	$548 M	$313 M	75.1%
Net margin	7.2%	4.8%	2.4 points
Net income per share—basic	$0.70	$0.40	75%
Net income per share—diluted	$0.67	$0.35	76.3%
Stockholders' equity	$6,675 M	$5,524 M	20.8%
Return on stockholders' equity	9.0%	5.9%	3.1 points
Revenue passengers carried	77,693,875	70,992,703	12.7%
Available seat miles	85,172,795	76,861,296	10.8%
Load factor	70.7%	69.5%	1.2 points

65 percent of its customers booked their flights on the Internet. (See Table 16.5.)

A pilot friend of mine, Captain Jim Cox of Scottsdale, Arizona, flew with Southwest for 20 years or more. Sadly, in 2002 he contracted kidney cancer and passed on in 2003. At his memorial I noticed that dozens of Southwest employees turned up in full company uniform. In his final letter as a tribute to his employer Southwest, he said how much he loved working there, how he thought he was "overpaid," and that Southwest had afforded him the best years of his life. Now Jim had flown planes on carriers in the U.S. Navy and knew excitement, but Southwest was his love. His colleagues cried over Jim's letter because they love the company, too! It's a service culture throughout the organization.

Happy, happy day.

Nokia (Finland, EU)

Nokia's history started with the wood pulp mill established by Fredrik Idestam in 1865. The turn of the century also saw the birth of two other

TABLE 16.6   Nokia Results Year End 2005

	2005	2004
Net sales	34,191	29,371
Cost of sales	22,209	18,179
Research and development expenses	3,825	3,776
Selling and marketing expenses	2,961	2,564
Administrative and general expenses	609	611
Other income and expenses	52	181
Amortization of goodwill	—	96
Operating profit	4,639	4,326
Share of results of associated companies	10	−26
Financial income and expenses	322	405
Profit before tax and minority interests	4,971	4,705
Tax	1,281	1,446
Profit before minority interests	3,690	3,259
Profit attributable to minority interests	−74	−67
Profit attributable to equity holders	3,616	3,192
Earnings per share, EUR		
Basic	0.83	0.69
Diluted	0.83	0.69

companies, the Finnish Rubber Works and Suomen Punomotehdas Oy, a wire and cable manufacturer. Nokia Ab also started generating electricity during the early years.

In the early 1900s, the companies grew in spite of external threats. In addition to the traditional forestry industry, the other industries also achieved a good position on the Finnish market. The period between and immediately after the two world wars was dedicated to developing the businesses. The 1960s, however, were more important as the start of Nokia's entry into the telecommunications market. A radiotelephone was developed in 1963 followed in 1965 by data modems—long before such items were even heard of by the public.

The changes in world economy led to the company's different

businesses having to concentrate on domestic markets. This would later be reversed as the company started shifting its focus onto international markets.

In 1994, CEO Jorma Ollila formulated the key elements of Nokia's new strategy: Leave old businesses and focus on telecommunications. The implementation of the new strategy helped the company's finances reach a sound standing, and created the basis for a successful conquer of the world markets. (See Table 16.6.)

For a company that is over 140 years old, its profit results are continuing positive due to diligence of the staff and leadership. Read Nokia's ethics and social responsibility statement on the Internet to see why. Nokia is Finland's number one company and in 2006 has over 50,000 employees worldwide in safe hands.

The Royal Bank of Scotland Group (United Kingdom)

The Royal Bank of Scotland Group, founded in 1727, is one of the world's leading financial service providers, and one of the oldest banks in the United Kingdom.

Following the takeover of National Westminster Bank in 2000, the Group has continued to grow its business around the globe and, in addition to its strong UK presence, has offices in Europe, the United States, and Asia. By the end of 2002, it was the second largest bank in Europe and the fifth largest in the world, by capitalization. (See Table 16.7.)

In the United Kingdom, the Royal Bank's branch network spans the nation and boasts a pedigree of great variety and distinction. Its history is very much the history of banking in the British Isles over the past four centuries, as the Royal Bank can trace its roots back to the sixteenth century through the amalgamation of more than 200 private and joint stock banks.

The Royal Bank of Scotland employs over 137,000 people worldwide. Enviable results and positive!

TABLE 16.7   Royal Bank of Scotland Results 2001–2005 (in Pounds)

2001 INCOME	2002 INCOME	2003 INCOME	2004 INCOME	2005 INCOME
14,558	17,016	19,251	22,754	25,569
Change over previous year	+16.9%	+13.1%	+18.2%	+11.3%
Profit				
4,252	4,852	6,076	6,917	7,936
29.2%	28.5%	31.6%	30.4%	31.0%
Change over previous year	+14.1%	+25.2%	+13.8%	+14.7%

Foster's Brewing (Australia)

Foster's is an amazing American/Australian success story little known to the person in the street in America or Australia. One fine day in 1887, two Americans of Irish extraction, William M. Foster and his brother Ralph R. Foster, stepped off a clipper ship in Melbourne. They had sailed from New York with the dream of starting a successful brewery "down under," which was in the middle of a gold rush. They set up the Foster's Brewing Company in 1888 in Rokeby Street, Collingwood, Melbourne, Victoria, which was the richest city in the world at the time because of the impact of 30 years of gold rush and the discovery of the world's largest nugget in Victoria.

The Foster's Brewing Company was largely responsible for the development of packaged beers, having been established with a German head brewer and ice-making machinery from the United States. This was the brothers' success story—if you bought a truckload of their beer they would give you free ice. What a marketing advantage they launched with! The first bottle of Foster's Lager was an immediate hit with drinkers who favored chilled beer during the hot Australian summer months. But the crash of 1893 resulted in a long economic recession in Australia. To help cut costs in the face of hard times, the Foster's Brewing Company and Carlton Brewery amalgamated with four other breweries to form Carlton and United Breweries (CUB). The two Foster brothers went back to the United States.

At the turn of the twentieth century, Foster's was still a small operation but it was already heading toward its current focus. It was selling beer to all Australian states and exporting to Samoa and South Africa. In 1908, not long after its amalgamation into CUB, the Foster's brewery was closed and the Foster's name was almost lost. CUB only continued to brew Foster's brand beer because of orders from Queensland and Western Australia.

Foster's Wine Estates controls more than 15,000 hectares of vineyards in the premium wine growing regions of Australia, California, New Zealand, Italy, and France, and operates more than 20 wineries across the world. It helped make Australia the world's number four wine exporting country. It has 13,400 employees. (See Table 16.8.)

Today Foster's beer is brewed in eight countries: Australia, Canada, China, England, Germany, Ireland, Spain, and Sweden. It is sold in over 135 countries and is the leading foreign beer in many markets. With a surname like Foster, wouldn't it be nice if I got a royalty of 1 cent per can or bottle! However, I do have an original 1889 green glass vintage bottle as a keepsake.

TABLE 16.8   Foster's Brewing Company—Recent Results

	FISCAL YEAR ENDING JUNE 30, 2005	FISCAL YEAR ENDING JUNE 30, 2004	PERCENT CHANGE
Income			
Net sales revenue	3,972.3	3,908.1	1.6%
EBITDA	895.8	885.1	1.2%
Net Profit after Tax	936.1	799.3	17.1%
Earnings per share	46.8¢	38.6¢	21.2%
Return on capital	13.9%	13.0%	0.9 points

Fisher & Paykel (New Zealand)

A New Zealand based international company, using innovation to develop a unique range of products and services for its customers around the world, Fisher & Paykel's historical base is as a marketer of white goods.

Sir Wolf Fisher and Maurice Paykel commenced business in 1934 as an importer of refrigerators and washing machines. In 1938 they started manufacturing appliances under license to several major international appliance companies. Driven by a desire to export, they moved to manufacturing products using in-house technology in the mid-1960s. Since then they have added health care, machinery, finance, and other allied businesses. Fisher & Paykel is a testament to the fact that size does not matter. The population of New Zealand is only 4 million, but that does not mean they cannot take on the world.

Their first manufacturing licenses were from American companies like Kelvinator, and now F&P markets appliances directly back into the United States. The exuberant leaders, Chairman Gary Paykel and the directors of this company, seek to distribute *to shareholders* 60 percent of net profit after tax, and 100 percent from the health care division. Recent Fisher & Paykel results are shown below in Table 16.9.

TABLE 16.9   Fisher & Paykel—Recent Results

OPERATING REVENUE	2005 ($000s)	2004 ($000s)	2003 ($000s)	2002 ($000s)
Totals	1,039	939	835	803
Profit after Tax	68.6	85.3	73.4	41.5
Earnings/share	0.26	0.33	0.28	1.13

My Seven Habits of Highly Effective Companies

To get the power of positive profit running in the business world, there are a number of improvements I would like to suggest.

First, education in math at the high school level needs vast improvement in the United States, Canada, the United Kingdom, Australia, and New Zealand if we want to maintain prosperity. This should be followed by improvement in business math—accounting, marketing, finance—at the tertiary levels of education. I would encourage young people to grasp the value of discipline and hard work and apply themselves to the appreciation of math, as do most Asians.

Second, for those already in business, whether corporate or their own business, I recommend detailed training on margin management, and teaching that shows the fallacy of the "sales volume at any cost" competitive strategy, taught without challenge in some Ivy League universities, which is severely eroding profits and families in the West. Study *MoneyMath*.

Third, inside all corporations, big or small, get started on balanced selling, balanced managing, and balanced marketing, with professional management of price and revenue right up there alongside management of sales and management of costs. The time-honored business formula has not changed: Profit equals revenue minus costs.

Fourth, the concept that it is *everybody's* job to improve the bottom line needs introducing everywhere. Entrepreneurs who hide their profits from employees kill off the next generation of entrepreneurs—those very employees!

Fifth, the use of software that helps manage the profit mix, with segmentation of customers, of products, and of margins, will greatly help the fine-tuning of a business toward profit.

Sixth, new employees need some simple math tests to see that they understand the fundamentals of generating profit in transactions (see the financial management test in Appendix B). They also need the vision, mission, values, and objectives of their employer shared with them in such a way that they enthusiastically desire to implement them. If their attitude is that they are only there 9 to 5, it is because they have perceived the senior management to be leeching the company to death without restraint. Don't blame employees for their lack of interest if that is the case.

Seventh, start competing on quality, not just price alone. It's a myth that everything only sells on price these days. Quality of product, quality of process, and quality of service can all add value to your customers. Study carefully why and how Toyota has overhauled the rest of the automotive world using quality, not just price.

Senior management and directors need tougher rules and guidelines when they deliver bad results. Governments may impose some rules, but the best discipline is a board and management that uphold truth in reporting, productive performance, innovation with ideas, and total commitment to the customers, both external and internal (shareholders are internal customers). Any social damage they cause should also apply in reverse to them. They should *lose any rewards* for poor performance. They also need goals like wanting to be listed as one of the 10 Best Boards of Directors in *BusinessWeek* magazine. Why can't directors have key performance indicators (KPIs) like the rest of the company?

The practice of the chairman of many companies also being the CEO needs reviewing. Outside directors who are appointed because of their expertise and wisdom are the balancing act needed in many boards. For companies with over $100 million turnover, there probably needs to be some recommended minimum number of directors, including a proportion of impartial outside directors who theoretically will have no conflicts of interest. Directors and managers doing deals with their own company is a clear conflict of interest that should be made illegal and visited with punitive measures worldwide. For companies with over $1 billion in revenue, there could be an appointed external public accountant who is not part of the auditing team nor a part of the accounting company that does the books. Maybe this third watchdog person would have the job of ensuring that accurate, true, and timely records are made and kept, separately from auditors.

Application

☑ Study the figures of profitable companies and see if you can uncover their success strategies. Similarly, study the reasons for failure of unprofitable organizations.

☑ Educate your staff in the math of buying and selling, and give them detailed help on margin.

☑ Read through the *MoneyMath* charts in Appendix A.

☑ Promote the idea that it is *everybody's* job to enhance the company profits, not just senior management's.

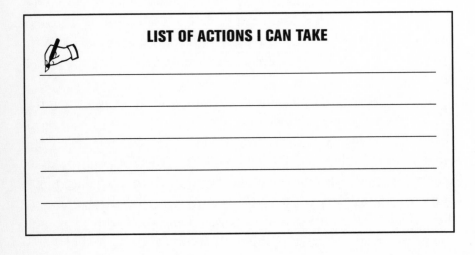

LIST OF ACTIONS I CAN TAKE

CHAPTER SEVENTEEN

Responsibilities Attached to Profit Making

We make a living by what we get,
We make a life by what we give.
— Winston Churchill (1874–1965)

Philanthropy and success, I believe, are blood brothers.

By 1900 the United States was a growing nation full of dreams and visions with moral virtue. It was creating millionaires, and none was richer than Andrew Carnegie (1837–1919). By the time Carnegie died in 1919, he had given away $350,695,653, which in today's values is equivalent to giving away $12 billion or more. At his death, the last $30,000,000 (1.05 billion today) was likewise given away to foundations, charities, and pensioners. His foundations are still donating today.

Andrew Carnegie saw himself as an amateur writer and opinion maker, and he often wrote to newspapers. As one of America's most successful businessmen and, perhaps, the world's then richest man, he felt his opinions were important because he had "made it." He loved seeing his own comments in print, and it fed his desire to write more.

He was a man of contradictions and was convinced of the merits of poverty in building character. His huge fortune, produced by "the toilers of Pittsburgh," he gave back to the city he loved, to America, to Scotland, to England, and to the world. He built 2,507 libraries around the world and rebuilt his home town of Dunfermline in Scotland. Seriously religious, he spoke in spiritual terms when expressing what he hoped his gifts would achieve in the lives of those employees whose labor had produced his wealth: "Man does not live by bread alone," he quoted.

Carnegie was deeply committed to the notion that education was the key to a successful life. Over the doors of the Carnegie Library of Pittsburgh, carved in stone, are his own words, "Free to the People." The Carnegie Library in Phoenix, Arizona (my hometown), still stands on Washington Avenue, a monument to his giving along with the other two and a half thousand libraries.

He commented about wealth a lot. "I have known millionaires starving for lack of the nutriment which alone can sustain all that is human in man, and I know workmen, and many so-called poor men, who revel in luxuries beyond the power of those millionaires to reach. It is the mind that makes the body rich. There is no class so pitiably wretched as that which possesses money and nothing else. Money can only be the useful drudge of things immeasurably higher than itself," he said in a speech for the presentation of the Carnegie Library to the people of Pittsburgh, November 5, 1895.

He wrote a treatise in 1889, "The Gospel of Wealth," in which he said that a rich man is only a *trustee* of his fortune—that it is his duty to spread it around "for the improvement of mankind."

He was under 5′6″ tall and sensitive about it, but he was a giant of a man philanthropically. His life spanned the industrialization of the United States and he was one of its leading entrepreneurs, the one who taught Mark Twain, "Put all your eggs in one basket and then watch that basket." He had an astonishing social conscience for a multimillionaire. "The man who dies thus rich, dies disgraced," he penned and practiced.

The spirit of Andrew Carnegie was his faith in the ability of individuals to better themselves and thus the society in which they live, and the families that they support. He is a role model who puts our current selfish generations to shame. You would think that the wealthy are planning to take their money with them when they pass on—a fond wish!

Ethics and Morality

With every responsibility comes accountability. The spate of corporate busts stemming from the 1990s shows again that human nature, when exposed to vast amounts of money, is tempted to steal some. This is why we have boards, directors, auditors, and so on, as third-party guides to ensure that the entity is running itself openly and honestly and that the books of account represent a fair and true record of transactions, of assets and liabilities, and of future security to the employees and investors who have placed their time and money into it.

In truth, profit is just a monetary thing that is the outcome of good products and services of value to one or more customers who describe themselves as satisfied. If I were pushed to decide between the importance of each, I would say that *people matter more than things*. That is to say, if you have a difference of opinion about the price of something, put the customer relationship first above the profit motive, because it is much harder to find new customers, and if you do lose a little bit of money at one point you can get it back later with a small price rise. The objective is to *keep your customers*.

However, the construction of hundreds of giant corporations in the United States and Europe, and soon Asia, has put particular ethical questions in front of us all regarding board, CEO, and senior executive behavior and remuneration.

In my opinion, it is fine for executive pay to be linked to results—it should be. Whether that is bottom line, share value, or any other measurement, go for it. However, it should be clear also that if results decline, then the remuneration will be *reduced* accordingly. Why should the shareholders reward bad performances?

Reports showed that CEO pay jumped 571 percent during the 1990s and that the average CEO at a major American firm now makes over 500 times more than the average factory worker. Early in this decade, the CEOs with the biggest paycheck also happened to lead firms that laid off the most workers in 2000: Disney's Michael Eisner garnered $72.8 million and laid off 4,000 workers; WorldCom's Bernard Ebbers (later jailed) laid off 6,000 while winning a $10 million bonus; Harvey Golub of American Express enjoyed a 22 percent pay raise and laid off 6,600 employees; and Cisco Systems' John Chambers took home $23.7 million and a 40 percent pay increase, and laid off 8,500 workers. How much food can one person eat, and how much house is enough?

Perception and Reality of Wealth

Back in the 1990s we saw a massive grab for power and wealth by corporate insiders. After all, it was the Clinton era of "anything goes," wasn't it? When all the smoke cleared, it was evident there had been a massive transfer of wealth to corporate insiders. In 1992 corporate CEOs held 2 percent of all stock in U.S. corporations while today it's a staggering 12 percent—a major shift. It was a strange kind of elite socialism at the top—CEOs achieved an almost cult celebrity status. Even better, if you had been a graduate of an Ivy League business school (or similar) you had a kind of free membership in an old boys club that would protect you despite poor performance both corporately and personally. The business press sucked up and worshiped at their shrine.

When a company hit an economic downturn, it might mean hard times and layoffs for some but understanding for the CEO. Kenneth Chenault at American Express saw his 2001 salary go up 86 percent to $30.2 million while shareholder return slumped 35 percent. Across the Atlantic in Britain, Shell CEO Sir Phillip Watts got a 55 percent increase while the share price slumped 27 percent and 4,000 staff were forced out. Man, how do you live with these kinds of results and sleep at night? A true leader, when things go really bad, has the guts to fall on his sword, or take a massive cut in pay for himself and all of the top leadership overhead before sacking the people who do the work.

It is clear that some CEOs of late are not only incompetent but also greedy and prepared to lift inordinate amounts of money out of corporations that they have personally wrecked. The popular stance is to blame market forces, currency exchange, acts of God, and any outside happening as an excuse for poor performance. These are all copouts for failure to accept responsibility for results. How many times have we heard 9/11 or Hurricane Katrina or the fuel hikes used as the excuse for poor performance?

How Much Profit Should We Be Making?

In my opinion, 5 percent is too small because there are any number of investments that will return 5 percent, so why go to all the trouble of setting up and running a company when you can invest the money in a bank and achieve a similar result? Wal-Mart boasts about being the biggest company, but its 3 percent net profit is absolutely pitiful and is achieved by screwing quality, suppliers, employees pay, customer service, competitors, and the communities in which it operates. It is a low-quality entity.

Good results depend very much on the industry you are in and the profit culture inside that industry. Some industries have traditionally attracted educated and experienced people who have known or learned how to generate profit. Other industries have attracted lower-quality staff who have struggled to understand the math behind profitability, and we often see the outcome of that ignorance. Then there are other industries that have screwed themselves into the ground through discounting; their low margins are what is deserved for their business behaviors.

Up to 5 percent return on sales would be a rock-bottom level of profit in my companies; 10 percent is a good result; 15 percent is an excellent result; 20 percent or more profitability comes from high-quality goods, services, and management all combined; 25 percent and beyond is absolutely outstanding and is probably on account of awesome products, technology, service, and management, or due to holding a monopoly position in the industry. Bill Gates regularly achieves 20 to 30 percent net profit.

Should the staff know what profit is generated? In my opinion, staff should be educated about margin and profit and what is a good outcome. How can it hurt them to know? If it's a private company and you are the owner, you may be protective about your figures, but your employees will perform better if they know the plan. If, on the other hand, they feel that all they are doing is putting you into a bigger luxury car and a bigger mansion on the other side of town, while not being told the plan, and being paid rock-bottom minimum wages to achieve this, there will be resentment within. I believe in educating staff in the profit motive, in understanding the way of freedom to operate in the market, and how they could go out and do it themselves if they wished.

Is there any difference between a public company and a private company regarding profit? A public company has stringent laws to follow. It has reporting and auditing standards different from those of a smaller, private company. In the United States a public company must report quarterly, which puts a lot of pressure on the management to come up with a great result every 12 weeks to satisfy Wall Street. In other countries the timeline is 12 months, which puts less pressure on management, while in Japan some projects are set so far out that the first profit may not appear until after 10 years of trading. This would not be acceptable to shareholders in the United States, hence the pressure on CEOs to deliver quickly.

The private company as an incorporated entity has a lot of flexibility. It can facilitate the lifestyle of its owners, and legitimate corporate expenses can be set as tax deductions against assessable income.

Some Guidelines for Success in Business

The two major reasons small companies fail are lack of capital and lack of management skills and experience. School teachers should understand that the profit motive is based in math, improvement, and the time value cost of money, not solely in greed. Profit is legitimate, healthy, desirable, and necessary for survival of corporations, governments, bureaucracies, nations, employees, families, churches with collections, charities, and shareholders. If educators teach an antagonistic, anti-profit philosophy along the lines of socialism and Marxism to their students, they will render those students unemployable. This imposes another cost on the business world of retraining and increasing the understanding of the math behind profitability to those new entrants into the workforce.

To represent the world of profit and capital as "the evil empire" to be destroyed by every means available is to sell the human race short. Different empires go through phases in their history, including conquest, consolidation of wealth, and then demise. This is the lesson of history that gets repeated over and over. One only has to read the history of the rise and fall of Rome to appreciate that they became wealthy and the society collapsed from within due to corruption, legalism, immorality, and materialism.

Parents have a role to teach their children how businesses work. When I was a child my brother and I were encouraged by our parents to initiate kids' businesses. We had a basement where we poured plaster of Paris molds, painted them, and then sold them to our relatives for a "profit." We were actually learning the free enterprise system in the marketplace.

Our parents bought us the board game Monopoly and we learned the rudiments of how business worked. We traded and bought properties, and while the money was only Monopoly money, the principles were life skills. One day my junior high school teacher asked us all what we wanted to do when we grew up. About 50 percent of the hands went up when she said "start my own business"! I wonder how many hands would go up for that in today's classrooms—5 percent?

When I was 16 my dear mother gave me a book entitled *Think and Grow Rich*, by Napoleon Hill (1936). This is still one of the best-selling motivational and personal development books of all time. It is another great legacy from Andrew Carnegie. In 1916 Carnegie thought that he would like the average person on the street to know how he had made his fortune, having come from Scotland at age 11 with basically nothing. He met a journalist who was a good researcher and writer, a man named Napoleon Hill, and he offered him a project: Carnegie would pay him for 20 years to interview the top 500 successful people in the world that Carnegie knew and discover the common thread that made them all successful. Hill was given introductions to people like Henry Ford, Thomas Edison, Gustav Eiffel, and hundreds of other entrepreneurs who had done well. Hill accepted the project and the book was published in 1936, 17 years after Carnegie's death.

I didn't read that book properly at age 16; because I knew everything there was to know at 16—of course! But by the time I reached 21 I noticed that my mother was catching up to me. And when I was 28 and I had no assets and growing responsibilities, I noticed that she had gone sailing right past me and knew heaps more than I did. It was then, at age 28, that I read Napoleon Hill's book thoroughly. You can still buy it and read it today because it is still a best-seller. Only one other book has had a more significant impact on my life, and that is the Holy Bible, which my mother gave me at age 11.

One of the jobs of corporate leaders and business owners is to be the role model of values in the company. If your values are materialistic or greedy or shady, the workers will spot this and you will attract people with the same values. The most powerful values in the world, I believe, are the Judeo-Christian values, which espouse hard work, honest trading, a fair day's pay for a fair day's work, and reasonable profits without abusing employees or customers. These are the values I support. The most prosperous countries in the world hold to these values to a greater or lesser degree. The United States was deliberately constituted on these values. You may or may not agree with those values, but I encourage you to go back to the source and check them out again.

If you are unsure of this, read Jim Collins' masterpiece, *Good to Great* (HarperCollins, 2001). This has to be one of the best-researched business books ever. It proves with empirical research that the show-pony managers who come charging in with big egos, big pay demands, and big plans are *not* the ones who get the great results. He describes the truly great managers as humble and steel-willed, full of unwavering values.

The role of personal values is critical as a part of the responsibilities attached to successful profit making. People run their lives and their work using their moral values. The Judeo-Christian profit values run this way: The view of wealth in the Bible is that wealth is a blessing from the one, true, living God. Abraham is put forward as an example of a wealthy, God-respecting man in Genesis 13:2. However, the generation and possession of profits and wealth bring with it the duty of philanthropy toward those in need, as shown in St. Paul's first letter to Timothy: "As for the rich in this present age, charge them not to be haughty, nor to set their hopes on the uncertainty of riches, but on God, who richly provides us with everything to enjoy. They are to do good, to be rich in good works, *to be generous and ready to share....*" (1 Timothy 6:17–18, English Standard Version).

True wealth and true riches are the spiritual blessings that God gives, rather than His material blessings. "For where your treasure is, there will your heart be also" (Luke 12:34). Andrew Carnegie well understood this scripture and happily parted with $350,000,000 of his hard-earned profits. My point here is that it is better to give than to get, but you have to know how to earn it and save it in the first place before you can give it away. The real benefit is in the *giving*, not in the *getting*.

Perhaps Carnegie knew well these words: "What will it profit a man if he gains the whole world and loses his own soul" (Matthew 16:26,

New King James Version). The responsibility attached to profit is to show yourself, your family, your work colleagues, your customers, and your shareholders that the trading results are important—that we own some money (in trust), but the money doesn't own us. When Pope John Paul II died in 2005 his will was simple: "I leave behind nothing to anybody!"

Just like the man voted the "Man of the Twentieth Century" said, "We make a living by what we get, we make a life by what we give" (Winston Churchill).

When you know how to turn a profit and how to deal with the rewards, all those around you will know the power of positive profit and safely keep their souls, while you keep yours.

Application

☑ Adopt *total* honesty as the best policy for your business dealings.

☑ Benjamin Franklin (1706–1790) said, "An honest man will receive neither money nor praise that is not due."

☑ Drive out dishonesty wherever you see it being practiced.

☑ All the business of your life uses your personal values. Reassess and strengthen your personal values where money and profit are concerned.

☑ Enjoy knowing and applying the math that connects money and numbers together. Be good at it.

☑ Don't be tempted—where big money abounds, so does corruption.

☑ If you have been successful and made some money either personally or corporately, start planning today to plow it back into the source from whence it came.

LIST OF ACTIONS I CAN TAKE

_____

_____

_____

_____

_____

APPENDIX A

MoneyMath Figures and Tables

Figure A.1 is fundamental to business life. Businesses run on margin. For sales managers the budgeted sales are the starting point; subtract the cost of goods and you have the gross profit margin. The cost of goods can be the manufactured cost or the purchase cost. For a service company it's the cost of provided services.

Concept of Margin

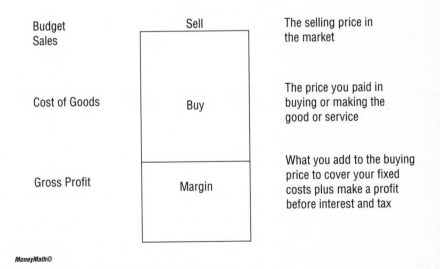

MoneyMath©

FIGURE A.1   Concept of Margin

Gross profit margin is added to the cost by the managers, the sales-people, or the costing staff. Terms like *gross profit margin*, *profit margin*, *margin*, and *gross profit* all mean the same thing and are used interchangeably. This can mislead some people. Teach your employees the meaning of the terms.

Always clarify the terms when speaking to a customer, a boss, a colleague. If you don't, significant loss of profit is possible.

In Table A.1, the error of confusing markup with margin is shown mathematically. If you need 20 percent margin you have to add 25 percent to the original number to achieve it: 25/125 equals 20 percent. You are adding it to the *cost* price, not to the selling price. Look again at Figure A.1—the margin is added to the buying or manufacturing cost and is a part of the sales price.

If you only add 20 percent markup it's 20/120, resulting in a 16.7 percent margin, which is a loss of 3.3 percent of margin. That could be

Markups for a Given Margin

Margin	Markup	Margin	Markup	Margin	Markup	Margin	Markup
1%	1.1%	20%	25%	27%	37%	35%	53.8%
2.5%	2.6%	21%	26.6%	28%	38.9%	40%	66.7%
5.0%	5.3%	22%	28.2%	29%	40.8%	45%	81.8%
7.5%	8.1%	23%	29.9%	30%	42.9%	50%	100%
10%	11.1%	24%	31.5%	31%	44.9%	55%	122%
12.5%	14.2%	25%	33.3%	32%	47%	60%	150%
15%	17.6%	26%	35.1%	33%	50%	70%	233%

MoneyMath©

TABLE A.1 Markups for a Given Margin

quite a chunk of your bottom line if you are in retail earning only a paltry 3 percent like Wal-Mart, for example. Low-margin discount retailers live on a precipice. Similarly, if you need more margin and you are going for a price increase, you use this chart. A margin increase of 5 percent needs a price increase of 5.3 percent (5.3/105.3 equals 5.0 percent). Many modern calculators have these tables built in now.

There are three or four mathematical ways you can calculate your markup percentage when you know the margin figure you want. I teach the K.I.S.S. method—"Keep It Simple, Stupid"—so that anyone can get it right. (See Figure A.2.) All you do is write the margin percentage you need in the bottom box, subtract it from 100, and put the remainder in the top part of the rectangle; then divide the bottom figure by the top figure and turn it into a percentage.

In the example in Figure A.2, 30 gets divided by 70, which gives us 0.429, or 42.9 percent markup. The math will never, ever change.

Calculating Markup

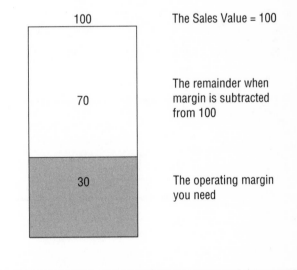

MoneyMath©

FIGURE A.2 Accurately Calculating Markup Percentage

Now the reverse situation using dollars is shown in Figure A.3. To calculate the margin you have obtained in a transaction, you divide the markup dollars by the selling price. Grab your calculator and divide $42.90 by $142.90, and it equals 0.3, or 30 percent, which was the margin figure we were seeking in the previous chart. If you make the mistake of dividing your $42.90 markup by your cost price of $100, you will erroneously believe you made 42.9 percent margin when in fact you generated 30 percent margin on the transaction.

So if you know your cost price and your sales price, you subtract the cost price from the sales price and divide the resulting difference by the sales price to obtain your margin percentage figure.

Markup and margin behave differently mathematically, as demonstrated in Figure A.4. Margin figures travel from 0 up to 99.99 percent, but the corresponding markup figures travel from 0 to 90,900 percent at

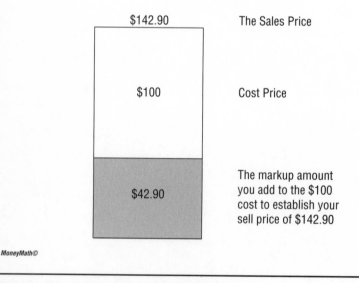

Calculating Margin

$142.90	The Sales Price
$100	Cost Price
$42.90	The markup amount you add to the $100 cost to establish your sell price of $142.90

MoneyMath©

FIGURE A.3   Accurately Calculating Markup Amount

Margin/Markup Divergence

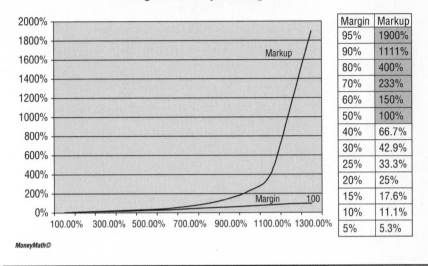

Margin	Markup
95%	1900%
90%	1111%
80%	400%
70%	233%
60%	150%
50%	100%
40%	66.7%
30%	42.9%
25%	33.3%
20%	25%
15%	17.6%
10%	11.1%
5%	5.3%

MoneyMath©

FIGURE A.4   Margin/Markup Divergence Chart

99.99 percent margin. Up to the 50 percent gross profit margin point, the corresponding markup figures behave themselves, but beyond 50 percent margin they appear to leap away exponentially while the margin numbers are a straight line to 100.

This characteristic of a markup calculation is interesting because the numerical values when applied to pricing are the same as margin, but markup equivalents beyond 50 percent margin are much, much higher. Study the side bar chart first, especially the shaded area markups. Check the math skills of your employees to ensure that they understand this.

To establish the margin of any transaction, divide the markup percentage by that same percentage plus 100. For example, for a 50 percent markup, divide by 150 percent, which yields 33.3 percent margin.

When markup and margin are confused in any pricing calculation, severe damage is made to the margins, which is what businesses need to run on—margin. The numbers going down diagonally in Table A.2 are

Percent Margin Lost When Confused with Markup

Margin Required within Selling Price Calculation

Markup	10%	15%	20%	25%	30%	40%	50%	60%
10%	−0.9%							
15%		−2.0%						
20%			−3.3%					
25%				−5.0%				
30%					−6.9%			
40%						−11.4%		
50%							−16.7%	
60%								−22.8%

MoneyMath©

TABLE A.2   Percent Margin Lost When Confused with Markup

the amount of margin lost on this miscalculation. The higher your margin aspiration, the bigger the damage when you make this error.

For example, a retail company targeting 25 percent gross margin and 10 percent net profit loses 5 percent of its margin, which is half of its profit. A manufacturer seeking 40 percent gross margin and 10 percent net profit loses 11.4 percent and goes backward on every sale by 1.4 percent. A pharmaceutical company on 60 percent gross margin seeking 20 percent net profit goes backward by 2.8 percent. The majority of industry and services operate in the 40 to 60 percent margin range. Retailers range from 20 to 40 percent, and few businesses can survive below 20 percent margin.

Table A.3 is the reverse of Table A.2. When you are considering increasing your margins with a price increase, you need to be careful with this distinction. If you are managing for margin and you need a 5 percent increase in your margins, and you increase prices by 5 percent (your

Margins for Given Markups

Markup	Margin	Markup	Margin	Markup	Margin	Markup	Margin
1%	0.99%	20%	16.6%	27%	21.3%	35%	25.9%
2.5%	2.43%	21%	17.4%	28%	21.9%	40%	28.6%
5.0%	4.76%	22%	18%	29%	22.5%	50%	33.3%
7.5%	6.98%	23%	18.7%	30%	23.1%	100%	50%
10%	9.1%	24%	19.4%	31%	23.7%	200%	66.7%
12.5%	11.1%	25%	20%	32%	24.2%	300%	75%
15%	13.0%	26%	20.6%	33%	24.8%	400%	80%

MoneyMath©

TABLE A.3   Margins for Given Markups

markup), you achieve only 4.76 percent margin, showing a small loss of 0.27 percent. You might say that isn't very much, but in a company with sales of $500 million that's an error of $1.35 million coming out of your margin and probably off the bottom line.

I recommend that all pricing calculations be taken to the first decimal point because of the amounts of money involved. Note that once markup goes beyond 100 percent its numbers leap away from the margin numbers exponentially, while margin numbers stop at 99.9 percent. Check that your staff understand that 80 percent margin means 400 percent markup, and that they coalesce with this philosophically and with this much higher markup percentage.

Okay, we have our margins set, and let's say our cost structure requires us to achieve a 40 percent margin. That margin of 40 percent contains two variables—the fixed costs (FC) and the net profit (NP). In Figure A.5, we have 30 percent for the fixed costs, and 10 percent is left

Turning Margin into Profit

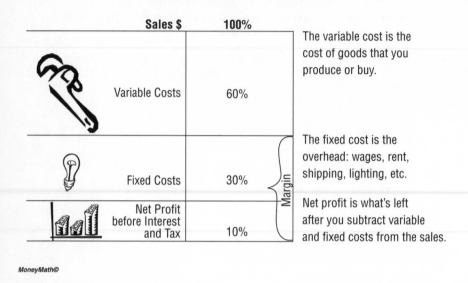

MoneyMath©

FIGURE A.5   Turning Margin into Profit

as net profit. There are lots of terms for net profit; a common one is EBIT, which means earnings before interest and taxes are taken out.

The other fundamental cost coming out of the sales value is the variable costs (VC). These costs vary up and down proportionally with the sales volume. If your sales go up 10 percent, your variable costs will also go up roughly 10 percent.

Because net profit or EBIT is buried inside the margins, I'm sure you can see why it is so important to run the business on margins and to calculate the pricing accurately. The fixed costs won't go away, so only your net profit is left to suffer. If you are a manager or seller in business, this is why you love math, the way a pilot loves his instruments.

Figure A.6 compares mathematically the relative effort needed to get an improvement in the bottom line, given that there are only three

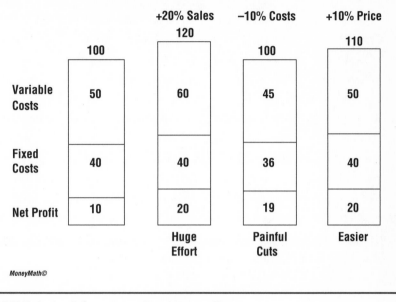

20% Sales Increase vs.
10% Cost Cuts vs. 10% Price Hike

FIGURE A.6   Sales versus Costs versus Price

overall strategies available: Increase sales (volume), cut costs, or increase price. In this chart, the model of cost stays constant for the exercise.

We introduce a 20 percent increase in sales, a 10 percent cut in all the costs, and a 10 percent increase in price. Notice the sales increase is double the price increase.

The 20 percent sales increase doubles the bottom line, but a mere 10 percent price increase does the same thing. The cost cutting delivers nearly the same gain. The point is that to increase sales by 20 percent requires massive effort by comparison to increasing the price by only 10 percent. The underlying philosophy of many businesses is sales volume (the Ivy League/GM strategy) and the price element is neglected. Why do so many people want to sell so hard for so little return when there are two other options available and beyond that a supreme strategy? Cost cutting can demoralize staff but it is an effective measure to improve the profitability.

Figure A.7 is astonishing to most when they first see it. The chart mathematically compares the relative effect of sales volume increase versus cost cuts versus price increase. Using a factory model of variable costs at 50, fixed costs at 40, and net profit of 10, we put a 10 percent increase into the sales, a 10 percent cut into the costs, and a 10 percent increase in price. Which strategy is going to have the biggest impact on the profits?

As this figure shows, the 10 percent sales increase adds 5 percent to the bottom line. That's good because selling more does increase profit. The 10 percent cost cutting of both variable and fixed costs adds 9 percent to the bottom line, so cost cuts are effective also. But look at what happens with the price: The 10 percent increase goes straight to the bottom line, making it 20 percent, a gain of the full 10 percent. This

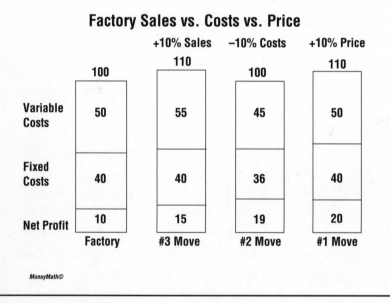

FIGURE A.7   Factory Sales versus Costs versus Price

one chart alone demonstrates the flaw in the Ivy League universities who teach you to maximize sales volume and market share using competitive advantage.

Nothing in industry has a bigger impact on your bottom line than a price increase—absolutely nothing!

Figure A.8 is the retail version of the previous figure, the only difference being the model of cost under which a retailer might operate. The chart mathematically compares the relative effect of increased retail sales volume versus cost cuts versus price increase in a retail model of variable cost 70, fixed cost 20, and net profit 10. We put a 10 percent increase into the sales, a 10 percent cut into the costs, and a 10 percent increase in price. Which is going to help the retailer the most?

The 10 percent sales increase adds 3 percent to the bottom line. The 10 percent cost cutting of both variable and fixed costs puts 9 percent on the bottom line. But once again, with the price, the 10 percent

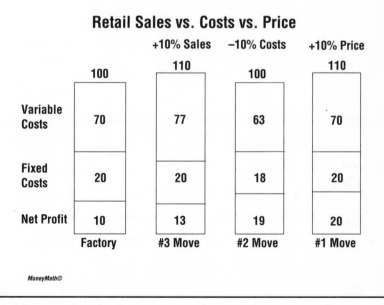

FIGURE A.8   Retail Sales versus Costs versus Price

increase goes straight to the bottom line, making it 20 percent, a gain of the full 10 percent.

Nothing in *retail* has a bigger impact on your bottom line than a price increase—nothing!

Service industries like accounting, the legal profession, and so on often need higher margins. Figure A.9 mathematically compares the relative effect of increased sales volume versus cost cuts versus price increase in a service industry model of variable costs 35, fixed costs 40, and net profit 25. We increase sales by 10 percent, cut costs by 10 percent, and increase the revenue by 10 percent. Which of these actions will have the biggest impact on the profits?

As with industry and retail, the 10 percent sales increase puts 6.5 percent on the bottom line. That is good because obtaining more clients does increase profit. The 10 percent cost cutting of both variable and fixed costs puts 7.5 percent on the bottom line. But the 10 percent in-

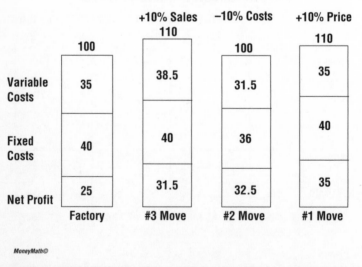

FIGURE A.9   Service Sales versus Costs versus Price

crease in price goes straight to the bottom line, making it 35 percent, a gain of the full 10 percent.

Nothing in *service industries* has a bigger impact on your bottom line than a price/fee/rate increase—nothing!

Table A.4 is well known around the world and shows the effect of discounting on margins and sales volumes. Look at the column labeled 40 percent margin. Let's say that's the amount of gross profit your company needs in order to operate satisfactorily. Now cut your prices across the board by a 10 percent discount. Follow across the 10 percent row and you can see mathematically that you now have to sell 33.3 percent more to make up for your discounting behavior. Question: Why would you want to work 33.3 percent harder for nothing?

If you look at retail margins (25 percent) and cut 10 percent off, they need a massive 66.7 percent increase to cover the discount. If you

Look Before You Cut Prices

Gross Profit Margin to Be Generated

Price Cut	5%	10%	15%	20%	25%	30%	35%	40%	50%	60%
−1%	25%	11.1%	7.1%	5.3%	4.2%	3.4%	2.9%	2.6%	2.04%	1.7%
−5%	—	100%	50%	33.3%	25%	20%	16.7%	14.3%	11.1%	9.1%
−10% (most popular)	—	—	200%	100%	66.7%	50%	40%	33.3%	25%	20%
−15%	—	—	—	300%	150%	100%	75%	60%	42.8%	33.3%
−20%	—	—	—	—	400%	200%	133%	100%	66.7%	50%

Sales Percent Increase Required to Maintain Same Gross Profit

MoneyMath©

TABLE A.4   Look Before You Cut Prices

don't get the increased volume from the discount, you have basically lost your shirt!

All discounts reduce your net profit!

Table A.5 is the king of *MoneyMath* charts. When managers, salespeople, and marketers see this they go ballistic. It should also give directors encouragement as well. The chart shows mathematically how much business you can afford to *lose* on a price increase. Most sales staff oppose price increases. Governments even legislate against them, so they must be a good thing to do!

To use this chart, let's use a 5 percent price increase. Follow that across until you land under 40 percent margin. The figure there is 11.1 percent. In a company whose gross profit margin is 40 percent you can risk losing up to 11.1 percent of your sales volume after a 5 percent price increase and still make a better profit. Of course, if you have good prod-

Look at What a Price Increase Does

Gross Profit Margin to Be Generated
(Providing Costs Remain the Same)

Price Increase	5%	10%	15%	20%	25%	30%	35%	40%	50%	60%
+1%	16.7%	9.1%	6.2%	4.8%	3.9%	3.2%	2.8%	2.4%	2.0%	1.6%
+5%	50%	33.3%	25%	20%	16.7%	14.3%	12.5%	11.1%	9.1%	7.7%
+10%	66.7%	50%	40%	33.3%	28.6%	25%	22.2%	20%	16.7%	14.3%
+15%	75%	60%	50%	42.9%	37.5%	33.3%	30%	27.3%	23.1%	20%
+20%	80%	66.7%	57.1%	50%	44.4%	40%	36.4%	33.3%	28.6%	25%

Sales Percent *Reduction* That Will Still Maintain Same Gross Profit

MoneyMath©

TABLE A.5　Look at What a Price Increase Does

ucts and service you will get some resentment over the increase but in a couple of weeks it will have all settled down again.

Nothing in *business* has a bigger impact on your bottom line than a price increase—absolutely nothing!

Table A.6 reminds us that for a given price increase we don't get the same percentage coming through in margin percentage increase. A 10 percent price increase will yield us a 9.09 percent margin increase.

Now you might say that's pretty close, so why worry! But every 0.1 percent of margin is important in business, particularly when you are trading up in the multimillion dollar category. By now you should understand: Nothing in business impacts your bottom line better than a price increase—nothing!

In Table A.7 we see how much margin comes through on your bottom line when you increase sales volume. Let's say you are a company needing 40 percent margin to operate and you enjoy a 5 percent increase

Margin Increase for Given Price Increases

Price Increase	Margin	Price Increase	Margin	Price Increase	Margin	Price Increase	Margin
1%	0.99%	8%	7.41%	15%	13.0%	22%	18%
2%	1.96%	9%	8.26%	16%	13.8%	23%	18.7%
3%	2.91%	10%	9.09%	17%	14.5%	24%	19.4%
4%	3.85%	11%	9.91%	18%	15.3%	25%	20%
5%	4.76%	12%	10.7%	19%	16%	26%	20.6%
6%	5.66%	13%	11.5%	20%	16.7%	27%	21.3%
7%	6.54%	14%	12.3%	21%	17.4%	28%	21.9%

MoneyMath©

TABLE A.6   Margin Increase for Given Price Increases

Look at What a Sales Increase Does

Current Gross Profit Margin
(Providing Fixed Costs Remain the Same)

Sales Up	5%	10%	15%	20%	25%	30%	35%	40%
1%	0.05%	0.1%	.15%	0.2%	.25%	0.3%	0.35%	0.4%
5%	0.25%	0.5%	0.75%	1%	1.25%	1.5%	1.75%	2%
10%	0.5%	1%	1.5%	2%	2.5%	3%	3.5%	4%
15%	0.75%	1.5%	2.25%	3%	3.75%	4.5%	5.25%	6%
20%	1%	2%	3%	4%	5%	6%	7%	8%

Contribution to Gross Profit Margin by Sales Increase

MoneyMath©

TABLE A.7   Look at What a Sales Increase Does

in sales volume. It's going to deliver a 2 percent increase into your margin. A 10 percent sales increase will deliver you a 4 percent margin increase. We need to secure every sale we can at healthy margins.

Selling huge increases in product volume is the goal in many companies, yet the massive effort involved in doing this doesn't put as much on the bottom line as we think, because generally when sales volume increases dramatically, say 15 to 20 percent, the fixed costs start to react because more sales staff are needed. Some companies increase sales and produce losses. There are other business strategies that build stronger bottom lines than the "Sell, sell, sell" approach only.

Table A.8 shows the percentage increase of your gross profit margin when you raise prices. Most price increases are going to fall in the 1 percent to 10 percent range. If your gross profit margin is 25 percent and you

How Price Increase Lifts Margin Percentage

Current Gross Profit Margin

Price Increase	5%	10%	15%	20%	25%	30%	35%	40%
1%	20%	10%	6.7%	5%	4%	3.3%	2.8%	2.5%
5%	100%	50%	33.3%	25%	20%	16.7%	14.3%	12.5%
10%	150%	100%	66.7%	50%	40%	33.3%	28.6%	25%
15%	300%	150%	100%	75%	60%	50%	42.9%	37.5%
20%	400%	200%	133%	100%	80%	66.7%	57.1%	50%

Percent Increase in Gross Profit Margin

MoneyMath©

TABLE A.8   How Price Increase Lifts Margin Percentage

raise prices by 10 percent price, that's lifting the 25 percent margin up by 40 percent.

This chart doesn't indicate an increase in the bottom line. It simply shows the relative margin uplift stemming from the price increase. That's worth repeating: It doesn't mean your bottom line has been lifted by this percentage. It means your *margin* has been lifted by that percentage.

Figure A.10 is a schematic that shows why the sales and marketing department in most organizations has the biggest impact on margins and net profit. The sales and marketing department controls two out of the three variables—they control the sales volumes sold in the marketplace and they control the prices obtained on those volumes. Everyone else in a business has a cost to control.

I have seen some business structures where the financial controller controls prices and signs off the work done by salespeople. This is not ideal; it means that the salespeople are either untrained or not trusted to

Why Sales and Marketing Staff
Affect Profit the Most

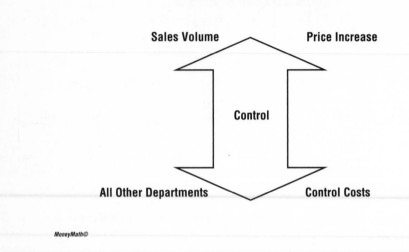

MoneyMath©

FIGURE A.10   Why Sales and Marketing Staff Affect Profit the Most

generate a margin in their selling. It would be best if they were taught about margins and remunerated for producing margin as well as volume. If the sales commission scheme rewards volume selling alone, then you know already what the sales team will do to your margins.

Let's look at what happens when sales are reduced by 10 percent due to a market downturn or a price war. (See Figure A.11.) If it's an industry downturn, everybody will be affected; if it's a price war, maybe a select few or you only are affected. The actions to maintain profit are similar. Sales are pushed down 10 percent, but variable costs will reduce proportionately; if you also cut out 10 percent of your fixed costs, your net profit will reduce down by 1 percentage point.

To keep the full 10 percent net profit, you will have to squeeze just a little bit more out of your variable costs and your fixed costs to find the extra 1 percent. *Do not cut your prices.* If you leave your costs untouched you will bleed (view the far right-hand column). Variable costs are the best place to start because the proportionate reduction there is due to

Comparisons in 10% War
or Downturn (Factory)

Sales	100%	100	90	90
Variable Costs	50%	50	45	45
Fixed Costs	40%	40	36	40
Net Profit before Interest and Tax	10%	10	9	5

Base Model of Cost ◤▶

MoneyMath©

FIGURE A.11   Comparisons in 10 Percent War or Downturn (Factory)

lesser sales volume. Request your suppliers to assist you with a better buying price; a reduction of 1 to 2 percent should not be too much to ask if the supplier/factory is apprised of your market difficulties. Share the pain! Keep in mind that they have a vested interest in keeping you going as their customer.

Table A.9 is about reducing your *total costs*, that is, variable and fixed costs together to preserve margin and net profit. When it gets tough, many businesses take the easy way out and just sack people, which reduces fixed costs if they are overhead staff and variable costs if they are linked to sales volume activity. However, it mathematically pulls back more profit if both the variable and the fixed costs are reduced together.

The combination of the variable costs and fixed costs is usually 75 percent to 90 percent of the total in the model of cost as in the shaded area, and if you are making an improvement to 90 percent of the argument it's a big slice when compared to, say, an improvement to the fixed costs alone, which may be only 40 percent of the total argument. Using

Total Costs Are Reduced

Total Costs (Variable Costs and Fixed Costs Combined)

Reduction	60%	65%	70%	75%	80%	85%	90%	95%
1%	0.6%	.65%	0.7%	.75%	0.8%	.85%	0.9%	.95%
2%	1.2%	1.3%	1.4%	1.5%	1.6%	1.7%	1.8%	1.9%
3%	1.8%	1.95%	2.1%	2.25%	2.4%	2.55%	2.7%	2.85%
4%	2.4%	2.6%	2.8%	3%	3.2%	3.4%	3.6%	3.8%
5%	3.0%	3.25%	3.5%	3.75%	4.0%	4.25%	4.5%	4.75%
10%	6%	6.5%	7%	7.5%	8%	8.5%	9%	9.5%
15%	9%	9.75%	10.5%	11.25%	12%	12.75%	13.5%	14.25%
20%	12%	13%	14%	15%	16%	17%	18%	19%

Percent Gross Profit Margin Regained through Cost Reduction

MoneyMath©

TABLE A.9   Percent Margin Gained When Total Costs Are Reduced

this chart, if your total costs (VC + FC) are 90 percent and you reduce them by 5 percent, you will pick up 4.5 percent of margin, and hopefully this will flow through to your net profit.

Let's look at this from a retail standpoint. In a retail downturn all traders will be affected; in a price war, maybe a select few or you only are affected. Either way, the actions to maintain profit are similar. As sales are pushed down 10 percent, variable costs will reduce proportionately. If you can also cut out 10 percent of your fixed costs (from 20 down to 18, in the example in Figure A.12), your net profit will drop by 0.5 percent point. If you leave your costs untouched you will bleed: The net profit

Comparisons in 10% War
or Downturn (Retail)

Sales	100%	100	90	90
Variable Costs	75%	75	67.5	67.5
Fixed Costs	20%	20	18	20
Net Profit before Interest and Tax	5%	5	4.5	2.5

Base Model of Cost ⬆

MoneyMath©

FIGURE A.12   Comparisons in 10 Percent War or Downturn (Retail)

falls by half from 5 to 2.5! Ask your suppliers to help by reducing your buying price 1 to 2 percent. Tell them of your retail market difficulties and remember that they have a vested interest in keeping you as a customer. Do not cut your prices; *cut your costs!*

Table A.10 is about reducing just your *fixed costs* (overhead) in order to preserve margin and net profit. For most companies, fixed costs travel in the 20 to 40 percent range (see the shaded area). Notice that a 10 percent reduction in fixed costs where the fixed costs are 25 percent potentially puts back only 2.5 percent on the bottom line. This activity often involves firing employees, your most valuable asset! If the employee cost was only half of the fixed costs of 25 percent, then you are actually only adding 1.25 percent to the bottom line. Not a lot, is it?

Such an action also leaves the remaining staff demoralized and unwilling to deliver the same levels of customer service as before. For so much pain and anxiety, it puts only a small amount of margin back. Of course, it is absolutely necessary sometimes to reduce staff, but make that

Percent Margin Gained When Only Fixed Costs Are Reduced

Fixed Costs Percentage

Reduction	15%	20%	25%	30%	35%	40%	50%	60%
1%	.15%	0.2%	.25%	0.3%	.35%	0.4%	0.5%	0.6%
2%	0.3%	0.4%	0.5%	0.6%	0.7%	0.8%	1.0%	1.2%
3%	.45%	0.6%	.75%	0.9%	1.05%	1.2%	1.5%	1.8%
4%	0.6%	0.8%	1%	1.2%	1.4%	1.6%	2%	2.4%
5%	0.75%	1%	1.25%	1.5%	1.65%	2%	2.5%	3%
10%	1.5%	2%	2.5%	3%	3.5%	4%	5%	6%
15%	2.25%	3%	3.75%	4.5%	5.25%	6%	7.5%	9%
20%	3%	4%	5%	6%	7%	8%	10%	12%

Margin Gained with Fixed Cost Reduction Only

MoneyMath©

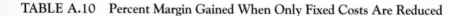

TABLE A.10   Percent Margin Gained When Only Fixed Costs Are Reduced

the last resort. Start with all the nonhuman items that build up over time in a company—subscriptions, power bills, rent, extra phones, and those ubiquitous cell phone accounts.

Figure A.13 looks at the same scenario in a service industry when sales are pushed down by 10 percent, due to either a market downturn or a price war. Assuming variable costs reduce proportionately, and you cut out 10 percent of your fixed costs (from 40 down to 36), your net profit will reduce down by 2.5 percent. If you leave your costs untouched you will lose 6.5 percent—the net profit falls from 25 to 18.5!

Comparisons in 10% War
or Downturn (Service Industry)

Sales	100%	100	90	90
Variable Costs	35%	35	31.5	31.5
Fixed Costs	40%	40	36	40
Net Profit before Interest and Tax	25%	25	22.5	18.5

Base Model of Cost ◄

MoneyMath©

FIGURE A.13   Comparisons in 10 Percent War or Downturn
(Service Industry)

This is the benefit of being in a professional service business. If bad times strike, your net profit will come down but your profit should still be in double digits. Pure service industries often survive a downturn more easily than other industries. Avoid cutting your prices—cut your costs.

Table A.11 explores what happens when a downturn in the marketplace hits your sales and takes a chunk of your gross margin percentage away. The assumption here is that fixed costs remain the same, and variable costs reduce proportionately to sales. In a downturn we are all tempted to cut prices immediately to regain some sales momentum. Don't do it! You *cut your costs* when you hit a market downturn.

The difference between a downturn and a price war is that *everybody* is affected by a downturn, so action to maintain profit is usually being taken by everyone in the market. You won't be alone.

Your goal will be to try and maintain *margin* first and maintain sales volume second. Demand has come down, but try to keep your share of

Look at What a Downturn Does

Current Gross Profit Margin

Sales Down	5%	10%	15%	20%	25%	30%	35%	40%
–1%	–.05%	–0.1%	–0.15%	–0.2%	–0.25%	–0.3%	–0.35%	–0.4%
–5%	–.25%	–0.5%	–0.75%	–1%	–1.25%	–1.5%	–1.75%	–2%
–10%	–0.5%	–1%	–1.5%	–2%	–2.5%	–3%	–3.5%	–4%
–15%	–0.75%	–1.5%	–2.25%	–3%	–3.75%	–4.5%	–5.25%	–6%
–20%	–1%	–2%	–3%	–4%	–5%	–6%	–7%	–8%

Loss of Gross Profit Margin

MoneyMath©

TABLE A.11   Look at What a Downturn Does

the declined market and you will be in good shape for the market recovery. The real damage is seen when you translate these lost margin percentages back into dollars and cents to feel the real effect.

Table A.12 is about a price war in the marketplace hitting your margins and taking away a percentage of your gross margin percentage. In a price war we are tempted to retaliate by cutting prices immediately to regain the sales volume and to make up for the lost margin. But you must *cut your costs* when you are in a price war.

You may strategically discount some of your competitors' major accounts to try and stop the war. In a price war not everyone is affected, so action to maintain profit is taken selectively and strategically. Your goal will be to try and maintain margin from your core customers. The damage is known when you translate your lost customers back into dollars and cents. The only winners in a price war are customers and lawyers. You may feed your ego running the war, but you won't feed the kids!

Look at What a Price War Does

Current Gross Profit Margin
(Providing Fixed Costs Remain the Same)

Price Down	5%	10%	15%	20%	25%	30%	35%	40%
−1%	20%	10%	6.7%	5%	4%	3.3%	2.9%	2.5%
−5%	100%	50%	33.3%	25%	20%	16.7%	14.3%	12.5%
−10%	—	100%	66.7%	50%	40%	33.3%	29%	25%
−15%	—	—	100%	75%	60%	50%	42.9%	37.5%
−20%	—	—	—	100%	80%	66.7%	57.1%	50%

Percent of Gross Profit Margin Percent Loss

MoneyMath©

TABLE A.12   Look at What a Price War Does

Now for the strategic solution—balance.

Figure A.14 is the mother of all *MoneyMath* charts. This is *the* solution for those businesses that only know "Sell, sell, sell!" This is how to make steady and growing profits.

If you were asked to increase your sales volume most years by only 1 percent, you would say, "No problem." If at the same time, leveraged, you were asked to shave your costs by 1 percent, you would say, "Piece of cake!" And if at the same time you were asked to increase your prices by 1 percent you would say, "Okay!"

Do all these three activities *together*, in *balance*, and watch the multiplier effect. The secret to profitability is to balance all the business—the selling, the marketing, and the management. In my opinion, 80 percent of companies don't reach their profit potential because they operate mostly in an unbalanced way—(60 percent of

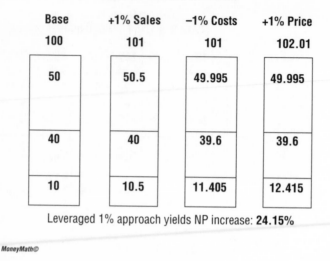

The Golden 1 Percent

Base	+1% Sales	−1% Costs	+1% Price
100	101	101	102.01
50	50.5	49.995	49.995
40	40	39.6	39.6
10	10.5	11.405	12.415

Leveraged 1% approach yields NP increase: **24.15%**

MoneyMath©

FIGURE A.14   The Golden 1 Percent

companies) by "Sell, sell, sell!" and others (20 percent of companies) by "Cut, cut, cut!"

Figure A.15 is the grandmother of all *MoneyMath* charts. This is *the* solution for those businesses that only know selling and chasing volume. If you tried the golden 1 percent, it's time to move up.

Increase your sales volume by only 2 percent; shave your costs by 2 percent, and increase your prices by 2 percent. Do all these three activities together, in a balanced way, and watch the multiplier effect. Profitability on this model climbs 48.6 percent from the original 10 percent up to 14.86.

The secret to profitability is to *balance the company*, and to do these activities professionally all the time. It will be unsuccessful in the long term to only aim at sales volume increase, market share increase, and obliterating competitors for the sake of being number one. You'll feed your ego but not the families who depend on your judgment and wisdom to manage profit.

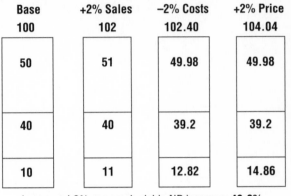

The Platinum 2 Percent

Base 100	+2% Sales 102	−2% Costs 102.40	+2% Price 104.04
50	51	49.98	49.98
40	40	39.2	39.2
10	11	12.82	14.86

Leveraged 2% approach yields NP increase: **48.6%**

MoneyMath©

FIGURE A.15 The Platinum 2 Percent

Figure A.16 is the biggest daddy of all *MoneyMath* charts. This is *the* solution for entrepreneurs who want to test their ability to push the envelope.

I do not recommend this 5 percent leveraged approach to new players or to those who haven't yet assured themselves of the balanced company approach using the golden 1 percent strategy first. This approach is for senior managers who have been in the game for some years and know the pitfalls and the nuances of their own operation like the back of their hand.

To achieve these results using sales alone would require a 25 percent increase in sales, and that doesn't factor in the additional sales costs that would be incurred with such a massive increase.

Figure A.17 is about segmenting your product mix into A, B, and C products based on the margins they generate—the 80-20 rule.

Sometimes a sales force will neglect the bread-and-butter lines

The Awesome 5 Percent

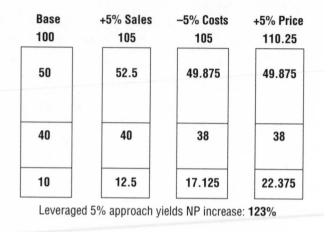

Base 100	+5% Sales 105	−5% Costs 105	+5% Price 110.25
50	52.5	49.875	49.875
40	40	38	38
10	12.5	17.125	22.375

Leveraged 5% approach yields NP increase: **123%**

MoneyMath©

FIGURE A.16   The Awesome 5 Percent

Margin Dangers in Product Mix

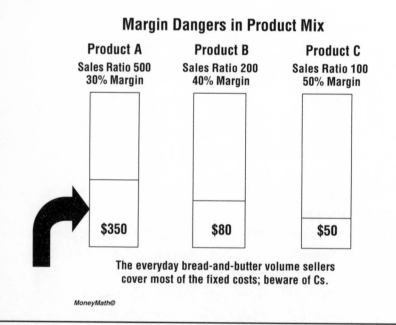

Product A	Product B	Product C
Sales Ratio 500 30% Margin	Sales Ratio 200 40% Margin	Sales Ratio 100 50% Margin
$350	$80	$50

The everyday bread-and-butter volume sellers
cover most of the fixed costs; beware of Cs.

MoneyMath©

FIGURE A.17   Margin Dangers in Product Mix

because they are boring and don't make high margins. But because of their large volume, when multiplied by their market share ratio, they pull in a lot of cash, which covers the overhead. You cannot bank margin percentage or market share, only cash.

In any company, there is a chance that an exotic new product will be included in the range because it has a high margin, say 50 percent. But what if it doesn't sell for two years? It sits in the warehouse, and at 1 percent interest per month the margin left is only 26 percent, which is lower than for the A product volume sellers.

You need new products coming on board, but if they don't look like they will become B's or A's, I would quit them early and move on to the next project.

Figure A.18 is about segmenting your *customers* into A, B, and C customers based on the amount of margin they generate—once again,

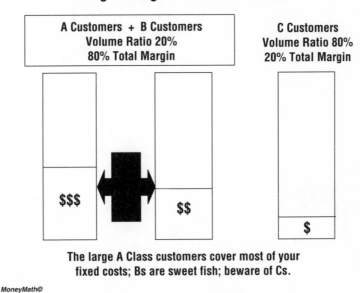

Margin Dangers in Customer Mix

| A Customers + B Customers
Volume Ratio 20%
80% Total Margin | C Customers
Volume Ratio 80%
20% Total Margin |

$$$ $$ $

The large A Class customers cover most of your fixed costs; Bs are sweet fish; beware of Cs.

MoneyMath©

FIGURE A.18   Margin Dangers in Customer Mix

the 80-20 principle. Sometimes a sales force will neglect the main customers and go chasing new business when the best profits are sitting right under their nose in the form of current customers. These A and B customers are boring and don't have any new jokes! But because of their large volume they pull in a lot of cash, and that cash usually covers the overhead of the company. You cannot bank margin or market share—only cash.

I have always recommended that 80 percent of the regular selling effort go into satisfying and maintaining the core A- and B-class customers who bring in most of the margin and only 20 percent be spent on new customers (C's) and new projects. Put a special team together for new projects while the main team keeps the margins healthy.

If you sell through dealers, Figure A.19 is useful in understanding that price, market share, and dealer margin form a profit cocktail

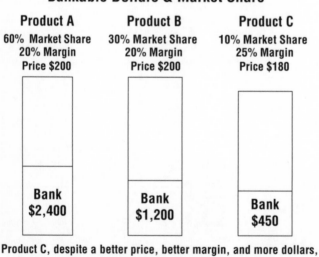

Bankable Dollars & Market Share

Product A	Product B	Product C
60% Market Share	30% Market Share	10% Market Share
20% Margin	20% Margin	25% Margin
Price $200	Price $200	Price $180
Bank $2,400	Bank $1,200	Bank $450

Product C, despite a better price, better margin, and more dollars, because of its lower market share generates less net profit.

MoneyMath©

FIGURE A.19   Bankable Dollars and Market Share

that will blow the dealer's mind if your product or service is the most profitable!

In this example, product C is lower priced than product A and it has a higher percentage margin, which yields more dollars per unit sale than product A—yet product A is more profitable. Why?

Because the market share figures for A are 6 times higher than for C. When multiplied by the higher unit sales in the same time period, the lower sales price actually yields the dealer more margin dollars. You cannot bank a low price, or margin percentage, or margin dollars—you can only bank net profit as cash. But with higher margin dollars, you have a better chance. In this chart the aggregate dollars for product A are higher than for product C, and that's why the "worse price, lower margin" item is more profitable. To use this math, you have to do careful *homework*.

Figure A.20 is about the effect of sales increases inside a factory model of cost 50/40/10. A 10 percent increase in sales can usually be absorbed readily in the sales structure without additional sales staff being

Sales Increase Effect (Factory)

Sales	100%	100	110	125
Variable Costs		50	55	62.5
Fixed Costs		40	40	42.5
Net Profit before Interest and Tax		10	15	20

Base Model of Cost ⬆

MoneyMath©

FIGURE A.20   Sales Increase Effect (Factory)

hired. So the benefits of sales volume increase at the lower end proportionately find their way into the bottom line.

However, a 25 percent hike in sales volume is a different matter.
Such a large increase requires extra staff to handle it, and this brings in additional fixed costs, which in turn erode some of that extra margin before it
reaches the bottom line. In Figure A.20, the profits could be 22.5 in the
right-hand column if the fixed costs didn't kick up with the 25 percent increase in volume. Notice that to double the net profit on this model using
sales alone, a huge 25 percent sales increase is required.

Similarly the next figure, Figure A.21, is about the effect of sales increases in a retail model of cost 75/20/5. The 10 percent increase in sales
is generally easily handled in the retail sales environment without additional sales staff. Again, the benefits of the increased sales volume are
proportionately reflected in the bottom line.

In retail, much of the cost is the inventory in the form of the cost of
goods, hence 75 is the variable cost in this example. The bottom line is

Sales Increase Effect (Retail)

Sales	100%	100	110	125
Variable Costs		75	82.5	93.8
Fixed Costs		20	20	22.5
Net Profit before Interest and Tax		5	7.5	8.7

Base Model of Cost ▪➔

MoneyMath©

FIGURE A.21   Sales Increase Effect (Retail)

so thin to begin with that increases represent huge percentage improvements. The 10 percent sales increase here achieved a 50 percent increase in net profit.

Always look at the net dollars and the percentage. Recently, by prostituting quality in most of what it does, discount retailer Wal-Mart has achieved some of the biggest revenues in the world but pathetic profits of only 3 percent.

Figure A.22 is about the effect of sales increases for service industry professionals, using model of cost 35/40/25. A 10 percent increase in work cannot be easily absorbed readily in the service structure without additional staff being needed. Still, the benefits of increased sales volume quickly work their way into the bottom line.

However, a 25 percent hike in professional work is a different matter. Such a large increase requires lots of extra staff to handle it, and this brings in additional fixed costs, which in turn erode the margin a little before the bottom line is reached. In this example, the profits could be 50 percent in the right-hand column if the variable and fixed costs didn't

Sales Increase Effect (Service Industry)

Sales	100%	100	110	125
Variable Costs		35	38.5	43.8
Fixed Costs		40	40	42.5
Net Profit before Interest and Tax		25	31.5	38.7

Base Model of Cost ◼▲

MoneyMath©

FIGURE A.22   Sales Increase Effect (Service Industry)

kick up so much with the increased volume. Even so, the margins are always nice and healthy in service, a good reason to add services to any struggling product lines you have in industry or retail.

Table A.13 is a tool to analyze a product or service by defining its benefits and their value. All the features of a product are listed in the left column, then categorized as major selling features (MSF) or unique selling features (USF). The fourth column tells which benefit a given feature provides, using the SPACED acronym from Chapter 7: Security, Performance, Appearance, Convenience, Economy, Durability. Ask the benefit questions of each feature in turn and list it.

For the "Value" column, ask the question, "What percentage or dollar amount is that feature/benefit worth within the price?" The answer can come from subjective or objective research, but *it is never nothing*!

How Perceived Value of Product Drives Up Margin

Feature	MSF	USF	Benefits (SPACED)	$ Value
1.				
2.				
3.				
4.				
5.				
6.				
7.				
8.				

Pacific Seminars International©

TABLE A.13   Universal Benefits Analysis Tool

These features were put into your cost structure to help make the product or service sell. If you don't explain to the customer their dollar value, how can they know?

Table A.14 lists, categorizes, and values the features of Coca-Cola. Coke is well differentiated from its competitors and can claim a value for that; its brand, leadership, and taste are all unique to Coke. Salespeople should constantly use this type of grid as preparation prior to making their presentations to customers.

Figure A.23 summarizes the key points in establishing the perceived value of a product.

How is perceived value deduced? By *customer research*, we mean professional, objective, external interview research which consultants provide along with a comprehensive report of customer satisfaction levels. *Subjective research* will be your own view of value, the customers' own

Product Example of Coke

Feature	MSF	USF	Benefits (SPACED)	$ Value
1. Coca-Cola Brand	—	X	S, A, C	3% = $0.03/can
2. Soft Drink Leader	—	X	S, E, D	0.5% = $0.005/can
3. International Company	—	—	S, C, D	—
4. Publicly Owned Company	X	—	S, C, D	—
5. 25 Configurations	X	—	S, C	—
6. Regular/Diet/Caffeine-Free	X	—	S, A, C, D	0.5% = $0.005/can
7. Secret Recipe (Taste)	—	X	S, D	1% = $0.01/can
			Total Perceived Value	
			= 5% = $0.05/can	

Pacific Seminars International©

TABLE A.14   Product Example of Coca-Cola

Establishing the Perceived Product Value % or $

- Some values will be objectively established from customer research.

- Sometimes the customer will offer it; if so, accept it immediately (subjective).

- Sometimes the staff perceive that their product has added value (subjective).

- But *it will never be nothing!*

- Communicate this value and you get margin.

- Remember the example of Coca-Cola.

- SPACED benefits are: Security, Performance, Appearance, Convenience, Economy, Durability.

MoneyMath©

FIGURE A.23   Establishing the Perceived Product Value

subjective view of value as expressed to you, and best of all (but impossible to get), your competitors' view of value.

These perceived values are inbuilt in the product, but also in the service, and it's the service that has the pulling power.

Always keep in mind that the value of these things *can never be nothing.* For profits, sell value instead of price alone.

Table A.15 analyzes the features of a Fortune 500 company.

Figure A.24 summarizes the key factors in establishing the perceived value of a service. Service, and specifically what we call customer service, is the most powerful differentiator today. When added to a me-too product, it makes the product competitive again.

Companies with legendary service rarely struggle to make profit. Of

How Perceived Value of Customer
Service Drives Margin Higher

Feature	MSF	USF	Benefits (SPACED)	$ Value
1. 73 Years Experience	X	—	S, D	2%
2. #1 Market Leader	—	X	S, E, D	0.5%
3. International (112 Countries)	—	—	S, P, C, E, D	0.5%
4. Technology Specialists	X	—	P, E	0.5%
5. NYSE-Listed Company	—	—	S	—
6. ISO9001 Manufacturer	—	—	S, C	0.5%
7. Web Site	X	—	P, A, C	—
8. 700 Offices Globally	—	—	C	—
9. Range 10,000 Products	X	—	S, C, E	1%
10. 6 Product Groups	—	—	S, C	—
11. E-Mail/Cell/Fax/Phone	—	—	C, E	—
12. Service 24 hours/7 days	X	—	S, C, D	2%
13. Highly Trained Staff	X	—	S, P, A, E	1%
14. G. Environmental Record	X	—	S, P, D	1%
15. 99% Inventory Level	X	—	S, C, E	1%
16. R&D = 7% Sales	X	—	S, D	1%

Total   11%
perceived value

Pacific Seminars International©

TABLE A.15   How Perceived Value Can Increase Margin

Establishing the Perceived
Service Value % or $

- You can change three things to get advantage:
  the quality of your product, process, or service.

- Some values will be objectively established
  from customer research (objective).

- Sometimes the customer will offer it; if so accept it
  immediately (subjective).

- Sometimes your staff perceive that the customer
  service has added value (subjective).

- But *it will never be nothing!*

- Communicate service values in dollars, and you get
  added value to your product margin.

MoneyMath©

FIGURE A.24 Establishing the Perceived Service Value

course they "struggle" in terms of effort, but they don't run scared. Generally the excellent external customer service is paralleled by excellent internal service, where everyone treats each other with respect and friendliness.

While service is not a mathematically measured ingredient, without awesome service the perception of value will be less and it will be harder to obtain higher prices. We recommend 24/7 service. Read my book *Where the Rubber Meets the Road: SERVICE!* for a more complete discussion of this essential component.

A word about tricks and taxes: Because two or three numbers are factors in one equation, caution is needed on things like discounts, rebates, and tax. For example, if you rebate a sale (delayed discount) by 10 percent, then the amount of tax applied to the original invoice is in all

Tax & Rebates

Sale including Tax

In many cases tax is a part of the selling price. If so, and a volume rebate or discount is involved later, and the tax has been forwarded already to the government, the tax will have been overpaid by the percent of the discount offered. Overpaid tax is a part of your margin and belongs to you. Get your accountant working now.
Define rebates as gross or net.

MoneyMath©

FIGURE A.25   Tax and Rebates

likelihood *overpaid*, also by 10 percent. (See Figure A.25.) This overpaid tax is recoverable from most tax agencies around the world. It will be a part of your hard-earned margin that is being returned to you and is *not* the government's money to keep. You overpaid tax by reducing the price a good while after the invoice was originally issued.

Ensure that your accountant is on to every angle of tax recovery. The statute of limitations usually applies to these claims, and that is seven years in most jurisdictions. The rebate is a gross rebate if the tax adjustment is included, and a net rebate if the tax adjustment is left separate.

Be alert to the workings of Murphy's law. No matter how hard you try, Murphy works in every organization and is waiting to throw a wrench in your profitability. You may be putting huge effort into sales and price increases, but Murphy works in the opposite direction. (See Figure A.26.)

Murphy's Law on Profit

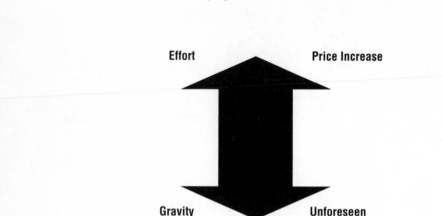

FIGURE A.26   Murphy's Law on Profit

In all my executive budgeting I allowed 5 percent for contingency—for Murphy, for the rainy day, for unforeseen costs. Who could have planned in their corporate budgets for the effect of the terrorist attacks of September 11, 2001?

This is why you should not feel bad when you make a little extra profit here and there, because it is surely going to be stripped away from you somehow by Murphy! What you don't need is sales staff, managers, or anyone else in your team feeling squeamish about making legal, reasonable, and ethical profits.

If you find that you cannot grow your sales sufficiently, that your cost reduction measures have been only partially effective, and that it is nearly impossible to institute a price increase, one useful solution is to merge with another player. (See Figure A.27.) When you merge, though, don't turn around and cut prices to teach other competitors a lesson. Concentrate on growing your profitability. Remember, it is better to be

How to Merge to Survive

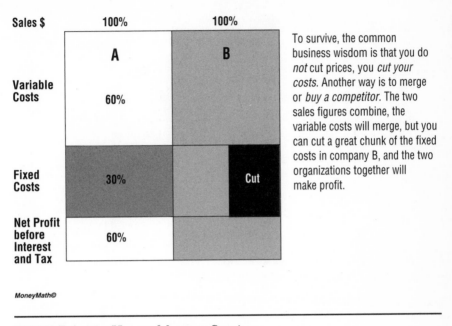

To survive, the common business wisdom is that you do *not* cut prices, you *cut your costs*. Another way is to merge or *buy a competitor*. The two sales figures combine, the variable costs will merge, but you can cut a great chunk of the fixed costs in company B, and the two organizations together will make profit.

MoneyMath©

FIGURE A.27   How to Merge to Survive

profitable and smaller than big and broke. Microsoft is a very profitable company, averaging around 27 percent net profit, but in 2006 it is only the 111th biggest in the world in revenue.

The attempt to be the biggest in the market via discounting is always mathematically doomed and nearly always makes low profit. Set a goal to be the most profitable in your industry.

A modern sales approach to make all this happen is to start out with the maximum sales of your core or basic product at optimum prices. Your prices may even have to be somewhat low. This is Level 1 in the Profit Selling Pyramid (see Figure A.28).

Having sold at Level 1, teach all your people to attempt add-on sales in every transaction at Level 2. McDonald's does it successfully—

Profit Selling Pyramid

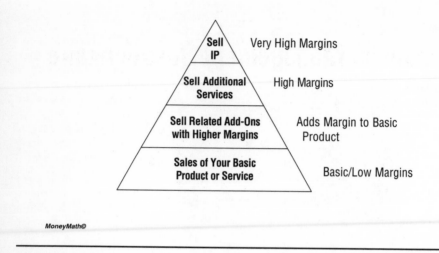

MoneyMath©

FIGURE A.28   Profit Selling Pyramid

why not you? Then with effective marketing move them up to additional service items that are unique and produce high margin at Level 3.

Continuing with effective marketing, get customers interested in buying your intellectual property (IP) via the Web, e-commerce, e-zines, products, services, subscriptions, and so on. This is Level 4 and is usually margin rich.

Ensure that all levels are defined, integrated, and taught inside your operation for a continuous, steady stream of profits from selling.

Financial Management Questionnaire

Name: _____

Perform calculations on this page if required.

1. Why is cash flow so important to our business?
   a. To control working capital levels.
   b. To generate cash for acquisitions.
   c. To raise capital for plant and equipment.
   d. To ensure profits are generated into cash flow.
   e. None of the above.
   f. All of the above.

2. Is markup the same as margin?
   a. Yes.
   b. No.
   c. Not sure.

3. What comprises working capital calculations?
   a. Inventory, debtors.
   b. Net inventory, net debtors, intercompany creditors.
   c. Net inventory, net debtors.
   d. None of the above.

4. What do the acronyms EBIT and NP stand for?

5. Which of the following sums up to EBIT and NP?
    a. Sales plus gross margin minus expenses.
    b. Sales minus cost of sales minus expenses.
    c. Sales plus cost of sales plus expenses.
    d. Sales minus cost of sales plus expenses.
    e. None of the above.

6. How is inventory stock turn calculated?
    a. Total inventory units divided by cost of sales units annualized.
    b. Total cost of sales dollars annualized divided by total inventory dollars on hand.
    c. Total stock level turned over by units issued.
    d. Stock valuation multiplied by cost of sales annualized.

7. If an item costs $100 Canadian to purchase plus 10 percent shipping costs and local costs estimated at 5 percent of landed cost, what would the standard cost be in U.S. dollars with an exchange rate of 0.65 Canadian to the U.S. dollar?
    a. $74.00
    b. $74.75
    c. $75.00
    d. $75.07

8. If an item costs $10 and sells for $15, what is the markup percentage?

9. What is the margin percentage in question 8?

10. Using compound interest calculations, what would $100 invested today be worth after three years at a rate of 10 percent interest per annum, rounded to the nearest dollar?

11. If an item sells for $165 including 10 percent sales tax, what is the sale value of the product excluding the tax?
    a. $148.50
    b. $150.00
    c. $165.00
    d. $181.50

12. Of the three things that can help profitability, which would you say has the most impact on profits?
    a. Increasing sales.
    b. Reducing costs.
    c. Raising prices.

13. If an item of stationery costs $220.00 inclusive of 10 percent tax, what would be the amount reflected in the profit and loss statement as an expense?

101 Price Management Questions

This list of questions forms a great agenda for your first Price Committee meeting. Attack five questions each week until they are all answered.

1. Which prices were increased in the last year (inflation percent is the minimum level of increase)?
2. Which prices have *not* been increased in the last two years?
3. Which prices have *not* been increased in the last five years?
4. Do you have a price committee?
5. Does the price committee meet monthly?
6. Does that meeting have a written agenda with input from all parties who can affect prices?
7. Is software used to calculate pricing?
8. Does the software algorithm use markup or margin in calculating prices?
9. Are you using a price list? With a fuel levy?
10. Is the price list current and given a specific printed date?
11. Is the price list regularly reviewed?
12. Have you differentiated your pricing by product A, B, and C?
13. Have you differentiated your customers by rank A, B, and C?
14. Do you increase prices differentially across products A, B, and C?
15. Do you increase prices differentially across customers A, B, and C?
16. Do you negotiate price increases with your A-class customers?

17. Do you have a market-based maximum list price?
18. Do you use the standard costs method to price? With what controls?
19. What latitude have you given in writing for staff to discount prices?
20. Do you manage the average margin needed across your product segments?
21. What margin variations are computer-tracked daily?
22. What margin variations are computer-tracked weekly?
23. What margin variations are computer-tracked monthly?
24. Do you know which managers consistently get poor margins?
25. Do you calculate your average margin needed across your customer segments?
26. Which sales representatives consistently sell at poor margins?
27. Which state or province operations consistently operate at poor margins?
28. Do you get a daily printout of the average margins obtained yesterday?
29. Do you get a monthly printout of the margins both real and average?
30. Do you have a margin plan?
31. What tax review controls are in place?
32. Do you have rebates involving third-level percentages, thereby involving tax refunds from the government?
33. In contracts do you have rise and fall clauses that are flagged chronologically?
34. Are your old contract prices removed from the computer at the end of the contract?
35. Does your accounting department have latitude to extend credit terms?
36. Do you measure your cash flow?
37. Do you measure your creditors and debtors against a standard?
38. What payment discounts do you run?
39. Are your terms and conditions printed and explained to your customers?

40. How many "no charge" invoices go through your books?

41. Does your company provide any freebies at no charge? Who is authorized to grant them?

42. Do you provide any specials at no charge?

43. Do you regularly take stock of your inventory?

44. Do you negotiate your bank terms annually?

45. What training is undertaken to train staff on price management?

46. Do your phone staff get trained to handle price queries coming in?

47. What deliveries attracted no delivery charge this month?

48. What no-charge urgent courier deliveries were made this month?

49. What error rate occurs with your order picking, leading to credits?

50. What error rate occurs with your invoicing, leading to reissues?

51. How many reissued invoices occurred last month?

52. What stock is held by customers on a "sale or return" basis?

53. What fire sales are held to clear slow-moving, high-margin stocks?

54. What negotiating is done with suppliers to obtain better input prices?

55. How frequently are supplier invoices checked for variations in prices?

56. What negotiation skills training is undertaken for senior executives?

57. Which staff members enjoy corporate credit cards or the use of fleet cars, corporate jets? Are they monitored?

58. What programs are being undertaken to get invoicing done the same day as the transaction?

59. Is the credit hotline number printed on your invoices?

60. What guidelines have been given to staff who price things in the field?

61. What guidelines have been given on credit note limits?

62. What staff purchase schemes are in operation?

63. What happens to the frequent flyer points generated by the employees, staff, and directors of the company?

64. What strategies are in place to lift margins inside high-volume projects with low margin in them?

65. What transactional strategies are in place to add value to each invoice?

66. What training is undertaken on value adding?
67. Are current competitors' price lists obtained regularly?
68. What comparative price analysis is undertaken?
69. What strategy is in place to combat low prices?
70. What training is undertaken to teach staff about price defense?
71. What are bonuses based on—sales volumes or margins, or net profit?
72. What is the general culture of the company—sales volume, cost cutting, or price management?
73. What plan is in place to balance out the company emphasis?
74. Who is responsible for the margins generated? Is it in their job description?
75. What program checks that three quotes are obtained for major company purchases?
76. What hourly labor rates are charged out at less than the applicable charge?
77. What charges are levied for traveling time? Waiting time?
78. What quality and price conditions have been applied to third-party suppliers of service?
79. Do you have a restocking fee?
80. What is your minimum invoice strategy?
81. What services do you provide at no charge and why?
82. What products are being sold illegally below invoice cost? Do you have a program to check on this?
83. What products are being accidentally charged out to customers at higher than your published list price?
84. Do you send out letters advising of price increases? Why? (not necessary)
85. Are prices reviewed more than once per year?
86. Do you raise some prices while leaving others?
87. Do you raise prices when your competitors raise theirs?
88. Do you use price reduction too often rather than quality as a market weapon?

89. Are your support staff trained in an understanding of margins and price?

90. What is your recovery strategy for customers who complain about your pricing?

91. Are all major quotes over a certain value vetted by a margin-conscious senior executive? And signed off?

92. Have all tax-related issues been covered by training in the sales team? And management team?

93. Is all software to do with pricing thoroughly understood?

94. Who is responsible for training regarding tax-related issues? For training in the use of your pricing software?

95. Are job descriptions worded in such a way as to encourage staff to manage money, margin, and prices as if it were all their own?

96. Do you have expert external advice available on revenue management?

97. Do you have call-out fees for field service staff to cover the fixed costs of running the business?

98. Are the field staff trained and skilled to be able to explain the value of their service?

99. What customer feedback mechanism on pricing is used?

100. What internal feedback mechanism is used to establish perception by staff of value for money?

101. Do you increase price when norms allow, such as in the event of an interest rate hike?

Acknowledgments

Among the many friends and acquaintances who stimulated me to write this book are, in no particular order:

- Anonymous persons—the donor and his/her family who donated the human heart valve to me in 1993 and made this book possible.
- Ted Shreve, my late father-in-law, who served on the USS *Haverfield* in World War II and founded Trautman & Shreve Inc., Denver, Colorado; he died October 11, 2005.
- Caroline Shreve, my mother-in-law, who graduated from the University of Colorado with a degree in chemistry.
- Warren Foster, my late brother, who was a founding director of Red Hot Canary Moulding Company; he passed away on January 26, 2005.
- Naomi Rhode of Phoenix, Arizona, my friend from 1995, mentor and co-founder of Smarthealth Inc., and past president of the National Speakers Association and International Federation of Speaking Professionals.
- Kerry Catell, ASEAN chairman and retired director of Foseco International, and without doubt a true Level 5 leader.
- Walter Reinhart PhD, professor of finance and academic director of the masters of science in finance program at Loyola College, Baltimore, Maryland, who decided *MoneyMath* is unique.

- John Sommer, my longtime friend and management consultant in Sydney, Australia; adviser to the Australian Institute of Management.

- Harold E. Cartwright, my first employer, boss, and mentor, who demonstrated product costing and integrity combined.

- Gordon Stenning, my favorite medical company entrepreneur in Australia.

- Adrian Diamond, the most survivable manager I have seen, co-owner of Fire Services Australia and chairman of the board of The Lakes Golf Club in Sydney.

- Barry Markoff and Peter Rosetti of ICMI Australia—they run the best nationwide speakers bureau down under.

- Jeff Richards, CPA and accounting guru in Los Angeles, California.

- Geoff Sargent, the nicest Kiwi profit builder I have known.

- Timothy Martin-Wright, my favorite Englishman, who in 1982 took on a project for me and has been a great friend in Liverpool, England, ever since.

- Les de Celis, a dedicated CEO in Sydney who truly puts all his people first in the automotive business and is another Level 5 leader.

- Leanne Christie, principal of Ovations, the best speakers bureau in Sydney, Australia.

- Dottie Walters of Glendora, California, the legendary author of *Speak and Grow Rich*, whose strategies helped open the door for me in the United States despite 9/11.

- Nancy and Bill Lauterbach of Five Star Speakers in Kansas City, Kansas, and past president of the International Association of Speakers Bureaus who exposed *MoneyMath* to their members in Washington, D.C., in 2004.

- Steve Gardner, president of Five Star Speakers Bureau in Kansas City, Kansas, who placed confidence in the message.

- Dr. Francisco Pena, my family doctor in Scottsdale, Arizona, who loves medicine more than money.

- Dr. Paul Mercer of Brisbane, Queensland—my family doctor, who helped save my life in 1993.

- Dr. Malcolm Davison, the eminent Brisbane cardiologist who keeps my heart ticking despite everything else failing!

- Dr. Mark O'Brien, the international cardiac valve surgeon (now retired) at Prince of Wales Hospital in Queensland, who extended my life in 1993.

- Michael Howes, CEO of Southwest Mechanical Services in Phoenix, Arizona, who cares more about customers than money.

- Gopal Padki, a totally amazing Indian CEO who speaks eight languages fluently and runs a very profitable business in Nanjing, China.

- Jeff Weekes, a fantastic South African CEO and director of Foseco who always makes double digit profits, and now leads the U.S. operations.

- Adrian Dart, my consulting colleague from Johannesburg, who shares leadership strategies to people who want more productive work lives.

- Dick Smith, adventurer and businessman, the first person to fly a helicopter solo around the world, and my first consulting customer in 1972.

- Gerry Harvey, the true retail genius of Southeast Asia, Australia, and New Zealand, who taught me entrepreneurialism.

- Jim Marsh, CEO of Burns Ferrall, Auckland, New Zealand, who applied *MoneyMath* and "11/10–24/7 Service" and rescued two companies.

- Jim Rhode, Arizona Entrepreneur of the Year 1999, co-founder of Smarthealth Inc. in Phoenix, Arizona.

- Duane Ward, president, and Brian Lord, vice president of Premiere Speakers Bureau in Nashville, Tennessee—they just love only quality in their business.

- Perry Scarfe, general manager of Tyres4U in New Zealand, who runs the best auto operation in New Zealand.

- Martin Roller, CEO of BMW Brisbane and former marketing director of BMW Australia.

- Kevin Steele, general manager of Schumacher European Mercedes in Scottsdale, Arizona, who became number one by always putting the customer first.

- Carl Sewell, principal of Sewell Motor Companies in Dallas, Texas, who kindly let me see inside his world's-best automotive operations.

- Andrew Young, CEO of Kleenmaid Australasia, who chairs a superior appliance marketing organization down under.

- Ian Percy of Ian Percy Corp., North Scottsdale, Arizona, who runs an awesome group (www.profitabletransformations.com).

- John Nevin, past CEO of World Book Encyclopedia, who first encouraged me to speak professionally.

- Jillian Moran, principal of Captive Audience Speakers Bureau, Auckland, New Zealand, who has the best bureau in the land of the long white cloud.

- Gale Ellsworth, CEO of Trailways Inc. in Fairfax, Virginia, who truly understands the importance of profits for entrepreneurs.

- Victoria Whitney of Whitney Bureau in Sydney, Australia; she knows the true value of relationships.

- Mark French, chairman and CEO of Leading Authorities, Washington, D.C.—an executive who saw *MoneyMath*, applied it in his business, and listed the author. He runs the best bureau on the East Coast.

- Frank Scammarcia, CEO of Spectrum Fire, a true believer in the balanced company concept using *MoneyMath*.

- Andrea Gold of Gold Stars speakers bureau, Tucson, Arizona, a believer in the power of *MoneyMath*.

- Zig Ziglar of Carrollton, Dallas, Texas, the motivational speaker who welcomed me to America at the National Speakers Association in 1997 and said, "Keep your accent." (What accent?)

Bibliography and Recommended Reading

Albrecht, Karl. *At America's Service*. New York: Warner Books, 1995.

Albrecht, Karl, and Lawrence Bradford. *The Service Advantage*. New York: Irwin Professional Publishers, 1989.

Carlzon, Jan. *Moments of Truth*. New York: HarperCollins, 1989.

Collins, Jim. *Good to Great*. New York: HarperCollins, 2001.

Doyle, Peter, and Phil Stern. *Marketing Management and Strategy*. Englewood Cliffs, NJ: Prentice Hall, 2006.

Foster, Graham. *Where the Rubber Meets the Road—Service!* Sevierville, TN: Insight Publishers, 2006.

Gates, Bill. *Business at the Speed of Thought*. New York: Warner Books, 2000.

Gerstner, Lou. *Who Says Elephants Can't Dance?* New York: HarperCollins, 2003.

Gross, Daniel. *Forbes—Greatest Business Stories of All Time*. New York: John Wiley & Sons, 1997.

Hill, Napoleon. *Think and Grow Rich*. New York: Ballantine, 1987.

The Holy Bible, English Standard Version (Wheaton, IL: Crossway Books, 2001) and New King James Version (Nashville, TN: Thomas Nelson, 1990).

Koch, Richard. *The 80/20 Principle*. New York: Doubleday, 1998.

Kotler, Philip, and Kevin Lane Keller. *Marketing Management*. Englewood Cliffs, NJ: Prentice Hall, 2005.

Label, Wayne. *Accounting for Non-Accountants*. Sourcebooks, Inc., 2006.

Liker, Jeffrey. *The Toyota Way*. New York: McGraw-Hill, 2004.

Maltz, Maxwell. *Psycho-Cybernetics*. New York: Simon & Schuster, 1989.

Peale, Norman Vincent. *The Power of Positive Thinking*. New York: Random House, 1956.

Sewell, Carl, and Paul Brown. *Customers for Life*. New York: Doubleday, 2002.

Spector, Robert, and Patrick McCarthy. *The Nordstrom Way*. New York: John Wiley & Sons, 1996.

Semler, Ricardo. *Maverick: The Success Story behind the World's Most Unusual Workplace*. New York: Warner Books, 1995.

Walters, Dottie, and Lillie Walters. *Speak and Grow Rich*. Englewood Cliffs, NJ: Prentice Hall, 1997.

Winkler, John. *Pricing for Results*. Bicester, England: Facts on File Publications, 1984.

Zemke, Ron, and Kristin Anderson. *Knock Your Socks Off Service*. New York: American Management Association, 1993.

Index

About the Author

Graham Foster is an author, business adviser, and keynote presenter. He speaks at conferences around the world and runs in-house seminars on the subject of profitability, customer service, and selling skills for profit. All those operational business elements that sustain profitability—margin, customer service, price salesmanship, market pricing, differentiated pricing, segmented marketing, relationship selling strategies, price elasticity, handling price wars, and more—are covered in his seminars.

As this book goes to press, Mr. Foster has made over 3,580 presentations in 44 countries. He is available to speak at your conference or to consult with your senior management. He is a CSP (Certified Speaking Professional) accredited with the National Speakers Association and is a current company director.

The profit improvement resources, both written and digital, are also available from Mr. Foster's two offices or from his Internet web site listed below.

Pacific Seminars International (Phoenix, Arizona)
www.pacificseminars.com
E-mail: GrahamHFoster@msn.com
GrahamHFoster@hotmail.com
Voice: 602-684-5644 (24/7 global)

Asia-Pacific (Brisbane, Australia)
Voice: 0409-361526 (24/7)
E-mail: gfoster@pacific.net.au
Skype ID: GrahamHFoster